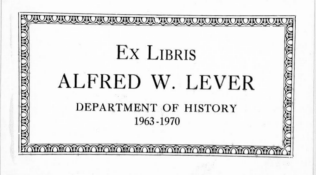

THE LAND OF DEEPENING SHADOW

D. Thomas Curtin

THE LAND OF DEEPENING SHADOW

GERMANY-AT-WAR

BY

D. THOMAS CURTIN

NEW YORK
GEORGE H. DORAN COMPANY

TO
LORD NORTHCLIFFE

CONTENTS

CONTENTS

THE LAND OF DEEPENING SHADOW

THE LAND OF
DEEPENING SHADOW

CHAPTER I

GETTING IN

E ARLY in November, 1915, I sailed from New York to Rotterdam.

I spent nearly a month in Holland completing my preparations, and at length one grey winter morning I took the step that I dreaded. I had left Germany six months before with a feeling that to enter it again and get safely out was hopeless, foolish, dangerous, impossible. But at any rate I was going to try.

At Zevenaar, while the Dutch customs officials were examining my baggage, I patronised the youth selling apple cakes and coffee, for after several months' absence from Germany my imagination had been kindled to contemplate living uncomfortably on short rations for some time as the least of my troubles. Furthermore, the editorial opinion vouchsafed in the Dutch newspaper which I had bought at Arnhem was that Austria's reply to the "Ancona" Note made a break with America almost a certainty. Consequently as the train rolled over the few remaining miles to the frontier I crammed down my apple cakes, resolved to face the unknown on a full stomach.

The wheels ground under the brakes, I pulled down the window with a bang and looked out no longer upon the soft rolled military cap of Holland but upon the business-like spiked helmet of Germany. I steeled myself. There was no backing out now. I had crossed the German frontier.

The few passengers filed into the customs room, where a corps of skilled mechanics prised open the contents of bags and trunks. Each man was an expert in his profession. A hand plunged into one of my bags and emerged with several bars of chocolate, the wrappers of which were shorn off before the chocolate was well out of the bag. A bottle of liniment, the brand that made us forget our sprains and bruises in college days, was brought to light, and with commendable dexterity the innocent label was removed in a twinkling with a specially constructed piece of steel. The label had a picture of a man with a very extensive moustache—the man who had made the liniment famous, or *vice versa*—but the trade name and proprietor must go unsung in the Fatherland, for the Government has decreed that travellers entering Germany may bring only three things containing printed matter, viz.: railroad tickets, money and passports.

When the baggage squad had finished its task and replaced all unsuspected articles, the bags were sealed and sent on to await the owner, whose real troubles now began.

I stepped into a small room where I was asked to hand over all printed matter on my person. Two reference books necessary for my work were tried and found not guilty, after which they were enclosed

in a large envelope and sent through the regular
censor.

Switched into a third room before I had a chance
even to bid good-bye to the examiners in the second,
I found myself standing before a small desk answering
questions about myself and my business asked tersely
by an inquisitor who read from a lengthy paper which
had to be filled in, and behind whom stood three officers
in uniform. These occasionally interpolated questions
and always glared into my very heart. When I
momentarily looked away from their riveted eyes it
was only to be held transfixed by the scrutinising orbs
of a sharp, neatly dressed man who had been a passenger
on the train. He plays the double rôle of detective-
interpreter, and he plays it in first-class fashion.

While the man behind the desk was writing my biography, the detective—or rather the interpreter, as I
prefer to think of him, because he spoke such perfect
English—cross-examined me in his own way. As the
grilling went on I did not know whether to be anxious
about the future or to glow with pride over the
profound interest which the land of Goethe and
Schiller was displaying in my life and literary
efforts.

Had I not a letter from Count Bernstorff?
I was not thus blessed.

Did I not have a birth certificate? Whom did I
know in Germany? Where did they live? On what
occasions had I visited Germany during my past life?
On what fronts had I already seen fighting? What
languages did I speak, and the degree of proficiency
in each?

Many of my answers to these and similar questions were carefully written down by the man at the desk, while his companions in the inquisition glared, always glared, and the room danced with soldiers passing through it.

At length my passport was folded and returned to me, but my credentials and reference books were sealed in an envelope. They would be returned to me later, I was told.

I was shunted along into an adjoining small room where nimble fingers dexterously ran through my clothing to find out if I had overlooked declaring anything.

Another shunting and I was in a large room. I rubbed elbows with more soldiers along the way, but nobody spoke. Miraculously I came to a halt before a huge desk, much as a bar of glowing iron, after gliding like a living thing along the floor of a rolling mill, halts suddenly at the bidding of a distant hand.

Behind the desk stood men in active service uniforms—men who had undoubtedly faced death for the land which I was seeking to enter. They fired further questions at me and took down the data on my passport, after which I wrote my signature for the official files. Attacks came hard and fast from the front and both flanks, while a silent soldier thumbed through a formidable card file, apparently to see if I were a *persona non grata,* or worse, in the records.

I became conscious of a silent power to my left, and turning my glance momentarily from the rapid-fire questioners at the desk, I looked into a pair of lynx eyes flashing up and down my person. Another detective, with probably the added rôle of interpreter, but as I was answering all questions in German he said not a word. Yet he looked volumes.

Through more soldiers to the platform, and then a swift and comparatively comfortable journey to Emmerich, accompanied by a soldier who carried my sealed envelope, the contents of which were subsequently returned to me after an examination by the censor.

At last I was alone! or rather I thought I was, for my innocent stroll about Emmerich was duly observed by a man who bore the unmistakable air of his profession, and who stepped into my compartment on the Cologne train as I sat mopping my brow waiting for it to start. He flashed his badge of detective authority, asked to see my papers, returned them to me politely, and bowed himself out.

My journey was through the heart of industrial Germany, a heart which throbs feverishly night and day, month in and month out, to drive the Teuton power east, west, north, and south.

Forests of lofty chimney-stacks in Wesel, Duisburg, Krefeld, Essen, Elberfeld and Düsseldorf belched smoke which hazed the landscape far and wide: smoke which made cities, villages, lone brick farmhouses, trees, and cattle appear blurred and indistinct, and which filtered into one's very clothing and into locked travelling bags.

But there was a strength and virility about everything, from the vulcanic pounding and crashing in mills and arsenals to the sturdy uniformed women who were pushing heavy trucks along railroad platforms or polishing railings and door knobs on the long lines of cars in the train yards.

Freight trains, military trains and passenger trains

were speeding over the network of rails without a hitch, soldiers and officers were crowding station platforms, and if there was any faltering of victory hopes among these men—as the atmosphere of the outside world may have at that time led one to believe—I utterly failed to detect it in their faces. They were either doggedly and determinedly moving in the direction of duty, or going happily home for a brief holiday respite, as an unmistakable brightness of expression, even when their faces were drawn from the strain of the trenches, clearly showed.

But it is the humming, beehive activity of these Rhenish-Westphalian cities and towns which crowd one another for space that impresses the traveller in this workshop section of Germany. He knows that the sea of smoke, the clirr and crash of countless foundries are the impelling force behind Germany's soldier millions, whether they are holding far-thrown lines in Russia, or smashing through the Near East, or desperately counter-attacking in the West.

In harmony with the scene the winter sun sank like a molten metal ball behind the smoke-stack forest, to set blood-red an hour later beyond the zigzag lines in France.

Maximilian Harden had just been widely reported as having said that Germany's great military conquests were in no way due to planning in higher circles, but are the work of the rank and file—of the Schultzs and the Schmidts. I liked to think of this as the train sped on at the close of the short winter afternoon, for my first business was to call upon a middle-class family on behalf of a German-American in New York, who wished me to take £100 to his relatives in a small Rhenish town.

Thus my first evening in Germany found me in a dark little town on the Rhine groping my way through crooked streets to a home, the threshold of which I no sooner crossed than I was made to feel that the arm of the police is long and that it stretches out into the remotest villages and hamlets.

The following incident, which was exactly typical of what would happen in nineteen German households out of twenty, may reveal one small aspect of German character to British and American people, who are as a rule completely unable to understand German psychology.

Although I had come far out of my way to bring what was for them a considerable sum of money, as well as some portraits of their long-absent relatives in the United States and interesting family news, my reception was as cold as the snow-blown air outside. I was not allowed to finish explaining my business when I was at first petulantly and then violently and angrily interrupted with:—

"Have you been to the police?"

"No," I said. "I did not think it was necessary to go to the police, as I am merely passing through here, and am not going to stay."

The lady of the house replied coldly, "Go to the police," and shut the door in my face.

I mastered my temper by reminding myself that whereas such treatment at home would have been sufficiently insulting to break off further relations, it was not intended as such in Germany.

It was a long walk for a tired man to the *Polizeiamt*. When I got there I was fortunate in encountering a lank, easy-going old fellow who had been commandeered for the job owing to the departure of all the local police for the war. He was clearly more interested in trying to find out something of *his* relations in some remote village in America, which he said was named after them, than in my business.

I returned to pay the £100 and deliver the photographs, and now that I had been officially "policed" was received with great cordiality and pressed to spend the evening.

Father, mother, grown-up daughters and brother-in-law all assured me that it was not owing to my personal appearance that I had been so coldly received, but that war is war and law is law and that everything must be done as the authorities decree.

Cigars and cigarettes were showered upon me and my glass was never allowed to be empty of Rhine wine. Good food was set before me and the stock generously replenished whenever necessary. It will be remembered that I had come unexpectedly and that I was not being entertained in a wealthy home, and this at a time when the only counter-attack on Germany's success in the Balkans was an increased amount of stories that she was starving.

Evidently the Schultzs and the Schmidts were not taking all the credit for Germany's position to themselves. They pointed with pride to a picture of the Emperor adorning one wall and then smiled with satisfaction as they indicated the portrait of von Hindenburg on the wall opposite. One of the daughters wore a huge silver medallion of the same renowned general on her neck. After nearly a year and a half of war these hard-working Germans were proud of their leaders and had absolute faith in them.

But this family had felt the war. One son had just been wounded, they knew not how severely, in France. If some unknown English soldier on the Yser had raised his rifle just a hairbreadth higher the other son would be sleeping in the blood-soaked soil of Flanders instead of doing garrison duty in Hanover while recovering from a bullet which had passed through his head just under the eyes.

CHAPTER II

THERE was one more passenger, making three, in our first-class compartment in the all-day express train from Cologne to Berlin after it left Hanover. He was a naval officer of about forty-five, clean-cut, alert, clearly an intelligent man. His manner was proud, but not objectionably so.

The same might be said of the manner of the major who had sat opposite me since the train left Düsseldorf. I had been in Germany less than thirty hours and was feeling my way carefully, so I made no attempt to enter into conversation. Just before lunch the jolting of the train deposited the major's coat at my feet. I picked it up and handed it to him. He received it with thanks and a trace of a smile. He was polite, but icily so. I was an American, he was a German officer. In his way of reasoning my country was unneutrally making ammunition to kill himself and his men. But for my country the war would have been over long ago. Therefore he hated me, but his training made him polite in his hate. That is the difference between the better class of army and naval officers and diplomats and the rest of the Germans.

When he left the compartment for the dining-car he saluted and bowed stiffly. When we met in the narrow corridor after our return from lunch, each stepped aside to let the other pass in first. I exchanged with him heel-click for heel-click, salute for salute, waist-bow for waist-bow, and after-you-my-dear-Alphonse sweep of the arm for you-go-first-my-dear-Gaston motion from him. The result was that we both started at once, collided, backed away and indulged in all the protestations and gymnastics necessary to beg another's pardon in military Germany. At length we entered, erected a screen of ice between us, and alternately looked from one another to the scenery hour after hour.

The entrance of the naval officer relieved the strain, for the two branches of the Kaiser's armed might were soon—after the usual gymnastics—engaged in conversation. They were not men to discuss their business before a stranger. Once I caught the word *Amerikaner* uttered in a low voice, but though their looks told that they regarded me as an intruder in their country they said nothing on that point.

At Stendal we got the Berlin evening papers, which had little of interest except a few lines about the *Ancona* affair between Washington and Vienna.

"Do you think Austria will grant the American demands?" the man in grey asked the man in blue.

"Austria will do what Germany thinks best. Personally, I hope that we take a firm stand. I do not believe in letting the United States tell us how to conduct the war. We are quite capable of conducting it and completing it in a manner satisfactory to ourselves."

The man in grey agreed with the man in blue.

Past the blazing munition works at Spandau, across the Havel, through the Tiergarten, running slowly now, to the *Friedrichstrasse Bahnhof*.

A bewildering swirl of thoughts rushed through my head as I stepped out on the platform. More than three months ago I had left London for my long, circuitous journey to Berlin. I had planned and feared, planned and hoped. The German spy system is the most elaborate in the world. Only through a miracle could the Wilhelmstrasse be ignorant of the fact that I had travelled all over Europe during the war for the hated British Press. I could only hope that the age of miracles had not passed.

The crowd was great, porters were as scarce as they used to be plentiful, I was waiting for somebody, so I stood still and took note of my surroundings.

Across the platform was a long train ready to start west, and from each window leaned officers and soldiers bidding good-bye to groups of friends. The train was marked *Hannover, Köln, Lille.* As though I had never known it before, I found myself saying, "Lille is in France, and those men ride there straight from here."

The train on which I had arrived had pulled out and another had taken its place. This was marked *Posen, Thorn, Insterburg, Stallupönen, Alexandrovo, Vilna.* As I stood on that platform I felt Germany's power in a peculiar but convincing way. I had been in Germany, in East Prussia, when the Russians were not only in possession of the last four places named, but about to threaten the first two.

Now the simple printed list of stations on the heavy train about to start from the capital of Germany to Vilna, deep in Russia, was an awe-inspiring tribute to the great military machine of the Fatherland. For a moment I believed in von Bethmann-Holweg's talk about the "map of Europe."

I was eager to see how much Berlin had changed, for I knew it at various stages of the war, but I cannot honestly say that the changes which I detected later, and which I shall deal with in subsequent chapters of this book—changes which are absorbingly interesting to study on the spot and vitally important in the progress and outcome of the war—were very apparent then.

In the dying days of 1915 I found the people of Berlin almost as supremely confident of victory, especially now since Bulgaria's entrance had made such sweeping changes in the Balkans, as they were on that day of cloudless blue, the first of August, 1914, when the dense mass swayed before the Royal Palace, to see William II. come out upon the balcony to bid his people rise to arms. Eyes sparkled, cheeks flushed, the buzz changed to cheering, the cheering swelled to a roar. The army which had been brought to the highest perfection, the army which would sweep Europe—at last the German people could see what it would do, would show the world what it would do. The anticipation intoxicated them.

An American friend told me of how he struggled toward the *Schloss,* but in the jam of humanity got only as far as the monument of Frederick the Great. There a youth threw his hat in the air and cried: *"Hoch der Krieg, Hoch der Krieg!"* (Hurrah for the war).

That was the spirit that raged like a prairie fire.

An old man next to him looked him full in the eyes. *"Der Krieg ist eine ernste Sache, Junge!"* (War is a serious matter, young man), he said and turned away.

He was in the crowd, but not of it. His note was discordant. They snarled at him and pushed him roughly.
They gloried in the thought of war. They were certain
that they were invincible. All that they had been
taught, all the influences on their lives convinced them
that nothing could stand before the *furor teutonicus*
once it was turned loose.

Delirious days when military bands blared regiment
after regiment through lines of cheering thousands;
whole companies deluged with flowers, long military
trains festooned with blossoms and greenery rolling
with clock-like regularity from the stations amid thunderous cheers. Sad partings were almost unknown, for,
of course, no earthly power could withstand the onslaughts of the Kaiser's troops. God was with them—
even their belts and helmets showed that. So, "Good-
bye for six weeks!"

The 2nd of September is Sedan Day, and in 1914 it
was celebrated as never before. A great parade was
scheduled, a parade which would show German prowess.
Though I arrived in "Unter den Linden" two hours
before the procession was due, I could not get anywhere
near the broad central avenue down which it would
pass. I chartered a taxi which had foundered in the
throng, and perched on top. The Government, always
attentive to the patriotic education of the children, had
given special orders for such occasions. The little ones
were brought to the front by the police, and boys were
even permitted to climb the sacred Linden trees that
they might better see what the Fatherland had done.

The triumphal column entered through the Kaiser
Arch of the Brandenburger Tor, and bedlam broke loose

during the passing of the captured cannon of Russia, France, and Belgium—these last cast by German workmen at Essen and fired by Belgian artillerists against German soldiers at Liége.

The gates of Paris! Then the clear-cut German official reports became vague for a few days about the West, but had much of Hindenburg and victory in the East. Democracies wash their dirty linen in public, while absolute governments tuck theirs out of sight, where it usually disappears, but sometimes unexpectedly develops spontaneous combustion.

Nobody—outside of the little circle—questioned the delay in entering Paris. Everything was going according to plan, was the saying. I suppose sheep entertain a somewhat similar attitude when their leader conducts them over a precipice. Antwerp must be taken first— that was the key to Paris and London. Such was the gossip when the scene was once more set in Belgium, and the great Skoda mortars pulverised forts which on paper were impregnable. Many a time during the first days of October I left my glass of beer or cup of tea half finished and rushed from café and restaurant with the crowd to see if the newspaper criers of headlines were announcing the fall of the fortress on the Scheldt. How those people discussed the terms of the coming early peace, terms which were not by any means easy! Berlin certainly had its thumbs turned down on the rest of Europe.

With two other Americans I sat with a group of prosperous Berliners in their luxurious club. Waiters moved noiselessly over costly rugs and glasses clinked, while these men seriously discussed the probable terms

Germany would soon impose on a conquered continent. Belgium would, of course, be incorporated into the German Empire, and Antwerp would be the chief outlet for Germany's commerce—and how that commerce would soon boom at the expense of Great Britain! France would now have an opportunity to develop her socialistic experiments, as she would be permitted to maintain only a very small army. The mistake of 1870 must not be repeated. This time there would be no paltry levy of five billion francs. A great German Empire would rise on the ruins of the British. Commercial gain was the theme. I did not gather from the conversation that anybody but Germany would be a party to the peace.

A man in close touch with things military entered at midnight. His eyes danced as he gave us new information about Antwerp. Clearly the city was doomed.

I did not sleep that night. I packed. Next evening I was in Holland. I saw a big story, hired a car, picked up a *Times* courier, and, after "fixing" things with the Dutch guards, dashed for Antwerp. The long story of a retreat with the rearguard of the Belgian Army has no place here. But there were scenes which contrasted with the boasting, confident, joyous capital I had left. Belgian horses drawing dejected families, weeping on their household goods, other families with everything they had saved bundled in a tablecloth or a handkerchief. Some had their belongings tied on a bicycle, others trundled wheel-barrows. Valuable draught dogs, harnessed, but drawing no cart, were led by their masters, while other dogs that nobody thought of just followed along. And tear-drenched faces everywhere.

Back in Bergen-op-Zoom and Putten I had seen chalk writing on brick walls saying that members of certain families had gone that way and would wait in certain designated places for other members who chanced to pass. On the road, now dark, and fringed with pines, I saw a faint light flicker. A group passed, four very old women tottering after a very old man, he holding a candle before him to light the way.

As I jotted down these things and handed them to my courier I thought of the happy faces back in Berlin, of jubilant crowds dashing from restaurants and cafés as each newspaper edition was shouted out, and I knew that the men in the luxurious club were figuring out to what extent they could mulct Belgium.

I pressed on in the dark and joined the Belgian army and the British Naval Brigade falling back before the Germans. I came upon an American, now captain of a Belgian company. "It's a damn shame, and I hate to admit it," he said, "but the Allies are done for." That is the way it looked to us in the black hours of the retreat.

Soldiers were walking in their sleep. Some sank, too exhausted to continue. An English sailor, a tireless young giant, trudged on mile after mile with a Belgian soldier on his back. Both the Belgian's feet had been shot off and tightly bound handkerchiefs failed to check the crimson trail.

London and Paris were gloomy, but Berlin was basking in the bright morning sunshine of the war.

Although the fronts were locked during the winter, the German authorities had good reason to feel optimistic about the coming spring campaign. They knew that they had increased their munition output enormously, and their spies told them that Russia had practically run out of ammunition, while England had not yet awakened to the realisation that this is a war of shells.

The public saw the result in the spring. The armies of the Tsar fell back all along the line, while in Germany the flags were waving and the bells of victory were pealing.

All through this there was *unity* in Germany, a unity that the Germans felt and gloried in. "No other nation acts as one man in this wonderful time as do we Germans," they told the stranger again and again. Unity and Germany became synonymous in my mind.

Love of country and bitterness against the enemy are intensified in a nation going to war. It is something more than this, however, which has imbued and sustained the flaming spirit of Germany during this war. In July, 1914, the Government deliberately set out to overcome two great forces. The first was the growing section of her anti-militaristic citizens, and the second was the combination of Great Powers which she made up her mind she must fight sooner or later if she would gain that place in the sun which had dazzled her so long.

Her success against the opposition within her was phenomenal. Germany was defending herself against treacherous attack—that was the watchword. The Social Democrats climbed upon the band-waggon along with the rest for the joy-ride to victory, and they re-

mained on the band-waggon for more than a year—
then some of them dropped off.

The story of how all Germans were made to think
as one man is a story of one of the greatest phenomena
of history. It is my purpose in the next few chapters
to show how the German Government creates unity.
Then, in later chapters, I will describe the forces tending to disintegrate that wonderful unity.

Germany entered the war with the Government in
control of all the forces affecting public opinion. The
only way in which newspaper editors, reporters, lec-
turers, professors, teachers, theatre managers, and pulpit preachers could hope to accomplish anything in the
world was to do something to please the Government.
To displease the Government meant to be silenced or to
experience something worse.

CHAPTER III

THE boys and girls of Germany play an important part in *die grosse Zeit* (this great wartime). Every atom of energy that can be dragged out of the children has been put to practical purpose.

Their little souls, cursed by "incubated hate," have been so worked upon by the State schoolmasters that they have redoubled their energies in the tasks imposed upon them of collecting gold, copper, nickel, brass, paper, acorns, blackberries, blueberries, rubber, woollen and war loan money.

All this summer on release from school, which commences at seven and closes at three in most parts of Germany, the hours varying in some districts, the children, in organised squads, have been put to these important purposes of State. They had much to do with the getting in of the harvest.

The schoolmaster has played his part in the training of the child to militarism, State worship, and enemy hatred as effectively as the professor and the clergyman.

Here are two German children's school songs, that are being sung daily. Both of them are creations of the war: both written by schoolmasters. The particularly offensive song about King Edward and England is principally sung by girls—the future mothers of Germany:—

O England, O England,
Wie gross sind Deine Lügen!
Ist Dein Verbrechen noch so gross,
Du schwindelst Dich vom Galgen los.
O Eduard, O Eduard, du Muster aller Fürsten,
Nichts hattest Du von einem Rex,
Du eitler Schlips—und Westenfex.

[*Oh, England, oh, England, how great are thy lies!
However great thy crimes, thou cheatest the gallows.
Oh, Edward, oh, Edward, thou model Prince! Thou
hadst nothing kindly in thee, thou vain fop!*]

Da drüben, da drüben liegt der Feind,
In feigen Schützengräben,
Wir greifen ihn an, und ein Hund, wer meint,
Heut' würde Pardon gegeben.
Schlagt alles tot, was um Gnade fleht,
Schiesst alles nieder wie Hunde,
Mehr Feinde, mehr Feinde! sei euer Gebet
In dieser Vergeltungsstunde.

[*Over there in the cowardly trenches lies the enemy.
We attack him, and only a dog will say that pardon
should be given to-day. Strike dead everything which
prays for mercy. Shoot everything down like dogs.
"More enemies, more enemies," be your prayer in this
hour of retribution.*]

The elementary schools, or *Volksschulen,* are free,
and attendance is compulsory from six to fourteen.
There are some 61,000 free public elementary schools
with over 10,000,000 pupils, and over 600 private elementary schools, with 42,000 pupils who pay fees.

Germany is a land of civil service, to enter which
a certificate from a secondary school is necessary. Some
authorities maintain that the only way to prevent being
flooded with candidates is to make the examinations
crushingly severe. Children are early made to realise

that all hope of succeeding in life rests upon the passing of these examinations. Thus the despair which often leads to suicide on the one hand and knowledge without keenness on the other.

Hardly any class has suffered more heavily in the war than the masters of the State schools, which are equivalent to English Council schools and American public schools. The thinning of their ranks is an eloquent proof of the heaviness of the German death toll. Their places have been taken by elderly men, but principally by women. It is a kind of Nemesis that they should have fallen in the very cause they have been propagating for at least a generation.

Those who knew only the old and pleasant Germany do not realise the speeding up of the hate machine that has taken place in the last decade. The protests against this State creation of hate grow less and less as the war proceeds. To-day only comparatively few members of the Social-Democrat Party raise objection to this horrible contamination of the minds of the coming generation of German men and women. Not much reflection is needed to see on what fruitful soil the great National Liberal Party, with its backing of capitalists, greedy merchants, chemists, bankers, ship and mine owners, is planting its seeds for the future. There is no cure for this evil state of affairs, but the practical proof, inflicted by big cannon, that the world will not tolerate a nation of which the very children are trained to hate the rest of the world, and taught that German *Kultur* must be spread by bloodshed and terror.

With the change in Germany has come a change in the family life. The good influence of some churches has gone completely. They are part of the great war machine. The position of the mother is not what it was. The old German Hausfrau of the three K's, which I will roughly translate by "Kids, Kitchen, and Kirk," has become even more a servant of the master of the house than she was. The State has taken control of the souls of her children, and she has not even that authority that she had twenty years ago. The father has become even more important than of yore. The natural tendency of a nation of which almost every man is a soldier, is to elevate the man at the expense of the woman, and the German woman has taken to her new position very readily. She plays her wonderful part in the production of munitions, not as in Britain in a spirit of equality, but with a sort of admitted inferiority difficult to describe exactly.

At four years of age the German male child begins to be a soldier. At six he is accustomed to walk in military formation. This system has a few advantages, but many disadvantages. A great concourse of infants can, for example, be marshalled through the streets of a city without any trouble at all. But that useful discipline is more than counterbalanced by the killing of individuality. German children, especially during the war, try to grow up to be little men and women as quickly as possible. They have shared the long working hours of the grown-ups, and late in the hot summer nights I have seen little Bavarian boys and girls who have been at school from seven and worked in the fields from three o'clock till dark, drinking their beer in the beer garden with a relish that showed they needed some stimulant. The beer is not Bass's ale, but it contains from two to five per cent. of alcohol. Unhealthy-looking little men are these German boys of from twelve to fifteen during the war. The overwork, and the lowering of the diet, has given them pasty faces and dark rings round their eyes. All games and amusements have been abandoned, and the only relaxation is corps marching through the streets at night, singing their hate songs and "Deutschland, Deutschland über Alles."

The girls, in like fashion, often spend their school interval in marching in columns of four, singing the same horrible chants.

Up to the time of the scarcity of woollen materials, the millions of little German schoolgirls produced their full output of comforts for the troops.

The practical result, from a military point of view, of training children to venerate the All-Highest War Lord and his family, together with his ancestors, was shown at the beginning of the war, when there came a great rush of volunteers (*Freiwillige*), many of them beneath the military age, many of them beyond it. In most of the calculations of German man-power, some ally and neutral military writers seem to have forgotten these volunteers, estimated at two millions.

A significant change in Germany is the cessation of the volunteer movement. Parents who gladly sent forth their boys as volunteers, are now endeavouring by every means in their power to postpone the evil day in the firm belief that peace will come before the age of military service has been reached. It is a change at least as significant as that which lies between the German's "We have won—the more enemies the better" of two years back, and the 'We must hold out" of to-day.

Of the school structures in modern Germany it would be idle to pretend that they are not excellent in every respect—perfect ventilation, sanitation, plenty of space, large numbers of class-rooms, and halls for the choral singing, which is part of the German system of education, and by which the "hate" songs have been so readily spread. The same halls are used for evening lectures for adults and night improvement schools.

It is significant that all the schools built between 1911 and 1914 were so arranged, not only in Germany, but throughout Austria, that they could be turned into hospitals with hardly any alteration. For this purpose, temporary partitions divided portions of the buildings, and an unusually large supply of water was laid on. Special entrances for ambulances were already in existence, baths had already been fitted in the wounded reception rooms, and in many cases sterilising sheds were already installed. The walls were made of a material that could be quickly whitewashed for the extermination of germs. If this obvious preparation for war is named to the average German, his reply is, "The growing jealousy of German culture and commerce throughout the world rendered necessary protective measures."

A total lack of sense of humour and sense of proportion among the Germans can be gathered from the fact that Mr. Haselden's famous cartoons of Big and Little Willie, which have a vogue among Americans and other neutrals in Germany, and are by no means unkind, are regarded by Germans as a sort of sacrilege. These same people do not hesitate to circulate the most horrible and indecent pictures of President Wilson,

King George, President Poincaré, and especially of Viscount Grey of Falloden. The Tsar is usually depicted covered with vermin. The King of Italy as an evil-looking dwarf with a dagger in his hand. Only those who have seen the virulence of the caricatures, circulated by picture postcard, can have any idea of the horrible material on which the German child is fed. The only protest I ever heard came from the Artists' Society of Munich, who objected to these loathsome educational efforts as being injurious to the reputation of artistic Germany and calculated to produce permanent damage to the juvenile mind.

The atmosphere of the German home is so different from that in which I have been brought up in the United States, and have seen in England, that the Germans are not at all shocked by topics of conversation never referred to in other countries. Subjects are discussed before German girls of eleven and twelve, and German boys of the same age, that make an Anglo-Saxon anxious to get out of the room. I do not know whether it is this or the over-education that leads to the notorious child suicides of Germany, upon which so many learned treatises have been written.

Just before the war it looked as though the German young man and woman were going to improve. Lawn tennis was spreading, despite old-fashioned prejudice. Football was coming in. Rowing was making some progress, as you may have learned at Henley. It was not the spontaneous sport of Anglo-Saxon countries, but a more concentrated effort to imitate and to excel.

Running races had become lately a German school amusement, but the results, as a rule, were that if there were five competitors, the four losers entered a protest against the winner. In any case, each of the four produced excellent excuses why he had lost, other than the fact that he had been properly beaten.

A learned American "exchange professor," who had returned from a German university, whom I met in Boston last year on my way from England to Germany, truly summed up the situation of athletics in German schools by saying, "German boys are bad-tempered losers and boastful winners."

Upon what kinds of history is the German child being brought up? The basis of it is the history of the House of Hohenzollern, with volumes devoted to the Danish and Austrian campaigns and minute descriptions of every phase of all the battles with France in 1870, written in a curious hysterical fashion.

The admixture of Biblical references and German boasting are typical of the lessons taught at German Sunday Schools, which play a great rôle in war propaganda. The schoolmaster having done his work for six days of the week, the pastor gives an extra virulent dose on the Sabbath. Sedan Day, which before the war was the culmination of hate lessons, often formed the occasion of Sunday School picnics, at which the children sang new anti-French songs.

There are some traits in German children most likeable. There are, for example, the respect for, and courtesy and kindness towards, anybody older than themselves. There are admiration for learning and ambition to excel in any particular task. There is a genuine love of music. On the other hand, there is much dishonesty, as may be witnessed by the proceed-

ings in the German police courts, and has been proved
in the gold and other collections.

The elimination of real religion in the education of
children and the substitution of worship of the State is,
in the minds of many impartial observers, something
approaching a national catastrophe. In any other community it would probably be accompanied by anarchy.
It certainly has swelled the calendar of German crime.
German statistics prove that every sort of horror has
been greatly on the increase in the last quarter of a
century.

I went to Germany the first time under the impression that the Anglo-Saxon had much to learn from
German education. I do not think that any observer
in Germany itself to-day would find anything valuable
to learn in the field of education, except when the German student comes to the time he takes up scentific research, to which the German mind, with its intense industry and regard for detail, is so eminently suited.
The German Government gives these young students
every advantage. They are not, as with us, obliged to
start money-making as soon as they leave school. As a
rule a German boy's career is marked out for him by
his parents and the schoolmaster at a very early age.
If he is to follow out any one of the thousand branches
of chemical research dealing with coal-tar products, for
example, he knows his fate at fourteen or fifteen, and his
eye is rarely averted from his goal until he has achieved
knowledge and experience likely to help him in the
great German trade success which has followed their
utilisation of applied science.

CHAPTER IV

PULPITS OF HATE

THE unpleasant part played by the clergy, and especially the Lutheran pastors, needs to be explained to those who regard clerics as necessarily men of peace.

The claim that the Almighty is on the side of Germany is not a new one. It was made as far back as the time of Frederick the Great. It was advanced in the war of 1870. It found strong voice at the time of the Boer War, when the pastors issued a united manifesto virulently attacking Great Britain.

These pastors are in communication with the German-American Lutherans in the United States, who exerted their influence to the utmost against the election of President Wilson, taking their instructions indirectly from the German Foreign Office.

The state of affairs in the German churches is so different from anything on the other side of the Atlantic, and in Great Britain, that it is almost as difficult to make people in England understand war-preaching ministers as it is to make them comprehend war-teaching schoolmasters.

My description of the poisoning by hate songs of the child mind of Germany at its most impressionable age came as a shock to many of my readers. But the hate songs of the children are not as fierce as the hate hymns and prayers of the pastors. Do the public here realise that of the original Zeppelin fund hundreds of thousands of marks were subscribed in churches and chapels, and that models of Zeppelins have formed portions of church decorations at festivals?

The pastors of the Prussian State Church are in one important respect the exact opposite of Martin Luther. He was thoroughly independent in spirit and rebelled against authority; they are abjectly submissive to it. As with the professor, so with the pastor, it is no mere accident that he is a puppet-tool of the State. The German Government leaves nothing to chance, and realising to the fullest the importance of docile and unified subjects both for interior rule and exterior conquest, it deliberately and artfully regulates those who create public opinion.

There are some Lutheran pastors in Germany who work for an ideal, who detest the propagation of hate. Why, one may naturally ask, do they not cry out against such a pernicious practice? They cannot, for they are muzzled. When a pastor enters this Church of which the Supreme War Lord is the head, his first oath is unqualified allegiance to his King and State. If he keeps his oath he can preach no reform, for the State, being a perfect institution, can have no flaw. If he breaks his oath, which happens when he raises his voice in the slightest criticism, he is silenced. This means that he must seek other means of earning a livelihood—a thing almost impossible in a land where training casts a man in a rigid mould. Thus these parsons have their choice between going on quietly with their work and being nonentities in the public eye or bespattering the non-

Germanic section of the world with the mire of hate. I regret to say that most of them choose the latter course.

While I was in Germany I read a lenghty and solicit-out letter from Pastor Winter, of Bruch, addressed to Admiral von Tirpitz, who had just retired for the ostensible reason that he was unwell, but whose illness was patently only diplomatic. The good pastor expressed the hope that his early recovery would permit the admiral to continue his noble work of olbiterating England. Pastor Falk, of Berlin, is a typical fire-eater. His Whitsuntide address was an attack upon Anglo-Saxon civilisation and the urgent German mission of smashing Britain and America. The Easter sermons of hate, one of which I heard at Stettin, were especially bloodthirsty. Congregations are larger than usual on that day, which is intended to commemorate a spirit quite the opposite to hate. The clergy are instructed not to attack France or Russia, and so it comes about that, as I have previously pointed out, in Prussia, Hanover, Schleswig-Holstein, Brandenburg, and Saxony, the pastors of the State Church preach hatred of Britain as violently in their pulpits as in their pastoral visits.

The pulpit orators, taking their tip from the Government, are also exhorting their congregations to "hold out and win the war." I know of one pastor in a good section of Berlin, however, who has recently lost considerable influence in his congregation. Sunday after Sunday his text has been, "Wir müssen durchhalten!" (We must hold out!) "No sacrifice should be too great for the Fatherland, no privation too arduous to be endured if one but has the spirit to conquer." He paid particular attention to the rapidly increasing number of people who grumble incessantly over the shortage of food. The good man was clearly losing patience with those who complained.

One day thieves broke into his home and got away with an enormous amount of hams and other edibles. I remind the reader that ham had ere this become unknown in Berlin. Less than three hundred pigs were being killed there per week where formerly twenty-five thousand were slaughtered. The Government had moreover taken a house-to-house inventory of food, and hoarding had been made punishable by law.

The story, of course, never appeared in the papers, since such divines are useful implements of the State, but the whole congregation heard of it, with the disastrous consequence that the good man's future sermons on self-denial fell upon stony ground.

One dear old lady, a widow, whose two sons had fallen in the war, told me that she had not gone to church for years, but after her second son fell she sought spiritual comfort in attending services every Sunday. "I am so lonesome now," she said, "and somehow I feel that when I hear the word of God I shall be nearer to my boys."

I met her some weeks later on her way home from church. "It is no use," she sighed, shaking her head sadly, "the church does not satisfy the longing in my heart. It is not for such as me. Nothing but war, war, war, and hate, hate, hate!"

The German Navy League, an aggressive body which had gathered around it more than a million members previous to the war, stirred up anti-British feeling by means of leaflets, newspaper articles, kinematograph exhibitions, and *sermons*. Among the bitterest of the preachers are returned missionaries from British possessions.

Although the social position of the pastor in a German village is less than that of a minor Government official, yet he and his wife wield considerable influence. The leading pastors receive each week many of the Government propaganda documents, including a digest carefully prepared for them by the Foreign Press Department. I obtained some copies of this weekly digest, but was unable to bring them out of Germany. What purport to be extracts from the London newspapers are ingenious distortions. Sometimes a portion of an article is reprinted with the omission of the context, thus entirely altering its meaning. The recipients of this carefully prepared sheet believe implicitly in its authenticity. Any chance remark of a political nobody in the House of Commons that seems favourable to Germany is quoted extensively. Mr. Ramsay Macdonald, in the eyes of the German village clergyman, ranks as one of the most important men in the British Empire. Mr. Stanton, M.P., in their view, is a low hireling of the British Government, doing dirty work in the hope of getting political preferment. The *Labour Leader,* which I have not seen in any house or hotel or on any newspaper stall, is, according to this digest, one of the leading English newspapers, and almost the only truthtelling organ of the Allies.

These people really believe this. When home-staying Englishmen talk to me about the German War party, I find it difficult to explain to them that the German War party is practically the whole country.

One or two better-travelled and better-educated pastors have expressed mild regret at the bloodthirsty attitude of their brethren in private conversation. But I never heard of one who had the courage to "speak out in open meeting."

The modern, material Germany has not much use for religion except as a factor in government. The notorious spread of extreme agnosticism in the last quarter of a century renders it essential for the clergy to hold their places by stooping to the violence of the Professors. Mixed with their attitude of hostility to Britain is a considerable amount of professional jealousy and envy. A number of German pastors paid a visit to London some two or three years before the outbreak of war, and I happened to meet one of them recently in Germany. So far from being impressed by what he had seen there, he had come to the conclusion that the English clergy, and especially the Nonconformists, were an overpaid and undisciplined body, with no other aim than their personal comfort. He had visited Westminster Abbey, St. Paul's, Spurgeon's Tabernacle, the City Temple, and had studied—so he told me—English Wesleyanism and Congregationalism in several provincial centres. He was particularly bitter about one Nonconformist who had accepted a large salary to go to the United States. He returned to Germany impressed with the idea that the Nonconformist and State Churches alike were a body of sycophants, sharing the general decadent state of the English. What struck him principally was what he referred to continually as the lack of discipline and uniformity. Each man seemed to take his own point of view, without any regard to the opinions of the particular religious denomination to which he belonged. All were grossly ignorant of science and chemistry, and all were very much overpaid. Here, I think, lay the sting of his envy, and it is part of the general jealousy of England, a country where everybody is supposed to be underworked and overpaid.

The only worse country in this respect from the German point of view is the United States, "where even the American Lutheran pastors have fallen victims to the lust for money." The particular Lutheran of whom I am speaking had been the guest of an English Nonconformist minister and his wife, who had evidently tried to be as hospitable as possible, and had no doubt put themselves out to take him for excursions and outings in the Shakespeare country.

"It was nothing but eating and drinking and sightseeing," remarked the Herr Pastor.

I suggested that he was a guest, to be looked after.

"I can assure you," he replied, "that Mr. —— had nothing to do all day but read the newspapers, and drink tea with his congregation. He did not take the trouble to grow his own vegetables, and all he had to do was to preach on Sundays and attend a very unruly Sunday school. His wife, too, was not dressed as one of ours."

He explained to me that his own life was very different. He eked out his minute salary by a small scientifically managed farm, and I gathered the impression that he was much more of a farmer than a pastor, for he deplored his inability to obtain imported nitrates owing to the blockade. The only question on which he was at all unorthodox was that of the Junkers and their regrettable power of holding potatoes, pigs, and other supplies while small men like him had been obliged to sell. He had a good collection of modern scientific agricultural works, of which the Germans have an abundance.

But while admiring the energy of the great capitalists and the National Liberal Party, the average clergyman tends towards sympathy with the Agrarians. The pastor of the small towns and villages, who is very much under the thumb of the local Junker or rich manufacturer, has as his highest ambition the hope that he and his wife may be invited to coffee at least twice a year. The pastor's wife is delighted to be condescendingly received by the great lady. Herr Pastor talks agriculture with Herr Baron, and Frau Pastor discusses past and coming incidents in the local birth rate with Frau Baron. Snobbery has no greater exemplification than in the relations of the local Lutheran pastor and the local landlord or millionaire.

A sidelight on German mentality is contained in a little conversation which I had with a clergyman in the Province of Posen. He knew England well, by residence and by matrimonial connections.

This is how he explained the battle of the Somme. I give his own words:—

"Many wounded men are coming back to our Church from the dreadful Western front. They have been fighting the British, and they find that so ignorant are the British of warfare that the British soldiers on the Somme refuse to surrender, not knowing that they are really beaten, with the result that terrible losses are inflicted upon our brave troops."

In this exact report of a conversation is summed up a great deal of German psychology.

For the Salvation Army a number of Germans have genuine respect, because it seems to be organised on some military basis. The Church of England they consider as degenerate as the Nonconformist. Both, they think, are mere refuges for money-making ecclesiastics.

CHAPTER V

THE professor, like the army officer, has long been a semi-deity in Germany. Not only in his university lectures does he influence the students, and particularly the prospective teachers of secondary schools who hang on his words, but he writes the bulk of the historical, economic and political literature of the daily Press, the magazines and the tons of pamphlets which flood the country.

Years before the war the Government corralled him for its own. It gave him social status, in return for which he would do his part to make the citizen an unquestioning, faithful and obedient servant of the State. As soon as he enters on his duties he becomes a civil servant, since the universities are State institutions. He takes an oath in which it is stipulated that he will not write or preach or do anything questioning the ways of the State. His only way to make progress in life, then, is to serve the State, to preach what it wishes preached, to teach history as it wishes history taught.

The history of Prussia is the history of the House of Hohenzollern, and the members of the House, generation after generation, must all be portrayed as heroes. There was a striking illustration of this in 1913 when the Kaiser had Hauptmann's historical play suppressed

48

because it represented Frederick William III. in true light, as putty in the hands of Napoleon.

There is a small group of German professors interested solely in scientific research, such as Professor Roentgen and the late Professor Ehrlich, which we exclude from the "puppet professors." Such men succeed through sheer ability and their results are their diplomas before the world. Neither shoulder-knots nor medals pinned in rows across their breasts would contribute one iota to their success, nor make that success the more glittering once it is achieved.

One of these, a Bavarian of the old school, a thoughtful, liberal man who had travelled widely, told me that he deplored the depths of mental slavery to which the mass of the German professors had sunk. "They are living on the reputation made by us scientists," he declared. "They write volumes and they go about preaching through the land, but they contribute nothing, absolutely nothing, to the uplifting of humanity and of the country." He told me of how Government spies before the war and during it watch professors who are suspected of having independent ways of thought, and for the slightest "offence" such as being in the audience of a Social Democratic lecture (this before the war, of course; such meetings are forbidden now) they are put on the official black-list and promotion is closed to them for ever.

In warring Germany I found professors vying with one another to sow hatred among the people, to show that Germany is always right, and that she is fighting a war of defence, which she tried to avoid by every means in her power, and that any methods employed to crush

Great Britain, the real instigator of the attack on Germany, are good methods.

With the pastors, they spread the idea that "Germany is the rock selected by Almighty God upon which to build His Empire." J. P. Bang, the able Danish Professor of Theology at the University of Copenhagen, writes clearly on this point. He says, when describing Emanuel Geibel:—

"He has succeeded in finding the classical formula for the German arrogance, which of necessity demands that Germanism shall be placed above everything else in the world, and at the same time in giving this arrogance such an expression that it shall not conflict with the German demand for moral justification. This has been achieved in the lines which have been quoted times without number in the newest German war literature:

Und es mag am deutschen Wesen
Einmal noch die Welt genesen!

(The world may yet again be healed by Germanism.)

"The hope here expressed has become a certainty for modern Germany, and the Germans see in this the moral basis for all their demands. Why must Germany be victorious, why must she have her place in the sun, why must her frontiers be extended, why is all opposition to Germany shameful, not to say devilish, why must Germany become a world-empire, why ought Germany and not Great Britain to become the great Colonial Power? Why, because it is through the medium of Germanism that the world is to be healed; it is upon Germanism that the salvation of the world depends. That is why all attacks against Germanism are against God's plans, in opposition to His designs for the world; in short, a sin against God. The Germans do not seem to be able to understand that other nations cannot be particularly delighted at being described as sickly shoots which can only be healed by coming under the influence of German fountains of health. Yet one would think that, if they would only reflect a little upon what the two lines quoted above imply, they would be able in some measure to understand the dislike for them, which they declare to be so incomprehensible.

"He also prophesied about the great master who would arise and create the unity of Germany. This prophecy was brilliantly fulfilled in Bismarck. After 1866 he loudly clamours for Alsace-Lorraine. This he cannot reasonably have expected to obtain without war; but when the war comes we hear exactly the same tale as now of the Germans' love of peace and the despicable deceitfulness of their enemies. 'And the peace shall be a *German peace;* now tremble before the sword of God and of Germany ye who are strong in impiety and fruitful in bloodguiltiness.'"

Hate lectures have been both fashionable and popular in Germany during the war. I was attracted to one in Munich by flaming red and yellow posters which announced that Professor Werner Sombart of the University of Berlin would speak at the Vierjahreszeiten Hall on "Unser Hass gegen England" (Our Hatred of England).

I sat among the élite of the Bavarian capital in a large hall with even the standing room filled, when a black-bearded professor stepped upon the stage amid a flutter of handclapping and proceeded to his task without any introduction. He was a Professor of

Hatred, and it soon became quite clear that he was full of his subject. His lank frame leaned over the foot-lights and he wound and unwound his long, thin fingers, while his lips sneered and his sharp black eyes gleamed venom as he instructed business men, bankers, smart young officers, lorgnetted dowagers and sweet-faced girls, in the duty of hating with the whole heart and the whole mind. I soon felt that if Lissauer is the Horace of Hate, Sombart is its Demosthenes.

"It is not our duty (*duty* is always a good catchword in German appeal) to hate individual Englishmen, such as Sir Edward Grey and Mr. Asquith and Mr. Lloyd George. No, we must go far beyond that. We must hate the very essence of everything English. We must hate the very soul of England. An abysmal gulf yawns between the two nations which can never, and must never, be bridged over. We need borrow *Kultur* from no nation on earth, for we ourselves have developed the highest *Kultur* in the world."

The professor continued in this strain for an hour and a half, and concluded with the rather striking statements that *hatred is the greatest force in the world to overcome tremendous obstacles,* and that *either one must hate or one must fear.*

The moral is, of course, obvious. Nobody wishes to be a coward, therefore the only alternative is to hate. Therefore, hate England!

I watched the audience during the lecture and did not fail to note the close attention shown the professor and the constant nods and sighs of assent of those about me. I was not, however, prepared for the wild tumult of applause at the finish. Indeed the admiring throng rushed to the stage to shower him with admiration.

"*Das war aber zu schön!*" sighed a dowager near me.

"*Ja, ja, wunderbar. Ein Berliner Professor!*" And the student with *Schmissen* (sabre cuts) across his close-cropped head smacked his lips with satisfaction over the words much as he might have done over his Stein at the Fürstenhof.

I investigated Professor Sombart and learned from authority which is beyond question that he was an out and out Government agent foisted on to the University of Berlin against the wishes of its faculty.

The name of Professor Joseph Kohler is known all over the world to men who have the slightest acquaintance with German jurisprudence. His literary output has been enormous and he has unquestionably made many valuable contributions to legal science. Even he, however, cannot do the impossible, and his "*Not kennt kein Gebot*" (Necessity knows no law), an attempt in the summer of 1915 to justify the German invasion of Belgium, makes Germany's case on this particular point appear worse than ever.

The Empire of Rome and the Empire of Napoleon worked upon the principle that necessity knows no law. Why should not the Empire of William II. ? That is the introductory theme. The reader then wades through page after page of classical philosophy, biblical philosophy, and modern German philosophy which support the theory that a sin may not always be a sin. One may steal, for example, if by so doing a life be saved. It naturally follows from this that when a nation is confronted by a problem which involves its very existence it may do anything which may work to its advantage. Thus Germany did right in attacking the little country she had solemnly sworn to defend, and history will later prove that the real barbarians of the war are the Americans, since they are so abjectly ignorant as to call the Germans barbarians for acting as they did. So argues Joseph Kohler, who certainly ranks among the first half-dozen professors of Germany.

There are a few professors of international law in Germany, however, who have preserved a legally-balanced attitude despite their sympathies. One of these wrote an article for a law periodical, many of the statements of which were in direct contradiction to statements in the German Press. The German people, for example, were being instructed—a not difficult task —that Britain was violating international law when her vessels hoisted a neutral flag during pursuit. This professor simply quoted paragraph 81 of the German Prize Code which showed that orders to German ships were precisely the same. Were this known to the German population one of the ten thousand hate tricks would be out of commission. Therefore, this and similar articles must be suppressed, not because they are not true, but because they would interfere with the delusion of hate which saturates the mind of the new Germany. I have seen articles returned to this distinguished writer with the censor stamp: *Not to be published till after the war*.

When a winning Germany began to grow angry at American munition deliveries I heard much talk of the indemnity which the United States would be compelled to pay after Europe had been duly disposed of. Professor Hermann Oncken, of the University of Heidelberg, made this his theme in a widely read booklet, entitled, *"Deutschlands Weltkrieg und die Deutsch-Ameri-kaner."*

Professor P. von Gast, of the Technical College of Aachen, does not appear to realise that his country has a sufficient job on her hands in Europe and Africa, but thinks the midst of a great war a suitable time to arouse his countrymen against the United States in Latin America. He explains that the Monroe Doctrine was simply an attempt on the part of the great Anglo-Saxon Republic to gobble up the whole continent to the south for herself. "All the world must oppose America in this attempt," he feels.

Then there is Professor Mendelssohn Bartholdy, who writes on reprisals in the *Juristenblatt* of July, 1916. It should be borne in mind that he is a professor of law and that he is writing in a book which is read by legal minds and not by the general public; all the more reason that we should expect something that would contain common sense. Professor Bartholdy, after expressing his profound horror over the French raid on Karlsruhe, hastens to explain that such methods can be of not the slightest military advantage to the French, but will only arouse Germany to fight all the harder. He deplores enemy attacks on unfortified districts, and claims that the French military powers confess that such acts are not glorious by their failure to pin decorations on the breasts of the aviators who perpetrate them, in the same way as the German Staff honours heroes like Boelke and Immelmann, who fight, as do all German aviators, like men.

There have been many incidents outside of Germany of which the professor apparently has never heard, or else his sense of humour is below the zero mark.

My talks with German professors impressed me with how little most of them keep in touch with the war situation from day to day and from month to month. A Berlin professor of repute with whom I sipped coffee one day in the Café Bauer expressed the greatest surprise when he heard that a neutral could actually get from America to Germany. I heard this opinion very often among the common people, but had supposed that doctors of philosophy were somewhat better informed.

During my conversation with another professor, whose war remarks have been circulated in the neutral countries by the Official News Service, he remarked that he read the London *Times* and other English newspapers regularly.

"Oh, so you get the English papers?" I asked, fully aware that one may do so in Germany.

"Not exactly," returned the professor. "The Government has a very nice arrangement by which condensed articles from the English newspapers are prepared and sent to us professors."

This was the final straw. I had always considered professors to be men who did research work, and I supposed that professors on political science and history consulted original sources when possible. Yet the German professor of the twentieth century is content to take what the Government gives him and only what the Government gives to him.

Thus we find that the professor is a great power in Germany in the control of the minds of the people, and that the Government controls the mind of the professor. He is simply one of the instruments in the German Government's Intellectual Blockade of the German people.

CHAPTER VI

A T the end of an absorbingly interesting reel showing the Kaiser reviewing his troops, a huge green
trade-mark globe revolved with a streamer fluttering
Berlin. The lights were turned on and the operator
looked over his assortment of reels.

An American had been granted permission to take
war films in Germany in the autumn of 1914, to be
exhibited in the United States. After he had arrived,
however, the authorities had refused to let him take
pictures with the army, but, like the proverbial druggist,
had offered him something "just as good." In London,
on his return journey home, he showed to a few newspaper correspondents the films which Germany had
foisted upon him.

"The next film, gentlemen, will depict scenes in East
Prussia," the operator announced.

Although I had probably seen most of these pictures
in Germany, my interest quickened, for I had been
through that devastated province during and after the
first invasion. Familiar scenes of ruined villages and
refugees scudding from the sulphur storm passed before
my eyes. Then came the ruined heap of a once stately
church tagged *Beautiful Church in Allenburg Destroyed
by the Russians.* The destruction seemed the more
heinous since a trace of former beauty lived through the

ruins, and you could not view this link of evidence against the Russians without a feeling of resentment. This out-of-the-way church was not architecturally important to the world as is Rheims Cathedral, to be sure, but the destruction seemed just as wanton.

The next picture flashed on the screen showed a Russian church intact, with the simple title, *Russian Church at Potetschki*. The moral of the sequence was clear. The German Government, up to the minute in all things, knows the vivid educative force of the kinema, and realises the effect of such a sequence of pictures upon her people at home and neutrals throughout the world. It enables them to see for themselves the difference between the barbarous Russians and the generous Germans.

The reel buzzed on, but I did not see the succeeding pictures, for my thoughts were of far-off East Prussia, of Allenburg, and of the true story of the ruined church by the Alle River.

Tannenberg had been fought, Samsanow had been decisively smashed in the swamps and plashy streams, and Hindenburg turned north-east to cut off Rennenkampf's army, which had advanced to the gates of Königsberg. The outside world had been horrified by stories of German crime in Belgium; whereupon Germany counter attacked with reports of terrible atrocities perpetrated by the Russians, of boys whose right hands had been cut off so that they could never serve in the army, of wanton murder, rapine and burnings. I read these stories in the Berlin papers, and they filled me with a deep feeling against Russia.

One of the most momentous battles of history was being fought in the West, and the Kaiser's armies were in full retreat from the Marne to the Aisne, but Berlin knew nothing of this. Refugees from East Prussia with white arm-bands filled the streets, Hindenburg and victory were on every tongue, Paris was forgotten, and all interest centred in the Eastern theatre of war.

That was in the good old days when the war was young, when armies were taking up positions, when the management of newspaper reporters was not developed to a fine art, when Europe was topsy-turvy, when it was quite the thing for war correspondents to outwit the authorities and see all they could.

I resolved to make an attempt to get into East Prussia, and as it was useless to wait for official permission —that is, if I was to see things while fresh—I determined to play the game and trust to luck.

Danzig seemed the end of my effort, for the railroad running east was choked with military trains, the transportation of troops and supplies in one direction and prisoners and wounded in the other. By good fortune, however, I booked passage on a boat for Königsberg.

The little steamer nosed its way through a long lock canal amid scenery decidedly Dutch, with old grey windmills dotting broad flat stretches, black and white cows looming large and distinct on the landscape, and fish nets along the water's edge. To the right the shore grew bolder after we entered the *Frishes Haff,* a broad lagoon separated from the Baltic by a narrow strip of pasture land. Red sails glowed in the clear sunshine, adding an Adriatic touch. Cumbersome junk-like boats flying the Red Cross passed west under full sail. Germany was using every man at her disposal to transport wounded and prisoners from the battle region which we were drawing near.

A smoky haze ahead indicated Königsberg. The mouth of the Pregel bustled with activity, new fortifications were being everywhere thrown up, while indistinct field-grey figures swarmed over the plain like ants. We glided through forests of masts and rigging and slid up to a pier opposite great sagging warehouses behind which the sun was setting.

As I picked up my bag to go ashore, a heavy hand fell on my shoulder and I was asked to wait until we were boarded from the police boat which was puffing alongside. My detainer, a government inspector, a man of massive frame with deep set eyes and a shaggy black beard, refused to say more than that the police wished to see me. They had been signalled and were coming to the boat expressly for that purpose.

American ammunition had not begun to play its part in German public opinion at that time, and, moreover, America was being hailed everywhere in Germany as a possible ally against Japan. Therefore, although only a few days previously Russian guns had been booming less than a dozen miles away, and Königsburg was now the base against Rennenkampf, my presence was tolerated, and I finally managed to get lodgings for the night after I had found two hotels turned into hospitals.

I spent the following day trying to obtain permission to pass the cordon of sentries outside the city, but I received only the advice to go back to Berlin and apply at the *Auswärtiges Amt* (Foreign Office). I did not wish to wait in Berlin until this campaign was over; I wished to follow on the heels of the army through the ruined land and catch up to the fighting if possible. American correspondents had done this in Belgium. I myself had done it with the Austrians against the Serbs, and I succeeded in East Prussia, but not through Berlin.

I was well aware that Germany was making a tremendous bid for neutral favour. I had furthermore heard so much of Russian atrocities that I was convinced that the stories were true; consequently I decided to play the rôle of an investigator of Muscovite crime. I won Herr Meyer of the Wolff Telegraph Bureau, who sent me along with his card to Commandant von Rauch, who at first refused to let me proceed, but after I had hovered outside his door for three days, finally gave me a pass to go to Tapiau, the high-water mark of the Russian invasion.

That night, "by chance," in the *Deutscher Hof,* I met the black-bearded official who had arrested me on the boat, and I told him that I had permission to go to Tapiau next morning. When he became convinced that I was a professional atrocity hunter who believed that the Russians had been brutal, his hospitality became boundless, and over copious steins of Munich beer he described the invaders in a manner which made Gladstone's exposé of the Turks in Bulgaria, the stories of Captain Kidd, and the tales of the Spanish Inquisition seem like essays on brotherly love. He was particularly incensed at the Russians because they had destroyed Allenburg, for Allenburg was his home. One of the stories on which he laid great stress was that a band of Cossacks had pillaged the church just outside of Allenburg on the road to Friedland, after they had driven sixty innocent maidens into it and outraged them there.

A train of the *Militär-Personenzug* variety bore me next morning through a country of barbed wire, gun emplacements and fields seamed with trenches to Tapiau, a town withered in the blast of war. Two ruined bridges in the Pregel bore silent testimony to the straits of the retreating Germans, for the remaining ends on the further shore were barricaded with scraps of iron and wood gathered from the wreckage.

Landsturm guards examined my pass, which was good only for Tapiau and return. I decided to miss the train back, however, and push on in the wake of the army to Wehlau. Outside of Tapiau I was challenged by a sentry, who, to my amazement, did not examine my now worthless pass when I pulled it from my pocket, but motioned me on.

The road ran through eye-tiring stretches of meadows pockmarked with great shell holes full of black water. I came upon the remains of an old brick farmhouse battered to dust in woods which were torn to splinters by shell, bullet and shrapnel. The Russians had bombarded Tapiau from here, and had in turn been shelled in the trenches which they had dug and chopped in the labyrinth of roots. Among the debris of tins, cases, knapsacks and cartridge clips were fragments of uniforms which had been blown off Russian bodies by German shells, while on a branch above my head a shrivelled human arm dangled in the light breeze of September.

I left the sickening atmosphere of the woods behind and pushed on to Wehlau, a primitive little town situated on the meadows where the Alle flows into the Pregel. Here my troubles began. Soldiers stared at

me as I walked through crooked, narrow streets un-
evenly paved with small stones in a manner that would
bring joy to the heart of a shoe manufacturer. The sun
sank in a cloudless blaze behind a line of trenches on
a gentle slope above the western shore when I entered
the *Gasthof Rabe,* where I hoped to get a room for the
night.

I had no sooner crossed the threshold, however, than
I was arrested and brought to the Etappen-Commandant
in the Pregelstrasse. I fully expected to be placed under arrest or be deported, but I determined to put up the
best bluff possible. A knowledge of Germans and their
respect for any authority above that invested in their
own individual selves led me to decide upon a bold
course of action, so I resolved to play the game with a
high hand and with an absolute exterior confidence of
manner.

Instead of waiting to be questioned when I was
brought into the presence of the stern old officer, I told
him at once that I had been looking for him. I informed
him that Herr von Meyer and Commandant Rauch in
Königsberg were in hearty sympathy with my search for
Russian atrocities, but although I succeeded in quieting
any suspicions which the Commandant may have entertained, I found winning permission to stay in Wehlau
an exceedingly difficult matter.

Orders were orders! He explained that the battle
was rolling eastward not far away and that I must go
back. To add weight to what he said he read me a set
of typewritten orders which had come from Berlin the
day before. "Journalists are not allowed with the army
or in the wake of the army in East Prussia. . . ."

he read, in a tone which indicated that he considered the last word said.

But I had become so fascinated with this battle-scarred, uncanny, out-of-the-way land that I resolved to try every means to stay. I declared that on this particular mission I was more of an investigator than a journalist, that I had the special task (self-imposed, to be sure) of investigating Russian atrocities; that if Berlin reports were to be given credence abroad they must be substantiated by some impartial observer. If Germany would supply the atrocities, I would supply the copy. That she wished to do so was evidenced by the permissions granted me by Herr von Meyer of the Wolff Telegraph Bureau and Commandant Rauch of the capital of the devastated province. (I had passed beyond the point where I was told that I could go, but at any rate their names carried weight.) Would it not seem strange if the Commandant at Wehlau had me sent back after these great men had set their seal of approval upon my investigations? After Germany had made such grave charges against the Russians, how would it impress American readers that the German Commandant at Wehlau could not make good and had sent me back?

Then, as a finishing stroke, I pulled my passport from my pocket and showed Berlin's approval of me stamped impressively in the right-hand corner. This visé was not at all unique with me. It had been affixed to the passports of thousands of Americans of all grades, and was merely to ensure passage from Germany into Holland. As I did not wish to impose upon the time of the Commandant I did not burden him with these extraneous details while he feasted his eyes on the magic words: *Gesehen, Berlin.* Mount Olympus, Mecca, Imperial and Ecclesiastical Rome all rolled into one— that is authoritative Berlin to the German of the province.

"Gesehen, Berlin," he repeated with reverence, carefully folded the passport and deferentially handed it back to me. I saw that I was winning, so I sought to rise to the occasion.

"And now, Herr Commandant," I began, "can you suggest where I may best begin my atrocity work tomorrow? Or first, would it not be well for me to get a more complete idea of the invasion by seeing on the map just what routes the Russians took coming in ?"

He unfolded a large military map of peerless German accuracy and regaled me for more than half an hour with the military features of the campaign.

"Just tell me the worst things that the Russians have done," I began, "and I will start investigating them tomorrow."

Then he anathematised the Russians and all things Russian, while his orderly stood stiffly and admiringly at attention and the other officers stopped in their tracks.

"First you should visit the ruins of the once beautiful old castle at Labiau destroyed by the beasts," he thundered. "And they also wantonly destroyed the magnificent old church near by."

He followed with an account of the history of the castle, and it was clear that he was deeply affected by the loss of these landscape embellishments which he had learned to love so much that they became part of his life, and that their destruction deeply enraged him against the enemy. Though I saw his point of view and sympathised with him, I questioned him in the hope of learning of some real atrocities. It was useless. Although he made general charges against the Russians, he always reverted, when pinned down to facts, with a fresh burst of anger, to the castle and church of Labiau as his pet atrocity.

The orderly had just been commanded to take me on a search for quarters for the night, when an automobile horn tooted beneath the window. Heavy steps on the stairs; a Staff Officer entered the room, looked surprised to see me, and asked who I was. The Commandant justified his permission to let me remain by eulogising the noble work upon which I was engaged, but though the Staff Officer's objections were hushed, he did not enthuse over my coming.

With intent to convince him that I was already hard at work I told him of the terrible destruction of the castle and church at Labiau, which I would visit on the following day.

"I have a sergeant below who was there, and I will have him come in," he said.

The sergeant entered, clicked his heels at attention; a doughty old warrior, small and wiry, not a civilian thrust into field-grey, but a soldier, every inch of him, a Prussian soldier, turned to stone in the presence of his superior officers, his sharp clear eyes strained on some point in space directly ahead. He might have stepped out of the pages of the Seven Years' War.

Nobody spoke. The pale yellow light of the oil lamp on the Commandant's desk fell on the military faces, figures and trappings of the men in the room. The shuffling tramp of soldiers in the dark street below died away in the direction of the river. I felt the military tenseness of the scene. I realised that I was inside the German lines on a bluff that was succeeding but might collapse at any moment.

Feeling that a good investigating committee should display initiative I broke the silence by questioning the little sergeant, and I began on a line which I felt would please the Commandant. "You were at Labiau during the fighting?" I asked.

"I was, sir!"

He did not move a muscle except those necessary for speech. His eyes were still rigid on that invisible something directly ahead. He clearly was conscious of the importance of his position as informant to a stranger before his superior officers.

"I have heard that the beautiful old castle and the magnificent old church were destroyed," I continued.

"You know of this, of course?"

"Ja, ja, that is true! Our wonderful artillery knocked them to pieces when we drove the Russians out in panic!"

The sergeant was not the only one looking into space now. The Staff Officer relieved the situation by dismissing him from the room, whereupon the Commandant sharply bade the orderly conduct me to my night lodgings.

"No Iron Cross for the little sergeant," I reflected, as we stumbled through the cooked old streets in the dark. Is it any wonder that the German Government insists that neutral correspondents be chaperoned by someone who can skilfully show them what is proper for them to see, and let them hear that which is proper for them to hear?

Everywhere in rooms lighted by oil lamps soldiers sat talking, drinking and playing cards. They were under every roof, and were also bivouacked on the flats along the river. In all three inns there was not even floor space available. The little brick town hall, too, was crowded with soldiers.

At the pontoon bridge we were sharply challenged by a sentry. The orderly answered and we passed on to a crowded beer hall above which I was fortunate to secure a room. By the flickering light of a candle I was conducted to a dusty attic furnished with ferruginous junk in one corner and a dilapidated bed in another. No such luxuries as bed clothing, of course; only a red mattress which had not been benefited in the least by Russian bayonet thrusts and sabre slashes in the quest. of concealed treasure. I could not wash unless I would go down to the river, for with the blowing up of the bridges the water mains had also been destroyed. The excellent organisation of the Germans was in evidence, however, for during my stay I witnessed their prompt and efficient measures to restore sanitation in order to avert disease.

I went downstairs and entered the large beer room, hazy with tobacco smoke, and filled for the most part with non-commissioned officers. They, like everybody else in the room, seemed to have heard of my arrival. I joined a group at a long table, a jovial crowd of men who chaffed good naturedly one of their number who said he wished to be home with his wife and little ones.

They looked at me and laughed, then pointing at him said, "He is no warrior!"

But it was their talk about the Russians which interested me most. There was no hate in their speech, only indifference and contempt for their Eastern enemy. Hindenburg was their hero, and they drank toast after toast to his health. The Russian menace was over, they felt; Britain and France would be easily smashed. They loved their Army, their Emperor, and Hindenburg, and believed implicitly in all three.

They sang a song of East Prussia and raised their foaming glasses at the last two lines:

"Es trinkt der Mensch, es säuft das Pferd,
In Ostpreussen ist das umgekehrt."

While they were singing a man in civilian clothes entered, approached me with an air of authority, and announced in a loud tone of voice that he had heard that I had said that I had come to East Prussia in search of Russian atrocities.

"My name is Curtin," I began, introducing myself, although I felt somewhat uneasy.

"Thomas!" was all he said.

"Good Heavens!" I thought. "Is this man looking for me? Am I in for serious trouble now?"

Instead, however, of *Thomas* being an interrogation as to my first name, it was his simple introduction of himself—a strange coincidence.

Although he was addressing his remarks to me, he exclaimed in a tone which could be heard all over the room that he was Chief of Police during the Russian occupation of Wehlau for three weeks, and took great pride in asserting that he was the man who could tell me all that I wished to know. He was highly elated because the Russians had employed him, given him a whistle and invested him with authority to summon aid if he detected any wrong-doing. They had furthermore paid him for his services. Although he now roundly tongue-lashed them in general terms, there was no definite personal accusation that he could make against them.

He told me of a sergeant who went into a house, ordered a meal and then demanded money, threatening the woman who had served him. A lieutenant entered at this moment, learned the particulars of the altercation, and struck the sergeant, whom he reproved for disobeying commands for good conduct which had come from Headquarters. "Just think of such lack of respect among officers," Thomas concluded. "One officer striking another for something done against a person in an enemy country. That is bad for discipline. Such a thing would never happen in the German Army."

The moral of the story as I saw it was quite different from what he had intended it to be.

A few days later I was again in the crowded beer hall when Herr Thomas entered. He liked to be in the limelight, and had a most extraordinary manner of apparently addressing his conversation to some selected individual, but carried it on in a tone which could be heard throughout the entire room. The Russian whistle which he still wore, and of which he was very proud, threatened to become a millstone about his neck, for returning refugees were accusing him of inefficiency during his reign, since they asserted that the Russians had stolen their goods from under his very nose.

After he had hurled the usual invectives against the invaders for my benefit, two splendid looking officers, captain and lieutenant, both perfect gentlemen, said that they hoped that I would not become so saturated with this talk that I would write unfairly about the Russians. They added that they had been impressed by the Russian officers in that region and the control which they had exercised over their men.

Early next morning I met the big man with the black beard who was either on my trail or had encountered me again by chance. When I said that I was going to Allenburg, of the destruction of which I had heard so much, he practically insisted that I go with him in his carriage. A mysterious stranger in brown was with him, who also assisted in the sight-seeing.

We road through a gently undulating farming and grazing country to the Alle River, where we boarded a little Government tug which threaded its way through dead cows, horses, pigs, dogs, and now and then a man floating down the stream. Battered trenches, ruined farmhouses, splintered woods, the hoof marks of Russian horses that had forded the stream under German fire, showed that the struggle had been intense along the river. The plan of battle formed in my mind. It was clear that the Germans had made the western bank a main line of defence, which, however, had been broken through.

"Just wait until we reach Allenburg," said the man in brown, "and you will see what beasts the murdering Russians are. Wait until you see how they have destroyed that innocent town!"

According to the course of the battle and the story

of the Russian destruction of Allenburg, I expected to find it on the western bank, but to my great surprise it is on the eastern, with a considerable stretch of road separating it from the river. We left the boat and walked along this road, on each side of which lay willows in perfect rows where they had been skilfully felled by the Russians. This sight evoked new assaults from my guides upon "the beasts" whom they accused of wanton and wilful violation of the arboreal beauty which the Allenburgers had loved.

I put myself in the place of the citizens of Allenburg, returning to their little town devastated by war; I understood their feelings and I sympathised with them. I was seeing the other side of Germany's page of conquest. The war map of Europe shows that she has done most of the invading, and during all the days I spent in the Fatherland I never heard a single word of pity for the people of the regions overrun by her armies—except, of course, the Pecksniffian variety used by her diplomats. It was now my rare privilege to return with German refugees to *their* ruined country, and they vied with one another when they talked to me in the presence of my guides in accusing the Russians of every crime under the sun. The war had been brought home to them, but in the meantime other Germans had brought the war home even more forcibly to the citizens of Belgium and northern France, but the thing could not balance in the minds of those affected.

I was conducted to a combination home and chemist's shop, the upper part of which had been wrecked by a shell. The Russians had looted the place of chemicals and had searched through all the letters in the owner's desk. These they had thrown upon the floor instead of putting them back neatly in the drawers.

My guides laid great stress on such crimes, but I took mental note of certain other things which were not pointed out to me. The beasts—as they always called them—had been quartered here for three weeks, but not a mirror had been cracked, not a scratch marred the highly polished black piano, and the well-stocked, exquisitely carved bookcase was precisely as it had been before the first Cossack patrol entered the city.

The owner viewed his loss philosophically. "When we have placed a war indemnity upon Russia I shall be paid in full," he declared in a voice of supreme confidence.

My guides never gave me an opportunity to talk alone with the few civilians in the place, and at the sausage and beer lunch the conversation was based on the "wanton destruction by the beasts of an innocent town."

After they had drunk so much beer that they both fell asleep I slipped quietly away and went about amid the ruins. I came upon human bodies burned to a crisp. Heaps of empty cartridge shells littered the ground, which I examined with astonishment for they were Russian, not German, shells, and must have been used by men defending the town.

I met a pretty girl of seventeen drawing water at a well, who had remained during the three weeks that the Russians were there to care for her invalid father, and had not suffered the slightest insult. Yet all my informants had told me that the Russians had spared none of the weaker sex who had remained in their path.

Further investigations had revealed that the Russians

had not fired a shot upon the town, but that the Germans had destroyed it driving them out.

I entered a little Roman Catholic church in the undamaged section of the town and noted with interest that nothing had apparently been disturbed—this the more significant since the Russians hold a different faith.

I walked back towards the river and strolled through the neat, well-shaded churchyard to the ruins of the large church, the dominating feature of the town. It was clear from what was left that the lines of the body and the spire had been of rare beauty for such an insignificant place as Allenburg.

"Too bad!" I remarked to a white-haired old man who was sitting on a bench mournfully contemplating the ruins.

"Sad, so sad!" he said in a voice full of grief. "And it seems sadder that it had to be done by our own people," he added.

"Were you here during the fighting?" I asked.

"I was," he answered. "I would rather die than leave this place, where I was born and where I have always lived."

I returned to the anxious guides and told them that I had visited the ruins of the church.

"A destruction which could serve no military purpose," declared the man in brown. "You see the methods of the people Germany is fighting."

I expressed a desire to seek only one more thing, the church on the road to Friedland which had been destroyed by the Russians after the sixty maidens had been driven into it. We went to it, but, alas! it had not been disturbed in the least. I somehow felt that my guides saw the lack of destruction with genuine regret. The big man with the black beard was at a loss to reconcile the story he told me at Königsberg with the actual facts found on the spot.

"Somebody must have made a mistake," was all he said.

My last view of Allenburg was from across the river with the long rays of the setting sun burnishing the ruins of the once beautiful church, the church I saw months later on the screen in the London display room, the church that has been shown all over the world as evidence of Russian methods in war.

I went all through East Prussia studying first hand the effects of the great campaign. My luck increased from day to day. I secured a military pass to visit all hospitals in the XXth Army Corps, which aided my investigations not a little. The prejudice which I had against the Russians died in East Prussia. It was buried forever the following winter when I was with the Russian Army in the memorable retreat through the Bukowina. In East Prussia I was in an entirely different position from a man investigating conditions in Belgium, for I was in the German's own country after he had driven out the invader. I tried to see some youth whose hand had been cut off, but could not find a single case, although everybody had heard of such mutilations. The fact that no doctor whom I questioned knew of any case was sufficient refutation, since a person whose hand had been cut off would need something more than a bandage tied on at home.

When the Russians entered the province they struck yellow and black posters everywhere announcing that it was annexed to Russia. In view of this the Russian officers were instructed to restrain their men and to treat the natives well. Isolated cases of violence, for the most part murder and robbery of the victim, had occurred where men had broken away from restraint, but they were surprisingly few.

After I returned to Berlin I met an American correspondent who was in East Prussia when I was. His sympathies were pro-German, but he was an open and fair-minded man, who, like me, had left Berlin with a deep feeling against the Russians, thanks to the excellent German propaganda. "I went especially to get some good stories of Russian atrocities," he said. "I thought that every mile would be blood-marked with evidence, but I came back defeated. Some petty larceny and robbery, a Red Cross flag torn to shreds by a Russian shell, two old men murdered and robbed by Cossacks, and a woman in the hospital at Soldau, who had been outraged by five Cossacks, was all that I could find, even though I was aided by the German Government."

My own first-hand investigations convinced me that it would be difficult for any army in the world to conduct a cleaner campaign than Russia conducted in her first invasion of East Prussia. I remind the reader that I am speaking of the *first* invasion, for I have no personal knowledge of the second. Subsequently in Germany when I spoke of the matter I was always told that it was the *second* invasion which was so bad. Perhaps! But I had been fooled when Berlin cried wolf the first time.

By a stroke of fortune while in East Prussia I became "assistant" for two days to a Government moving picture photographer who had a pass for himself and assistant in those happy days of inexactitude. We formed the kind of close comradeship which men form who are suffocated but unhurt by a shell which kills and maims others all about them. That had been our experience. He had, moreover, been over much of the ground covered by me behind the front.

"I am instructed to get four kinds of pictures," he explained. "(1) Pictures which show German patriotism and unity. (2) Pictures which show German organisation and efficiency. (3) Pictures which show evidence of humanity in the German Army. (4) Pictures which show destruction by the enemy. Some of my pictures are kept by the *Kriegsministerium* for purposes of studying the war. The greater part, however, are used for propaganda both at home and abroad. Furthermore, I must be careful to keep an accurate record of what each picture is. The pictures are then arranged and given suitable titles in Berlin."

I thought of all this in the London display-room when the familiar picture of the ruined church flashed before my eyes with the title *Beautiful Church at Allenburg Destroyed by the Russians*—a deliberate lie on the film.

I have nothing to say against the Germans for knocking their own town to pieces or against the British and French for knocking French towns to pieces. That is one of the misfortunes of war.

The point is, that the propaganda department of the

Wilhelmstrasse fully understands that people who do not see the war, especially neutrals, are shocked at the destruction of churches. The Germans have been taught an unpleasant lesson in this in the case of Rheims. Therefore they answer by falsifying a film when it suits their purpose with just as little compunction as they repudiate promises.

"A little thing!" you might say.

That adds to its importance, for it is attention to detail which characterises modern Germany. It is the subtle things which are difficult to detect. The Government neglects nothing which will aid in the ownership of public opinion at home and the influencing of neutrals throughout the world.

CHAPTER VII

THE IDEA FACTORY

A GROUP of diplomats and newspaper correspondents were gathered at lunch in a German city early in the war, when one of the latter, an American, asked how a certain proposition which was being discussed would suit public opinion. "Will public opinion favour such a move?" he questioned.

"Public opinion! Public opinion!" a member of the German Foreign Office repeated in a tone which showed that he was honestly perplexed. "Why, we create it!"

He spoke the truth. They certainly do.

The State-controlled professor, parson and moving-picture producer appeal to limited audiences in halls and churches, but the newspaper is ubiquitous, particularly in a country where illiteracy is practically unknown, and where regulations bidding and forbidding are constantly appearing in the newspapers—the reading of which is thus absolutely necessary if one would avoid friction with the authorities.

In a free Press, like that of the United States or Great Britain, the truth on any question of public interest is reasonably certain to come to light sooner or later. Competition is keen, and if one paper does not dig up and publish the facts, a rival is likely to do so. The German Press was gaining a limited degree of freedom before the war, but that has been wiped away.

As in other belligerent countries news of a military nature must quite properly pass the censor. But in Germany, unlike Great Britain, for example, all other
topics must be written in a manner to please the Government, or trouble ensues for the writer and his paper.
To a certain extent the Press is a little unmuzzled during the sittings of the Reichstag—not much, but somewhat, for the reports of the Reichstag proceedings are
strictly censored. The famous speech of Deputy Bauer
in May, 1916, was a striking example, for not a word
of his speech, the truth of which was not questioned,
was allowed to appear in a single German newspaper.
The suppression of most of Herr Hoffmann's speech in
the Prussian Diet in January, 1917, is another important case in point. This is in striking contrast to the
British Parliament, which is supreme, and over whose
reports the Press Bureau has no control. The German
Press Bureau, on the other hand, revises and even suppresses the publication of speeches. When necessary, it
specially transmits speeches by telegram and wireless to
foreign countries if it thinks those speeches will help
German propaganda.

The Berlin and provincial editors are summoned
from time to time to meetings, when they are addressed
by members of the Government as to what it is wise
for them to say and not to say. These meetings constitute a hint that if the editors are indiscreet, if they,
for example, publish matter "calculated to promote disunity," they may be subject to the increasingly severe
penalties now administered. If a newspaper shows a
tendency to kick over the traces, a Government emissary
waits upon the editor, calls his attention to any offend-

ing article or paragraph, and suggests a correction. If a newspaper still offends, it is liable to a suspension for a day or even a week, or it may be suppressed altogether.

But in peace, as well as in war, editors all over Germany were instructed as to the topic on which to lay accent for a limited period, and just how to treat that topic. For example, during the three months preceding the war, Russia was bitterly attacked in the German Press. From August 1 to August 4, 1914, the German people had it crammed down their throats that she was the sole cause of the war. On August 4 the Government marshalled the editors and professors and ordered them to throw all the responsibility on Britain, and the hate was switched from one to the other with the speed and ease of a stage electrician throwing the lever from red to blue.

How do the editors like being mere clerks for the Government? The limited numbers of editors of independent thought, such as the "relentless" Count Reventlow, Maximilian Harden, and Theodor Wolff, detest such a rôle, and struggle against it. After sincere and thorough investigation, however, I am convinced the average German editor or reporter, like the average professor, prefers to have his news handed to him to digging it up for himself.

In this connection the remark made to me by the editor of a little paper in East Prussia is interesting. After the Russians had fallen back he told me of two boys in a neighbouring village whose hands had been cut off. He said that he was going to run the story, and suggested that I also use it. I proposed that we make a little trip of investigation, as we could do so in a couple of hours.

He looked surprised. "Why, we have the story already," he declared.

"But I am not going to write it unless I can prove it," I replied.

A moment later I heard him sigh with despair as he half whispered to a cavalry captain: "Yes, yes, alas, over there the Press is in the hands of the people!"

Many newspaper readers run more or less carelessly through articles, and many more simply read the headlines and headings. The Official Press Bureau, for which no detail is too minute, realises this perfectly, with the result that German newspaper headings are constructed, less with a view to sensationalism, as in some British and American papers, or with a view to condense accurately the chief news feature of the day, as to impress the reader—or the hearer, since the headlines are cried shrilly in Berlin and other cities—with the idea that Germany is always making progress towards ultimate victory. The daily reports of the General Staff have been excellent, with a few notable exceptions such as the Battle of the Marne and the Battle of the Somme. During reverses, however, they have shown a tendency to pack unpalatable truths in plenty of "shock absorber," with the result that the public mind, as I know from my personal investigations, is completely befogged as to the significance of military operations which did not go in a manner satisfactory to the German leaders. In all this the headline never failed to cheer. When the Russians were smashing the Austrians in the East, while the British and French were making important gains and inflicting much more important losses on the Somme, the old reliable headline—TERRIBLE RUSSIAN LOSSES—was used until it was worn threadbare.

What would you think, you who live in London or New York, if you woke up some morning to find every newspaper in the city with the same headlines? And would you not be surprised to learn that nearly every newspaper throughout your country had the same headlines that day? You would conclude that there was wonderful central control somewhere, would you not?

Yet that is what happens in Germany repeatedly. It is of special significance on "total days." Those are the days when the Government, in the absence of fresh victories, adds the totals of prisoners taken for a given period, and as only the totals appear in the headlines the casual reader feels nearer a victorious peace. On the morning of March 13, 1916, most of the papers had "total" headlines for Verdun.

Not so the *Tageblatt*. Theodor Wolff, its editor, has had so much journalistic experience, outside of Germany, and is, moreover, a man of such marked ability, that he is striving to be something more than a sycophantic clerk of the Government. He is not a grumbler, not a dissatisfied extremist, not unpatriotic, but possesses a breadth of outlook patriotic in the highest sense. On the morning after the Liebknecht riots in the Potsdamer Platz, his paper did not appear. The reason given by the Commandant of the Mark of Brandenburg was that he had threatened the *Burgfriede* by charging certain interests in Germany with attempting to make the war a profitable institution. But there are those who say that the police were very watchful in the newspaper offices that night, and that the *Tageblatt* did not appear because of its attempt to print some of the happenings in the Potsdamer Platz.

It has been the custom of Herr Wolff to write a front-page article every Monday morning signed T. W. On the last Monday morning in July, 1916, in a brilliantly written article, the first part of which patted the Government on the back for some things, he delicately expressed a desire for reform in diplomatic methods which would render war-making less easy. Then he added that if some statesman, such as Prince Bülow, had been called as adviser in July, 1914, a way to avert the war might have been found.

This so angered the Government, which has successfully convinced its great human sheep-fold that Germany is the innocent victim of attack, that the *Tageblatt* was suppressed for nearly a week, and, like the ex-Socialist paper *Vorwaerts,* was permitted to reappear only after it promised "to be good." Theodor Wolff was personally silenced for several months. This was his greatest but not his only offence. All over Germany the people have been officially taught to regard this great war time as *die grosse Zeit.* Wolff, however, sarcastically set the expression in inverted commas—thereby committing a sacrilege against the State.

Throughout Germany monuments have been reared and nails driven into emblems marked DIE GROSSE ZEIT. I have often wondered just what thoughts these monuments will arouse in the German's mind if his country is finally beaten and all his bloodshed and food deprivation will have been in vain.

The Press has, of course, been the chief instrument, reinforced by the schoolmaster, professor and parson, in spreading the doctrine of scientific hatred. It is not generally known that Deputy Cohn, speaking in the Reichstag on April 8, 1916, sharply criticised the method of interning British civilians at Ruhleben. He went on to say that, "reports of the persecutions of Germans in England were magnified and to some extent invented by the German Press in order to stir up war feeling against England."

I saw a brilliant example of the German Press Bureau's attention to details in the late autumn of 1914. I was on a point of vantage half way up the Schlossberg behind Freiburg during the first aerial attack by the French in that region. In broad daylight a solitary airman flew directly over the town and went on until he was directly over the extensive barracks just outside. Freiburg is a compact city of 85,000 inhabitants, and it would have been easy to have caused damage, and probably loss of life to the civilian population. It was clear to me in my front-row position and to the natives, with many of whom I afterwards discussed the matter, that the Frenchman was careful to avoid damaging the town, and circled directly over the barracks on which he dropped all his bombs. The Freiburg papers said little about the raid, but to my surprise when I reached Frankfurt and Cologne a week later, newspaper notices were still stuck about the cities calling upon Germans to witness again the dastardly methods of the enemy who attack the inhabitants of peaceful towns outside of the zone of operations.

The French very properly and effectively practised

reprisals later, but the Germans believe that the shoe is on the other foot. And so it is in everything connected with the war. The Germans tell you that they use poisonous gas because the French used it; in fact, only their good luck in capturing some of the French gas generators enabled them to learn the method. Britain, not Germany, violates the laws of the sea. It was the Belgians who were cruel to German troops, especially the Belgian women and the Belgian children.

When the Verdun offensive came to a standstill a spirit of restlessness developed which was reflected in the Reichstag, where a few Social Democrats attacked the Government because they believed that Germany could now make peace if she wished, and that further bloodshed would be for a war of conquest, advocated by the annexationists.

During the succession of German military victories, especially in the first part of the war, there was plenty of "front copy" both as news and filler. Some of the accounts were excellent. The reader seldom got the idea, however, that German soldiers were being killed and wounded, and after a time most of the battle descriptions contained much of soft nocturnal breezes whispering in the moonlight, but precious few real live details of fighting.

Regarding this point, a German of exceptional information of the world outside his own country expressed to me his utter amazement at the accounts appearing in the British Press of the hard life in the trenches. "I don't see how they hope to get men to enlist when they write such discouraging stuff," he said.

After the Battle of the Somme opened, the German

newspapers used to print extracts from the London papers in which British correspondents vividly described how their own men were mown down by German machine-guns after they had passed them, so well was the enemy entrenched. On that occasion one of the manipulators of public opinion said to me, "The British Government is mad to permit such descriptions to appear in the Press. They will have only themselves to blame if their soldiers soon refuse to fight!"

This is one of the many instances which I shall cite throughout this book to show that because the German authorities know other countries they do not necessarily know other subjects.

As weeks of war became months and months became years, the censorship screws were twisted tighter than ever, with the result that docile editors were often at their wits' end to provide even filler.

On July 14, for example, with battles of colossal magnitude raging east and west, the *Berliner Morgenpost* found news so scarce that it had to devote most of the front page to the review of a book called "Paris and the French Front," by Nils Christiernssen, a Swedish writer. I had read the book months before, as the Propaganda Department of the Foreign Office had sent it to all foreign correspondents.

It became noticeable, however, that as food portions diminished, soothing-syrup doses for the public increased. Whenever a wave of complaints over food shortage began to rise the Press would build a dyke of accounts of the trials of meatless days in Russia, of England's scarcity of things to eat, and of the dread in France of another winter. The professors writing in the Press grew particularly comforting. Thus on June 30 one of them comforted the public in a lengthy and serious article in the evening edition of the *Vossische Zeitung* with "the revelation that over-eating is a cause of baldness."

The cheering news of enemy privations continued to such an extent that many Americans were asked by the more credulous if there were bread-tickets in New York and other American cities. In short, Germany is being run on the principle that when you are down with small-pox it is comforting to know that your neighbour has cholera.

The key-note of the German Press, however, has been to show that the war was forced on peace-loving Germany. Of the Government's success in its propaganda among its own people I saw evidence every day. The people go even one step farther than the Government, for the Government sought merely to show that it was forced to declare war upon Russia and France. Most of the German people are labouring under the delusion that Russia and France actually declared war on Germany. This misconception, no doubt, is partly due to the accounts in the German papers during the first days of August, 1914, describing how the Russians and French crossed the frontier to attack Germany before any declaration of war.

A German girl who was in England at the outbreak of war, and who subsequently returned to her own country, asked her obstinate, hard-headed Saxon uncle, a wealthy manufacturer, if Germany did not declare war on Russia and France. She insisted that Germany did, for she had become convinced not only in England but in Holland. Her uncle, in a rage, dismissed the matter with: *Du bist falsch unterrichtet*. (You are falsely informed.)

An American in Berlin had a clause in his apartment lease that his obligations were abruptly and automatically terminated should Germany be in a state of war. Yet when he wished to pack up and go his German landlord took the case to court on the ground that Germany had not declared war.

The hypnotic effect of the German newspapers on the German is not apprehended either in Great Britain or in the United States. Those papers, all directed from the Foreign Office in the Wilhelmstrasse, can manipulate the thoughts of these docile people, and turn their attention to any particular part of the war with the same celerity as the operator of a searchlight can direct his beam at any part of the sky he chooses. For the moment the whole German nation looks at that beam and at nothing else.

* * * * *

In the late afternoon of an autumnal day I stopped at a little wayside inn near Hildesheim. The place had an empty look, and the woman who came in at the sound of my footsteps bore unmistakable lines of trouble and anxiety.

No meat that day, no cheese either, except for the household. She could not even give me bread without a bread-ticket—nothing but diluted beer.

Before the war business had been good. Then came one misfortune after another. Her husband was a prisoner in Russia, and her eldest son had died with von Kluck's Army almost in sight of the Eiffel Tower.

"You must find it hard to get along," I said.

"I do," she sighed. "But, then, when fodder got scarce we killed all the pigs, so bother with them is over now."

"You are not downhearted about the war?" I asked.

"I know that Germany cannot be defeated," she replied. "But we do so long for peace."

"You do not think your Government responsible at all for the war?" I ventured.

"I don't, and the rest of us do not," was her unhesitating reply. "We all know that our Kaiser wanted only peace. Everybody knows that England caused all this misery." Then she looked squarely and honestly into my eyes and said in a tone I shall never forget: "Do you think that if our Government were responsible for the war that we should be willing to bear all these terrible sacrifices?"

I thought of that banquet table more than two years before, and the remark about creating public opinion. I realised that the road is long which winds from it to the little wayside inn near Hildesheim, but that it is a road on which live both the diplomat and the lonely, war-weary woman. They live on different ends, that is all,

CHAPTER VIII

CORRESPONDENTS IN SHACKLES

TOWARDS the end of 1915 the neutral newspaper correspondents in Berlin were summoned to the *Kriegs-Presse-Bureau* (War Press Bureau) of the Great General Staff. The official in charge, Major Nicolai, notified them that the German Government desired their signature to an agreement respecting their future activities in the war. It had been decided, Major Nicolai stated, to allow the American journalists to visit the German fronts at more or less regular intervals, but before this was done it would be necessary for them to enter into certain pledges. These were, mainly :—

1. To remain in Germany for the duration of the war, unless given special permission to leave by the German authorities.
2. To guarantee that dispatches would be published in the United States precisely as sent from Germany, that is to say, as edited and passed by the military censorship.
3. To supply their own headlines for their dispatches, and to guarantee that these, and none others, would be printed.

After labouring in vain to instruct Major Nicolai that with the best of intentions on the part of the correspondents it was beyond their power to say in exactly what form the *Omaha Bee* or the *New Orleans Picayune* would publish their "copy," they affixed their signatures to the weird document laid before them. It was signed, without exception, by all the important correspondents permanently stationed in Berlin. Two or three who did not desire to hand over the control of their personal movements to the German Government for an unlimited number of years did not "take the pledge," with the result that they were not invited to join the personally conducted junkets to the fronts which were subsequently organised.

Nothing that has happened in Germany during the war illustrates so well the vassalage to which neutral correspondents have been reduced as the humiliating pledges extorted from them by the German Government as the price of their remaining in Berlin for the practice of their profession.

It was undoubtedly this episode which inspired the American Ambassador, Mr. Gerard, to tell the American correspondents last summer that they would do well to obtain their freedom from the German censorship before invoking the Embassy's good offices to break down the alleged interference with their dispatches by the British censorship. When the Germans learned of the rebuff which Mr. Gerard had administered to his journalistic compatriots, the Berlin Press launched one of those violent attacks against the Ambassador to which he has constantly been subject in Germany during the war.

As I have shown in a previous chapter the German Government attaches so much importance to the control and manufacture of public opinion through the Press that it is drastic in the regulation of German newspapers. It is therefore comprehensible that it should strive to enlist to the fullest possible extent the Press of other countries. At least one paper in practically every neutral country is directly subsidised by the German Foreign Office, which does not, however, stop at this. The attempt to seduce the newspapers of other nations into interpreting the Fatherland as the Wilhelmstrasse wishes it to be interpreted leads the investigators to a subterranean labyrinth of schemes which would fill a volume.

Archduke Franz Ferdinand was assassinated on June 28, 1914. Long before that Dr. Hammann, head of the *Nachrichtendienst* of the German Foreign Office, had organised a plan for the successful influencing of the Press of the world. In May, 1914, the work of a special bureau under his direction and presided over by a woman of international reputation was in full operation.

The following incident, which is one of the many I might cite, throws interesting light on one method of procedure. The head of the special bureau asked one of the best known woman newspaper reporters of Norway if she would like to do some easy work which would take up very little of her time and for which she would be well paid.

The Norwegian reporter was interested and asked for particulars.

"Germany wishes to educate other countries to a true appreciation of things German. Within a year, or at most within two years, we shall be doing this by sending to foreign newspapers articles which will instruct the world about Germany. Of course, it is not advisable to send them directly from our own bureau; it is much better to have them appear to come from the correspondents of the various foreign newspapers. Thus, we shall send you articles which you need only copy or translate and sign."

This has been the practice in German journalism for years, and its extension to other countries was merely a chain in the link of Germany's deliberate and thorough preparations for the war.

With a few exceptions, German reporters and correspondents are underpaid sycophants, mere putty in the hands of the Government. Therefore, the chagrin of the officials over the independence and ability of the majority of the American correspondents is easy to understand. The Wilhelmstrasse determined to control them, and through them to influence the American Press. Hence the rules given above.

When a man signs an agreement that he will not leave Germany until the end of the war, without special dispensation, he has bound himself to earn his livelihood in that country. He cannot do this without the consent of the Government, for if he does not write in a manner to please them they can slash his copy, delay it, and prevent him from going on trips to such an extent that he will be a failure with his newspaper at home. His whole success depends therefore upon his being "good" much after the manner in which a German editor must be "good." If he expresses a wish to leave Germany before the end of the war and the wish is granted, he feels that a great favour has been conferred upon him and he is supposed to feel himself morally bound to be "good" to Germany in the future.

The American journalistic colony in Germany is an entirely different thing from what it used to be in pre-war days. Before 1914 it consisted merely of the representatives of the Associated Press and United Press, half a dozen New York papers (including the notorious *New-Yorker Staats-Zeitung*), and the well-known and important Western journal, the *Chicago Daily News*. To-day many papers published in the United States are represented in Berlin by special correspondents. The influx of newcomers has been mostly from German-language papers, printed in such Teutonic centres as Chicago, Cincinnati, St. Louis, Milwaukee, etc. Journals like the *Illinoiser Staats-zeitung,* of Chicago, which for years past has barely been able to keep its head above water, have suddenly found themselves affluent enough to maintain correspondents in Europe who, for their part, scorn lodgings less pretentious than those of the *de luxe* Hotel Adlon in Unter den Linden.

The bright star in the American journalistic firmament in Berlin is Karl Heinrich von Wiegand, the special representative of the *New York World*. The *New York World* is not pro-German, but von Wiegand is of direct and noble German origin. Apart from his admitted talents as a newspaper man, his Prussian "von" is of no inconsiderable value to any newspaper which employs him. Von Wiegand, I believe, is a native of California. Persons unfriendly to him assert that he is really a native of Prussia, who went to the United States when a child. Wherever he was born, he is now typically American, and speaks German with an unmistakable Transatlantic accent. He is a bookseller by origin, and his little shop in San Francisco was wiped out by the earthquake. About forty-five years of age, he is a man of medium build, conspicuously near-sighted, wears inordinately thick "Teddy Roosevelt eye-glasses," and is in his whole bearing a "real" Westerner of unusually affable personality. Von Wiegand claims, when taunted with being a Press agent of the German Government, that he is nothing but an enter-prising correspondent of the *New York World*. I did not find this opinion of himself fully shared in Ger-many. There are many people who will tell you that if von Wiegand is not an actual attaché of the German Press Bureau, his "enterprise" almost always takes the form of very effective Press agent work for the Kaiser's cause. He certainly comes and goes at all official head-quarters in Germany on terms of welcome and intimacy, and is a close friend of the notorious Count Reventlow.

My personal opinion, however, is that he is above all a journalist, and an exceedingly able one.

Von Wiegand's *liaison* with the powers that be in Berlin has long been a standing joke among his Ameri-can colleagues. Shortly after the fall of Warsaw in August, 1915, when the stage in Poland was set for exhibition to the neutral world, he was roused from his slumbers in his suite at the Adlon by a midnight tele-phone message, apprising him that if he would be at Friedrichstrasse Station at 4.30 the next morning, with packed bags, he would be the only correspondent to be taken on a staff trip to Warsaw. Wiegand was there at the appointed hour, but was astonished to discover that he had been hoaxed. The perpetrators of the "rag" were some of his U. S. *confrères*.

Von Wiegand for nearly two years has been the recipient of such marked and exclusive favours in Berlin that Mr. Hearst's *New York American* (the chief rival of the *New York World,* and the head of the "International News Service" which has been suppressed in Great Britain, where it has been proved to have maliciously lied on divers occasions) decided to send to Germany a special correspondent who would also have a place in the sun. The gentleman appointed to crowd Mr. von Wiegand out of the limelight was a former clergyman named Dr. William Bayard Hale, a gifted writer and speaker, who obtained some international notoriety eight years ago by interviewing the Kaiser. That interview was so full of blazing political indiscretions that the German Government suppressed it at great cost by buying up the entire issue of the New York magazine in which the explosion was about to take place. Enough of the contents of the interview subsequently leaked out to indicate that its main feature was the German Emperor's insane animosity to Great Britain and Japan and his determination to go to war with them.

Dr. Hale also enjoyed the prestige of having once been an intimate of President Wilson. He had written the latter's biography, and later represented him in Mexico as a special emissary. Shortly before the war he married a New York German woman, who is, I believe, a sister or near relative of Herr Muschenheim, the owner of the Hotel Astor, which in 1914 and 1915 was inhabited by the German propaganda bureau, or one of the many bureaus maintained in New York City. From the date of his German matrimonial alliance Dr.

Hale became an ardent protagonist of *Kultur*. One of his last activities before going to Germany was to edit a huge "yellow book" which summarised "Great Britain's violations of international law" and the acrimonious correspondence on contraband and shipping controversies between the British and American Governments. This publication was financed by the German publicity organisation and widely circulated in the United States and all neutral countries.

Dr. Hale, a tall, dark, keen-looking, smooth-shaven, and smooth-spoken American, received in Berlin on his arrival a welcome customarily extended only to a newcoming foreign Ambassador. He came, of course, provided with the warmest credentials Count Bernstorff could supply. Long before Hale had a chance to present himself at the Foreign Office, the Foreign Office presented itself to him, an emissary from the Imperial Chancellor having, according to the story current in Berlin, left his compliments at Dr. Hale's hotel. He had not been in Berlin many days before an interview with Bethmann-Hollweg was handed to him on a silver plate. Forthwith the *New York American* began to be deluged with the journalistic sweetmeats—Ministerial interviews, Departmental statements, and exclusive news tit-bits—with which Karl Heinrich von Wiegand had so long and alone been distinguishing himself.

I have told in detail these facts about von Wiegand and Hale because between them the two men are able to flood the American public with a torrent of German-made news and views, whose volume and influence are tremendous. The *New York World's* European news is "syndicated" to scores of newspapers throughout the

American continent, and the service has "featured" von Wiegand's Berlin dispatches to the exclusion, or at least almost to the eclipse, of the *World's* other war news. Hale's dispatches to the Hearst Press have been published all the way across the Republic, not only in the dailies of vast circulation owned by Mr. Hearst in New York, Boston, Chicago, San Francisco, Los Angeles, and elsewhere, but also in a great many other papers like the prominent *Philadelphia North American,* which subscribed to the "International News Service."

The German authorities understand all this perfectly well. That explains their unceasing attentions to von Wiegand and Hale, and to other valuable correspondents. One of these recently undertook to compile a book on Belgium in war-time for the purpose of whitewashing Germans in American estimation. Accompanied by his wife, he was motored and wined and dined through the conquered country under the watchful chaperonage of German officers. He has returned to Berlin to write his book, although it is common knowledge there that during his entire stay in Belgium he was not permitted to talk to a single Belgian.

Although nominally catered to and fawned upon by the German authorities, the American correspondents cut on the whole a humiliating figure, although not all of them realise it. It is notorious they are spied upon day and night. They are even at times ruthlessly scorned by their benefactors in the Wilhelmstrasse. One of the Americans who essays to be independent, was some time ago a member of a journalistic party

conducted to Lille. He left the party long enough to
stroll into a jeweller's shop to purchase a new glass for
his watch. While making the purchase he asked the
Frenchman who waited on him how he liked the Germans. "They are very harsh, but just," was the reply.
A couple of weeks later, when the correspondents were
back in Berlin, Major Nicolai, of the War Press
Bureau, sent for the correspondent, said to him that he
knew of the occasion on which the American journalist
had "left the party" in Lille, and demanded to know
what had occurred in the watchmaker's shop. The
correspondent repeated precisely what the Frenchman
had said. "Well," snarled Major Nicolai, "why didn't
you send that to your papers?" I may mention here
that these parties of neutral correspondents are herded
rather than conducted when on tour.

The American correspondents had a sample of the
actual contempt in which the German authorities hold
them on the day when the commercial submarine
Deutschland returned to Bremen, August 23. For purposes of glorifying the *Deutschland's* achievement in
the United States, the American correspondents in Berlin were dispatched to Bremen, where they were told
that elaborate special arrangements for their reception
and entertainment had been completed. Count Zeppelin,
two airship commanders, who had just raided England,
and a number of other national heroes would be present, together with the Grand Duke of Oldenburg at the
head of a galaxy of civil, military, and naval digni-
taries. The grand climax of the *Deutschland* joy carnival was to be a magnificent banquet with plenty of
that rare luxury, bread and butter, at the famous

Bremen *Rathaus* accompanied by both oratorical and pyrotechnical fireworks. The correspondents were given an opportunity to watch the triumphal progess of the *Deutschland* through the Weser into Bremen harbour, but at night, when they looked for their places at the *Rathaus* feast, they were informed that there was no room for them. An overflow banquet had been arranged in their special honour in a neighbouring tavern. This was too much even for some of the War Press Bureau's best American friends, and the overflow dinner party was served at a table which contained many vacant chairs. Their intended occupiers had taken the first train back to Berlin, thoroughly disgusted.

It is fair to say that several of the principal American correspondents in Berlin are making a serious effort to practise independent journalism, *but it is a difficult and hopeless struggle.* They are shackled and controlled from one end of the week to the other. They could not if they wished send the unadorned truth to the United States. *All they are permitted to report is that portion of the truth which reflects Germany in the light in which it is useful for Germany to appear from time to time.*

Germany has organised news for neutrals in the most intricate fashion. A certain kind of news is doled out for the United States, a totally different kind for Spain, and still a different brand, when emergency demands, for Switzerland, Brazil, or China. There is a Chinese correspondent among the other "neutrals" in Germany. The "news" prepared for him by Major Nicolai's department would be very amusing reading in the columns of Mr. von Wiegand's or Dr. Hale's papers.

There is a celebrated and pro-Ally newspaper in New York whose motto is "All the news that's fit to print." The motto of the German War Press Bureau is "All the news that's safe to print."

CHAPTER IX

WHILE I was at home on a few weeks' visit in October, 1915, I read in the newspapers a simple announcement cabled from Europe that Anton Lang of Oberammergau had been killed in the great French offensive in Champagne. This came as a shock to many Americans, for the name of this wonderful character who had inspired people of all shades of opinion and religious belief in his masterful impersonation of Christ in the decennial Passion Play was almost as well known in the United States and in England as in his native Bavaria, and better, I found than in Prussia.

British and American tourist agencies had put Oberammergau on the map of the world. The interest in America after the Passion Play of 1910 was so great, in fact, that some newspapers ran extensive series of illustrated articles describing it. The man who played the part of Christ was idealised, everybody who had seen him liked him, respected him and admired him. Thousands had said that somehow a person felt better after he had seen Anton Lang. As a supreme test of his popularity, American vaudeville managers asked him to name his own terms for a theatrical tour.

And now the man who had imbued his life with that of the Prince of Peace had thrown the past aside, and with the spiked helmet in place of the Crown of Thorns had gone to his death trying not to save but to slaughter his fellow-men.

Truly, the changes wrought by war are great!

*   *   *   *   *

In Berlin I inquired into the circumstances of Anton Lang's death. Nobody knew anything definite. Berlin knew little of him in life, much less than London, New York or Montreal.

Munich is different. There his name is a household word. Herr von Meinl, then Director of the Bavarian Ministry, now member of the Bundesrat, told me that he believed that there was a mistake in the report that Anton had been killed.

Later, when tramping through the Bavarian Highlands, I walked one winter day from Partenkirchen to Oberammergau, for I had a whim to know the truth of the matter.

On the lonely mountain road that winds sharply up from Oberau I overtook a Benedictine monk who was walking to the monastery at Ettal. We talked of the war in general and of the Russian prisoners we had seen in the saw-mills at Untermberg. I was curious to hear his views upon the war, and I soon saw that not even the thick walls of a monastery are proof against the idea-machine in the Wilhelmstrasse. Despite Cardinal Mercier's denunciation of German methods in Belgium, this monk's views were the same as the rest of the Kaiser's subjects. He did, however, admit that he was sorry for the Belgians, although, in true German fashion, he did not consider Germany to blame. He sighed to think that "the Belgian King had so treacherously betrayed his people by abandoning his neutrality and entering into a secret agreement with France and Great Britain." He recited the regular story of the secret military letters found by the Germans after they had invaded Belgium, the all-important marginal notes of which were maliciously left untranslated in the German Press.

We parted at Ettal, and I pushed on down the narrow valley to Oberammergau. The road ahead was now in shadow, but behind me the mountain mass was dazzling white in the rays of the setting sun. "What a pity," I thought, "that the peasant must depart from these beautiful mountains and valleys to die in the slime of the trenches."

The day was closing in quiet and grandeur, yet all the time the shadow of death was darkening the peaceful valley of the Ammer. I became aware of it first as I passed the silent churchyard with its grey stones rising from the snow. For there, on the other side of the old stone wall that marks the road, was a monument on which the Reaper hacks the toll of death. The list for 1870 was small, indeed, compared with that of *die grosse Zeit*. I looked for Lang and found it, for Hans had died, as had also Richard.

I passed groups of men cutting wood and hauling ice and grading roads, men with rounder faces and flatter noses than the Bavarians, still wearing the yellowish-brown uniform of Russia. That is, most of them wore it. Some, whose uniforms had long since gone to tatters, were dressed in ordinary clothing, with flaming red R's painted on trousers and jackets.

An old woman with a heavy basket on her back was trudging past a group of these. "How do you like them ?" I asked. "We shall really miss them when they go," she said. "They seem part of the village now. The poor fellows, it must be sad for them so far from home."

Evidently the spirit of new Germany had not saturated her.

I went through crooked streets, bordered with houses brightly frescoed with biblical scenes, to the *Pension Daheim,* the home of the man I wished to see. As he rose from his pottery bench to welcome me, I felt that beneath his great blue apron and rough garb of the working man was true nobility. I did not need to ask if he was Anton Lang. I had seen his picture and had often been told that his face was the image of His Who died on the Cross. I expected much, but found infinitely more. I felt that life had been breathed into a Rubens masterpiece. No photograph can do him justice, for no lens can catch the wondrous light in his clear blue eyes.

I was the only guest at the *Pension Daheim;* indeed, I was the only stranger in Oberammergau. I sat beside Anton Lang in his work room as his steady hands fashioned things of clay, I ate at table with him, and in the evening we pulled up our chairs to the comfortable fireside, where we talked of his country and of my country, of the Passion Play and of the war.

I had been sceptical about him until I met him. I wondered if he was self-conscious about his goodness, or if he was a dreamer who could not get down to the realities of this world, or if he had been spoiled by flattery, or if piety was part of his profession.

When I finally went from there I felt that I really

understood him. His life has been without an atom of
reproach, yet he never poses as pious. He does not
preach or stand aloof, or try to make you feel that he
is better than you, but down in your heart you know
that he is. He has been honoured by royalty and men
of state, yet he remains simple and unaffected, though
quietly dignified in manner. He is truly Nature's
Nobleman, with a mind that is pure and a face the mirror of his mind.

To play well his rôle of *Christus* is the dominating
passion of his life. Not the make-up box, but his own
thoughts must mould his features for the rôle, which
has been his in 1890, 1900 and 1910.

His travels include journeys to Rome and to the Holy
Land. He is well read, an interesting talker, and an
interested listener. He commented upon the great
change in the spirit of the people, a change from the
intoxicating enthusiasm of victory to a war-weary feeling of trying to hold out through a sense of duty. To
my question as to when he thought the war would end,
he answered: "When Great Britain and Germany both
realise that each must make concessions. Neither can
crush the other."

The doctrine that "only through hate can the greatest
obstacles in life be overcome" has not reached his home,
nor was there hanging on the wall, as in so many German homes, the famous order of the day of Crown
Prince Rupert of Bavaria, which commences with "Soldiers of the army! Before you are the English!" in
which he exhorts his troops with all the tricky sophistry
of hate.

Anton Lang has worked long hard hours to bring up

his family, rather than accept fabulous offers for a theatrical tour of America. He refused these offers through no mere caprice.

"I admit that the temptation is great," he said to me. "Here I must always work hard and remain poor; there I quickly could have grown rich. But the Passion Play is not a business," he continued earnestly. "Nearly three hundred years ago, when a terrible plague raged over the land, the people of Oberammergau vowed to Almighty God that if He would save their village, they would perform every ten years in His glory the Passion of His Divine Son. The village was saved and Oberammergau has kept its promise. You see, if I had accepted those theatrical offers I could never again live in my native village, and that would break my heart."

There is carefully preserved in the town hall at Oberammergau an old chronicle which tells of the plague. There will undoubtedly be preserved in the family of Lang a new chronicle, a product of the war, printed in another country, a chronicle which did not rest content with a notice of Anton's obituary, but told the details of his death in battle.

Frau Lang showed me this chronicle. She seemed to have something on her mind of which she wished to speak, after I told her that I was an American journalist. At length one evening, after the three younger children had gone to bed, and the eldest was industriously studying his lessons for the next day, she ventured. "American newspapers tell stories which are not at all true, don't they?" she half stated, half asked.

My natural inclination was to defend American journalism by attacking that of Germany, but something restrained me, I did not know what. "Of course," I explained, "in a country such as ours where the Press is free, evils sometimes arise. We have all kinds of newspapers. A few are very yellow, but the vast majority seek to be accurate, for accuracy pays in the long run in self-respecting journalism." I thought that perhaps she was referring to the announcement of the death of the man who was sitting with us in the room. We both agreed, however, that such a mistake was perfectly natural since two Langs of Oberammergau had already been killed. In fact, Anton had read of his own death notice in a Munich paper. The American correspondent who had cabled the news on two occasions had presumably simply "lifted" the announcement from the German papers. Frau Lang could understand that very well when I explained, but how about the stories that Anton had been serving a machine-gun and other details which were pure fiction?

She had trump cards which she played at this point. Two gaudily coloured "Sunday Supplements" of a certain newspaper combination in the United States were spread before me. The first told of how Anton Lang had become a machine-gunner of marked ability, and that he served his deadly weapon with determination. Could the Oberammergau Passion Play ever exert the old influence again, after this? was the query at the end of the article.

A second had all the details of Anton's death and was profusely illustrated. The story started with Anton going years ago into the mountains to try out his voice in order to develop it for his histrionic task. There was a brief account of how he had followed in the path of the Prince of Peace, and of the tremendous effect he had upon his audiences.

Then came the war, which tore him from his humble home. The battle raged, the Bavarians charged the French lines, and the spot-light of the story was played upon a soldier from Oberammergau who lay wounded in "No-Man's Land." Another charging wave swept by this soldier, and as he looked up he saw the face of the man he had respected and loved more than all other men, the face of Anton Lang, the *Christus* of Oberammergau. The soldier covered his eyes with his hands, for never had Anton Lang looked as he did then. The eyes which had always been so beautiful, so compassionate, had murder in them now.

The scene shifted. A French sergeant and private crouched by their machine-gun ready to repel the charge, the mutual relationship being apparently somewhat that of a plumber and his assistant. They sprayed the oncoming Bavarians with a shower of steel and piled the dead high outside the French trenches. The charge had failed, and the sergeant began to act strangely. At length he broke the silence. "Did you see that last *boche,* Jean?" he asked. "Did you see that face?" Jean confessed that he did not. "You are fortunate, Jean," said the sergeant. "Never have I seen such a face before. I felt as if there was something supernatural about it. I felt that it was wrong to kill that man. I hated to do it, Jean.—But then the butcher was coming at us with a knife two feet long."

I finished reading and looked up at the questioning eyes of Frau Lang and at the wonderful, indescribable blue eyes of the "butcher" across the table, who, I may

add, is fifty-two years of age, and has not had a day's
military training in his life.

"And look," said Frau Lang, "these men are not even
Oberammergauers."

She pointed to one of the illustrations which depicted a small group of rather vicious-looking Prussians, with rifles ready peering over the rim of a trench.
The picture was labelled "Four apostles now serving at
the Front."

"And see," continued the perplexed woman, "there is
Johann Zwinck, the Judas in the play. It says that he
is at the front. Why, he is sixty-nine years old, and is
still the village painter. Only yesterday I heard him
complain that the war was making it difficult for him
to get sufficient oil to mix his paint."

I was at a loss for words. "When one compares such
terrible untruths with our German White Book," declared Frau Lang, "it is indeed difficult for the American people to understand the true situation."

I felt that it would be useless for me at that moment
to explain certain very important omissions in the German White Book. Anything would look *white* in comparison with the yellow journal I had just read. But
I knew, and tried to explain that the particular newspaper combination which printed such rubbish was well
known in America for its inaccuracies and fabrications,
and although it was pro-German, it would sacrifice anything for sensation. But the good woman, being a German, and consequently accustomed to standardisation,
could not dissociate this newspaper from the real Press.

CHAPTER X

THE German submarines are standardised. The draughts and blue prints of the most important machinery are multiplied and sent, if necessary, to twenty different factories, while all the minor stampings are produced at one or other main factory. The "assembling" of the submarines, therefore, is not difficult. During the war submarine parts have been assembled at Trieste, Zeebrugge, Kiel, Bremerhaven, Stettin, and half a dozen other places in Germany unnecessary to relate. With commendable foresight, Germany sent submarine parts packed as machinery to South America, where they are being assembled somewhere on the west coast.

The improvement, enlargement, and simplification of the submarine has progressed with great rapidity.

When I was in England after a former visit to Germany I met a number of seafolk who pooh-poohed extensive future submarining, by saying that, no matter how many submarines the Germans might be able to produce, the training of submarine officers and crew was such a difficult task that the "submarine menace," as it was then called in England, need not be taken too seriously.

The difficulty is not so great. German submarine officers and men are trained by the simple process of double or treble banking of the crews of submarines on more or less active service. Submarine crews are therefore multiplied probably a great deal faster than the war destroys them. These double or treble crews, who rarely go far away from German waters, and are mostly trained in the safe Baltic, are generally composed of young but experienced seamen. There are, however, an increasing number of cases of soldiers being transferred abruptly to the U-boat service.

The education of submarine officers and crew begins in thorough German fashion on land or in docks, in dummy or disused submarines, accompanied by much lecture work and drill. Submarine life is not so uncomfortable as we think. With the exception of the deprivation of his beer, which is not allowed in submarines, or, indeed, any form of alcohol, except a small quantity of brandy, which is kept under the captain's lock and key, Hans in his submarine is quite as comfortable as Johann in his destroyer.

Extra comforts are forwarded to submarine men, which consist of gramophone records (mostly Viennese waltzes), chocolate, sausages, smoked eels, margarine, cigars, cigarettes, and tobacco, a small and treasured quantity of real coffee, jam, marmalade, and sugar. All these, I was proudly told, were extras. There is no shortage in the German Navy.

I learned nothing of value about the largest German submarines, except that everybody in Germany knew they were being built, and by the time the gossip of them reached Berlin the impression there was that they were at least as large as Atlantic liners.

Now as to German submarine policies. The part

that has to do with winning the war will be dealt with in the next chapter. But there is also a definite policy in connection with the use of submarines for winning the "war after the war."

The National Liberal Party, of which Tirpitz is the god, is at the head of the vast, gradually solidifying mammoth trust, which embraces Krupps, the mines, shipbuilding yards, and the manufactures. Now and then a little of its growth leaks out, such as the linking up of Krupps with the new shipbuilding.

The scheme is brutally simple and is going on under the eyes of the British every day. These people believe that *by building ships themselves and destroying enemy and neutral shipping,* they will be the world's shipping masters at the termination of the war. In their attitude towards Norwegian shipping, you will notice that they make the flimsiest excuse for the destruction of as much tonnage as they can sink. It was confidently stated to me by a member of the National Liberal Party, and by no means an unimportant one, that Germany is building ships as rapidly as she is sinking them. That I do not believe; but that a great part of her effort is devoted to the construction of mercantile vessels I ascertained beyond the shadow of a doubt.

I have met people in England who refuse to believe that Germany, battling on long lines east and west, and constructing with feverish haste war vessels of every description, can find sufficient surplus energy to build ships which will not be of the slightest use until after the war is finished. I can only say that I personally have seen the recently completed Hamburg-America liners *Cap Polonio* and *Cap Finisterre* anchored in the

Elbe off Altona. They are beautiful boats of 20,000 and 16,000 tons, a credit to the German shipbuilding industry, which has made such phenomenal strides in recent years. At Stettin I passed almost under the stern of the brand new 21,000 ton Hamburg-South America liner, *Tirpitz*—which for obvious business reasons may be re-named after the war.

Both at Hamburg and Lübeck, where the rattle of the pneumatic riveter was as incessant as in any American city in course of construction, I was amazed at the number of vessels of five or six thousand tons which I saw being built. Furthermore, the giant North German Lloyd liner, *Hindenburg,* is nearing completion, while the *Bismarck,* of the Hamburg-America Line will be ready for her maiden trip in the early days of peace.

Another part of the National Liberals' policy is the keeping alive of all German businesses, banks and others, in enemy countries. Some people in England seem to think that the Germans are anxious to keep these businesses alive in order to make money. Many Germans regard John Bull as extremely simple, but not so simple as to allow them to do that. So long as the businesses are kept going until after the war, when they can again start out with redoubled energy, the Germans desire nothing more. The Deutsche Bank, for example, which bears no comparison to an English or American bank, but which is an institution for promoting both political and industrial enterprise, is entrenched behind so powerful an Anglo-German backing in London, I was informed on many occasions, that the British Government dare not close it down. The mixture of spying and propaganda with banking, with export, with manufacture, seems so foreign to Anglo-Saxon ways as to be almost inconceivable.

Coincident with the destruction of foreign shipping, and the maintenance of their businesses in enemy countries (England and Italy especially) is the exploitation of the coal and other mines, oil wells, and forests in occupied enemy territory. The French and Belgian coalfields are being worked to the utmost, together with the iron mines at Longwy and Brieux. Poland is being deforested to such an extent that the climate is actually altering.

It is a vast and definite scheme, with such able leaders as Herr Bassermann, the real leader of the National Liberal Party, Herr Stresemann, and Herr Hirsch, of Essen. "We have powerful friends, not only in London, Milan, Rome, Madrid, New York, and Montreal, but throughout the whole of South America, and everywhere except in Australia where that *verdammter Hooges* (Hughes) played into the hands of our feeble, so-called leader, von Bethmann-Hollweg, by warning the people that the British people would follow Hughes' lead."

So much for the commercial part of submarining.

U-boating close to England has long ceased to be a popular amusement with the German submarine flotilla, who have a thoroughly healthy appreciation of the various devices by which so many of them have been destroyed. The National Liberals believe that the British will not be able to tackle long-distance submarines operating in the Atlantic and elsewhere. Their radius of action is undoubtedly increasing almost month by month. From remarks made to me I do not believe that these submarines have many land bases at great distances—certainly none in the United States. They may have floating bases; but this I do know—that their petrol-carrying capacity altogether exceeds that of any earlier type of submarine, and that their surface speed, at any rate in official tests, runs up to nearly 20 knots.

The trip of the *Deutschland* was not only for the purpose of bringing a few tons of nickel and rubber, but for thoroughly testing the new engines (designed by Maybach), for bringing back a hundred reports of the effects of submersion in such cold waters as are to be found off the banks of Newfoundland, for ascertaining how many days' submerged or surface travelling is likely to be experienced, and, indeed, for making such a trial trip across the Atlantic and back as was usual in the early days of steamships.

CHAPTER XI

THE EAGLE AND THE VULTURE

AN enthusiastic, war-mad crowd had gathered about an impromptu speaker in the Ringstrasse, not far from the Hotel Bristol, in Vienna, one pleasant August evening in 1914. His theme was the military prowess of Austria-Hungary and Germany.

"And now," he concluded, "Japan has treacherously joined our enemies. Yet we should not be disturbed, for her entrance will but serve to bring *us* another ally too. You all know of the ill-feeling between the United States and Japan. At any moment we may hear that the great Republic has declared war." He called for cheers, and the Ringstrasse echoed with *Hoch! Hoch! Hoch!* for the United States of America.

That was my introduction to European opinion of my country during the war. During my four weeks in the Austro-Serbian zone of hostilities, I had heard no mention of anything but the purely military business at hand.

The following evening from the window of an "American-Tourist-Special Train" I looked down on the happy Austrians who jammed the platform, determined to give the Americans a grand send-off, which they did with flag-waving and cheers. A stranger on the platform thrust a lengthy typewritten document into my hands, with the urgent request that I should give it to the Press in New York. It was a stirring appeal to Americans to "witness the righteousness of the cause of the Central Powers in this war which had been forced upon them." Three prominent citizens of Vienna had signed it, one of whom was the famous Doctor Lorenz.

Berlin, in an ecstasy of joyful anticipation of the rapid and triumphal entrance into Paris, was a repetition of Vienna. True, in the beginning, Americans, mistaken for Englishmen by some of the undiscerning, had been roughly treated, but a hint from those in high authority changed that. In like manner, well-meaning patriots who persisted in indiscriminately mobbing all members of the yellow race were urged to differentiate between Chinese and Japanese.

So I found festive Berlin patting Americans on the back, cheering Americans in German-American meetings, and prettily intertwining the Stars and Stripes and the German flag.

"Now is your opportunity to take Canada," said the man in the street. In fact, it was utterly incomprehensible to the average German that we should not indulge in some neighbouring land-grabbing while Britain was so busy with affairs in Europe.

The German Foreign Office was, of course, under no such delusion, although it had cherished the equally absurd belief that England's colonies would rebel at the first opportunity. The Wilhelmstrasse was, however, hard at work taking the propaganda which it had so successfully crammed down the throats of the German citizen and translating it into English to be crammed down the throats of the people in America. This was simply one of the Wilhelmstrasse's numerous mistakes in the psychological analysis of other people. But the Wilhelmstrasse possesses the two estimable qualities of perseverance and willingness to learn, with the result that its recent propaganda in the United States has been much more subtle and very much more effective.

The American newspapers which reached Germany after the outbreak of war gave that country its first intimation that her rush through Belgium was decidedly unpopular on the other side of the Atlantic. Furthermore, many American newspapers depicted the Kaiser and the Crown Prince in a light quite new to German readers, who with their heads full of Divine Right ideas considered the slightest caricature of their imperial family as brutally sacrilegious.

But the vast majority of Germans never saw an American newspaper. How is it, then, that they began to hate the United States so intensely? The answer is simple. In the early winter of 1914-15, the German Government with its centralised control of public opinion turned on the current of hatred against everything American as it had already done against everything British, for the war had come to a temporary stalemate on both fronts, and the Wilhelmstrasse had to excuse their failure to win the short, sharp pleasant war into which the people had jumped with anticipation of easy victory. "If it were not for American ammunition the war would have been finished long ago!" became the key-note of the new gospel of hate, a gospel which has been preached down to the present.

Just before I left Germany the "Reklam Book Company" of Leipzig issued an anti-American circular which flooded the country. The request that people

should enclose it in all their private letters was slavishly followed with the same zest with which the Germans had previously attached *Gott strafe England*
stickers to their correspondence.

The circular represented a 7000-ton steamer ready
to take on board the cargo of ammunition which was
arranged neatly on the pier in the foreground. The
background was occupied by German troops, black lines
dividing them into three parts, tagged respectively—
30,000 *killed,* 40,000 *slightly wounded,* 40,000 *seriously wounded.* This, then, is the graphic illustration
of the casualties inflicted upon the German Army by a
single cargo of one moderate-sized liner.

Since at such a rate, it would take less than two hundred cargoes of this astoundingly effective ammunition
to put the entire German Army out of action, one wonders why Britain troubles herself to convert her industries.

Ere the first winter of war drew to a close the official
manipulators of the public opinion battery had successfully electrified the nation into a hate against the United
States second only to that bestowed on Great Britain.
And so it came about that the Government had the solid
support of the people when the original submarine manifesto of February 4th, 1915, warning neutral vessels
to keep out of the war zone, threatened a rupture with
the United States. When two weeks later Washington
sent a sharp note of protest to Berlin, the Germans became choleric every time they spoke of America or met
an American.

"Why should we let America interfere with our plan
to starve England?" was the question I heard repeat-

edly. Their belief that they could starve England was absolute. What could be simpler than putting a ring of U-boats round the British Isles and cutting off all trade until the pangs of hunger should compel Britain to yield? I heard no talk then about the "base crime of starving women and children," which became their whine a year later when the knife began to cut the other way.

In 1915 it was immaterial to the mass of Germans whether America joined their enemies or not. Their training had led them to think in army corps, and they frankly and sneeringly asked us, "What could you do?" They were still in the stage where they freely applied to enemies and possible enemies the expression, "They are afraid of us." "The more enemies, the more glory," was the inane motto so popular early in the war that it was even printed on post cards.

The *Gulflight,* flying the Stars and Stripes, was torpedoed in the reign of submarine anarchy immediately inaugurated. But two can play most games, and when the British Navy made it increasingly difficult for U-boats to operate in the waters near the British Isles, the German Foreign Office and the German Admiralty began to entertain divergent opinions concerning the advisability of pushing the submarine campaign to a point which would drag the United States into the war.

Only a few people in Germany know that von Bethmann-Hollweg strenuously opposed the plan to sink the *Lusitania.* That is, he opposed it up to a point. The advertisement from the German Embassy at Washington which appeared in American newspapers warning Americans could not have appeared without his sanction. In the last days of July, 1914, backed by the Kaiser, he had opposed the mobilisation order sufficient to cause a three days' delay—which his military opponents in German politics claim was the chief cause of the failure to take Paris—but in the case of the *Lusitania* he was even more powerless against rampant militarism.

For nearly a year after the colossal blunder of the *Lusitania* there existed in the deep undercurrents of German politics a most remarkable whirlpool of discord, in which the policy of von Tirpitz was a severe tax on the patience of von Bethmann-Hollweg and the Foreign Office, for it was they who had to invent all sorts of plausible excuses to placate various neutral Powers.

The Kaiser after disastrously meddling with the General Staff during the first month of the war, subsequently took no active hand in military, naval and political policies unless conflicts between his chosen chieftains forced him to do so.

One striking instance of this occurred when the Wilhelmstrasse discovered that Washington was in possession of information in the *"Arabic* incident" which made the official excuses palpably too thin. After the German authorities became convinced that their failure to guarantee that unresisting merchantmen would not be sunk until passengers and crew were removed to a place of safety would cause a break with the United States, Tirpitz asserted that the disadvantages to Germany from America as an enemy would be slight in comparison with the advantages from the relentless submarining which in his opinion would defeat Britain.

He therefore advocated that no concessions be made to Washington. Von Bethmann-Hollweg was of the opposite opinion. A deadlock resulted, which was broken when the Kaiser summoned both men to separate and secret conferences. He decided in favour of the Chancellor, whereupon Washington received the famous "*Arabic* Guarantees." It is highly significant that these were never made known to the German people.

Then followed six months of "frightfulness," broken pledges, notes, crises, semi-crises, and finally the great crisis *de luxe* in the case of the *Sussex*. When, a few days after my return to England from Germany, I used the expression "*Sussex* Crisis" to a leading Englishman, he expressed surprise at the term "crisis." "We did not get the impression in England that the affair was a real crisis," he said.

My experiences in Germany during the last week in April and the first four days in May, 1916, left no doubt in my mind that I was living through a crisis, the outcome of which would have a tremendous effect upon the subsequent course of the war. Previous dealings with Washington had convinced the German Government as well as the German people that the American Government would stand for anything. Thus the extraordinary explanation of the German Foreign Office that the *Sussex* was not torpedoed by a German submarine, since the only U-boat commander who had fired a torpedo in the channel waters on the fateful day had made a sketch of the vessel which he had attacked, which, according to the sketch, was not the *Sussex*.

The German people were so supremely satisfied with this explanation that they displayed chagrin which quickly changed to ugliness when the German Press was allowed to print enough of the news from Washington to prepare the public mind for something sharp from across the Atlantic. I have seen Berlin joyful, serious, and sad during the war; I have seen it on many memorable days; but never have I seen it exactly as on Saturday, April 22nd, the day when the *Sussex* Ultimatum was made known through the Press. The news was headlined in the afternoon editions. The eager crowds snapped them up, stood still in their tracks, and then one and all expressed their amazement to anybody near them. "President Wilson began by shaking his fist at Germany, and ended by shaking his finger," was the way one of the President's political opponents summarised his Notes. That was the opinion in Germany. And now he had "pulled a gun." The Germans could not understand it. When they encountered any of the few Americans left in their country they either foamed in rage at them, or, in blank amazement, asked them what it was all about.

It was extremely interesting to the student of the war to see that the people really did not understand what it was all about. Theodor Wolff, the brilliant editor of the *Berliner Tageblatt,* with great daring for a German editor, raised this point in the edition in which the Ultimatum was printed. He asserted that the German people did not understand the case because they purposely had been left in the dark by the Government. He said, among other things, that his countrymen were in no position to understand the feeling of resentment in the United States, because the meagre reports permitted in the German Press never described such details as the death agonies of women and children struggling helplessly in the water.

This article in the *Tageblatt* was the striking exception to the rest of the Press comment throughout Germany, for the German Government made one of its typical moves at this point. "To climb down or not to climb down," was a question which would take several days to decide. Public opinion was already sufficiently enraged against America to give the Government united support in case of a break, but it must be made more enraged and consequently more united. Thus on Easter Sunday the full current of hate was turned on in the German Press. President Wilson was violently attacked for working in the interest of the Allies, whom he wished to save. Germany would not bow to this injustice, she would fight, and America, too, would be made to feel what it means to go to war with Germany. The German Press did its part to inflame a united German sentiment, and the Foreign Office, which believes in playing the game both ways when it is of advantage to do so, with characteristic thoroughness did not permit the American correspondents to cable to their papers the virulent lies, such as those in the *Tägliche Rundschau,* about the affair in general and President Wilson in particular. These papers were furthermore not allowed to leave Germany.

On the evening preceding the publication of the Ultimatum, Maximilian Harden's most famous number of the *Zukunft* appeared with the title "If I Were Wilson." On Saturday morning it was advertised on yellow and black posters throughout Berlin, and was quickly bought by a feverish public to whom anything pertaining to German-American relations was of the sharpest interest. The remarkable article was directly at variance with all the manufactured ideas which had been storming in German brains for more than a year. The British sea policy was represented in a light quite different from the officially incubated German conception of it. President Wilson was correctly portrayed as strictly neutral in all his official acts. This staggered Harden's readers quite as much as his attacks on the brutal submarine policy of his country.

A careless censor had allowed "If I Were Wilson," to appear. But a vigilant Government, ever watchful of the food for the minds of its children, hastened with the usual police methods to correct the mistake. The *Zukunft* was *beschlagnahmt,* which means that the police hastily gathered up all unsold copies at the publishers, kiosks, and wherever else they were to be found. If a policeman saw one in a man's pocket he took it away.

Why did the Government do everything in its power to suppress this article? The Government fully understood that there was nothing in it that was not true, nothing in it of a revolutionary character. It divulged no military or naval secrets. It was a simple statement of political truths. But the German great Idea Factory in the Wilhelmstrasse does not judge printed matter from its truth or falsity. The forming of the public mind in the mould in which it will best serve the interests of the State is the sole consideration. While the Directors of Thought were deliberating on the relative disadvantages of a curtailment of submarine activity and America as an enemy, and the order of the day was to instill hatred, no matter how, they decided that it would be inadvisable for the people to read the true statements of Harden.

One American correspondent began to cable five thousand words of "If I Were Wilson" to his paper. The Censor stopped him after he had sent thirteen hundred. A rival correspondent, when he glanced at the article immediately after it had appeared, decided that it was more suitable for mail matter than cable matter, put it in an envelope, and actually scored a scoop over all opponents.

During the following days, when the leaders of Germany were in conference at the Headquarters of the General Staff, I travelled as much as possible to find out German sentiment. The people were intoxicated with the successes against Verdun, and were angrily in favour of a break. One German editor said to me, "The Government has educated them to believe that the U-boat can win the war. Their belief is so firm that it will be difficult for the authorities to explain a back-down to Wilson."

It was not. The Government can explain anything to the German people. The back-down came, causing sentiments which can be divided into three groups. One, "We were very good to give in to America. England would not be so good." Two, "Americans put us in a bad position. To curtail our submarine weapon means a lengthening of the war. On the other hand, to add America to the list of our enemies would lengthen the war still more." Three, "We shall wait our opportunity and pay back America for what she has done to us." I heard the latter expression everywhere, particularly among the upper classes. It was the expression of Doctor Drechsler, head of the Amerika-Institut in Berlin, and one of the powerful propaganda triumvirate composed of himself, Doctor Bertling, and the late Professor Münsterberg.

With the increasing deterioration inside the German Empire the resolve of the Chancellor to avoid a clash with the United States strengthened daily. His opponents, however, most of the great Agrarians and National Liberals, the men behind Tirpitz, continue to work for a new submarine campaign in which all neutrals will be warned that their vessels will be sunk without notice if bound to or from the ports of Germany's enemies. They are practical men, who believe that only through the unrestricted use of the submarine can Britain, whom they call the keystone of the opposition, be beaten. The Chancellor is also a practical man, who believes that the entrance of America on the side of the Entente would seal the fate of Germany. He is supported by Herr Helfferich, the Vice-Chancellor, and Herr Zimmermann, the Foreign Secretary, men with a deep insight into the questions of trade and treaties. They believe that peace will be made across the table and not at the point of the sword, and they realise that it is much better for Germany not to have the United States at the table as an enemy.

In September, 1916, the Chancellor began to lay the wires for a new campaign, a campaign to enlist the services of Uncle Sam in a move for peace. It is significant, however, that he and his Government continue to play the game both ways. While Germany presses her official friendship on the United States, and conducts propaganda there to bring the two nations closer together, she at the same time keeps up the propaganda of hate at home against America, in order to have the support of the people in case of emergency.

The attacks against Washington in the *Continental Times* show which way the wind blows, for this paper is subsidised by the German Foreign Office through the simple device of buying 30,000 copies of each issue—it appears three times weekly—at $2\frac{1}{2}d.$ per copy. The editors are Aubrey Stanhope, an Englishman who even before the war could not return to his native country for reasons of his own, and R. L. Orchelle, whose real name is Hermann Scheffauer, who claims to be an American, but is not known as such at the American Embassy in Berlin. He has specialised in attacks against Great Britain in the United States. Some of the vicious onslaughts against Washington in Germany were made by him.

American flags are scarce in Berlin to-day, but one always waves from the window of 48, Potsdamerstrasse. It is a snare for the unwary, but the League uses it here as in countless other instances as a cloak for its warfare against the U.S.A.

The League started early in the war by issuing booklets by the ton for distribution in Germany and America. Subscription blanks were scattered broadcast for contributions for the cause of light and truth. Donations soon poured in, some of them very large, from Germans and German-Americans who wished, many of them sincerely, to have what they considered the truth told about Germany.

The ways of the League, however, being crooked, some of the charter members began to fall away from one another and many of the doings of the ringleaders are now coming to light.

The League must be doing well financially, as William Martin, the chief of the Potsdamerstrasse office, jubilantly declared that no matter how the war ended he would come out of it with a million.

Any real American, whether at home or abroad, deeply resents the degradation of his flag. Yet the League of Truth in Berlin has consistently dragged the Stars and Stripes in the mire, and that in a country which boasts that the police are not only omniscient but omnipotent.

A constant attempt, in accordance with the policy of most German newspapers, I may add, is made to depict us as a spineless jelly-fish nation. They have regarded principles of international custom as little as the manipulators of submarines under the reign of Tirpitz.

Last fourth of July, Charles Mueller, a pseudo-American, hung from his home in the busy Kurfürstendamm a huge American flag with a deep border of black that Berlin might see a "real American's" symbol of humiliation. On the same day, dear to the hearts of Americans, a four-page flyer was spread broadcast through the German capital with a black border on the front page enclosing a black cross. The Declaration of Independence was bordered with black inside and an ode to American degradation by John L. Stoddard completed the slap in the face.

The League selected January 27th, 1916, the Kaiser's birthday, as a suitable occasion for Mueller and Marten, not even hyphenates, solemnly and in the presence of a great crowd to place an immense wreath at the base of the statue of Frederick the Great on the Linden, with the inscription "Wilson and his Press are not America."

The stern Police Department of Berlin does not permit the promiscuous scattering of floral decorations and advertising matter on the statues of German gods, and the fact that the wreath remained there month after month proved that somebody high up was sanctioning the methods of the League.

The protests of the American Ambassador were of no avail, until he determined to make an end of the humiliation, after three months, by threatening to go down to this busy section of Berlin, near the Royal Palace, and remove the wreath himself. Force is the only argument which impresses the Prussians, and we are extremely fortunate that our Ambassador to Germany is a man of force.

The League, however, had printed a picture of the wreath in its issue of *Light and Truth,* which it endeavours to circulate everywhere.

Stoddard, mentioned above, is the famous lecturer. He has written booklets for the League, one of which I read in America. His last pamphlet, however, is a most scurrilous attack against his country. He raves against America, and, after throwing the facts of international law to the winds, he shrieks for the impeachment of Wilson to stop this slaughter for which he has sold himself.

It is no secret in Berlin that the League have systematically hounded Mr. Gerard. I do not know why they hate him, unless it is because he is a member of the American Government. I have heard it said that one way to get at Wilson was through his Ambassador.

Their threats and abuse became so great that he and one of the American newspaper correspondents went to 48, Potsdamerstrasse during the *Sussex* crisis to warn the leaders. They answered by swearing out a warrant against Mr. Gerard with the Berlin police—paying no heed to international customs in such matters—and circulating copies of the charge broadcast.

Readers who are familiar with Germany know that if a man does not instantly defend himself against *Beleidigung* society judges him guilty. Thus this and countless other printed circulations of falsehood against Mr. Gerard have cruelly hurt him throughout Germany, as I know from personal investigation. Next to Mr. Wilson and a few men in England he is the most hated man among the German people. He finally felt obliged to deny in the German Press some of the absurd stories circulated about him, such as that of Mrs. Gerard putting a German decoration he received on her dog.

Mueller, however, was not content with mere printed attacks, but has made threats against the life of the American Ambassador. A prominent American has sworn an affidavit to this effect, but Mueller still pursues his easy way. On the night that the farewell dinner was being given to a departing secretary at our Embassay, Mueller and a German officer went about Berlin seeking Mr. Gerard for the professed purpose of picking a fight with him. They went to Richards' Restaurant, where the dinner was being given, but fortunately missed the Ambassador.

The trickery of the League would fill a volume, for Marten especially is particularly clever. He leapt into fame in Berlin by going to Belgium "at his own risk," as he says, to refute the charges of German cruelty there. His book on Belgium, and a later one claiming to refute the Bryce report, are unimpressive since they fail to introduce facts, and the writer contents himself for the main part with soliloquies on Belgian battle-fields, in which he attacks Russian aggression and Britain's perfidy in entering the war. The Belgians, we gather, are more or less delighted with the change from Albert to Wilhelm.

Marten prints testimonials of the book from leading Germans, most of whom, such as General Falkenhayn, content themselves with acknowledgment of receipt with thanks and statement of having read the work. Count Zeppelin goes further, and hopes that the volume will find a wide circulation, particularly in neutral countries.

And now for the vice-president of this anti-American organisation. He is St. John Gaffney, former American Consul-General to Munich. He belongs to the modern martyr series of the German of to-day. All over Germany I was told that he was dismissed by Mr. Wilson because he sympathised with Germany. The Germans as a mass know nothing further, but I can state from unimpeachable authority that he used rooms of the American Hospital in Munich, while a member of the board of that hospital and an officer in the consular service of the United States, for propaganda purposes. His presence became so objectionable to the heads of the hospital, excellent people whose sole aim is to aid suffering humanity, that he was ousted.

He returned from his American trip after his dismissal last year and gave a widely quoted interview upon arrival in Germany which sought to discredit America—through hitting Mr. Wilson and the Press—in the most tense point of our last altercation in February with Germany over the *Lusitania*. Such men as Gaffney are greatly to blame for many German delusions.

Mr. Gerard is not the only official whose path has not been strewn with roses in Germany. Our military attaché has not been permitted to go to the German front for nearly a year, and the snub is apparent in the newspaper and Government circles of Berlin. He is probably the only one left behind.

The big Press does not use League of Truth material and certain other anti-American copy which would be bad for Germany, to reach foreign critics' attacks. Many provincial papers, however, furiously protested against the recent trip of the American military attaché through industrial Germany. It was only the American, not other foreign attachés, to whom they objected.

All this is useful to the German Government, for it keeps the populace in the right frame of mind for two purposes. In the first place, a hatred of America inspired by the belief that she is really an enemy, gives the German Government greater power over the people. Secondly, should the Wilhelmstrasse decide to play the relentless submarine warfare as its last hand it will have practically united support.

CHAPTER XII

THERE is only one way to realise the distress in Germany, and that is to go there and travel as widely as possible—preferably on foot. The truth about the food situation and the growing discontent cannot be told by the neutral correspondent *in* Germany. It must be memorised and carried across the frontier in the brain, for the searching process extends to the very skin of the traveller. If he has an umbrella or a stick it is likely to be broken for examination. The heels are taken from his boots lest they may conceal writings. This does not happen in every case, but it takes place frequently. Many travellers are in addition given an acid bath to develop any possible writing in invisible ink.

In Germany, as it is no longer possible to conceal the actual state of affairs from any but highly placed and carefully attended neutrals travelling therein, the utmost pains are being taken to mislead the outside world. The foreign correspondents are not allowed to send anything the Government does not wish to get out. They are, moreover, regularly dosed with propaganda distributed by the *Nachrichtendienst* (Publicity Service of the Foreign Office).

One of the books handed round to the neutrals when I was in Berlin was a treatise on the German industrial and economic situation by Professor Cassell, of the University of Upsala, Sweden.

He came upon the invitation of the German authorities for a three weeks' study of conditions. In his preface he artlessly mentions that he was enabled to accomplish so much in three weeks owing to the praiseworthy way in which everything was arranged for him. He compiled his work from information discreetly imparted at interviews with officials, from printed statistics, and from observations made on carefully shepherded expeditions. Neutral correspondents are expected to use this sort of thing, which is turned out by the hundredweight, as the basis of their communications to their newspapers. We were supplied with a similar volume on the "Great German naval victory of Jutland."

One feels in Germany that the great drama of the war is the drama of the food supply—the struggle of a whole nation to prevent itself being exhausted through hunger and shortage of raw materials.

After six months of war the bread ticket was introduced, which guaranteed thirty-eight ordinary sized rolls or equivalent each week to everybody throughout the Empire. In the autumn of 1915 Tuesday and Friday became meatless days. The butter lines had become an institution towards the close of the year. There was little discomfort, however.

For seventeen months Germany laughed at the attempt to starve her out. Then, early in 1916 came a change. An economic decline was noticeable, a decline which was rapid and continuous during each succeeding month. Pork disappeared from the menu, beef became scarcer and scarcer, but veal was plentiful until April. In March sugar could be obtained in only small quantities, six months later the unnutritious saccharine had almost completely replaced it. Fish continued in abundance, but became increasingly expensive. A shortage in meat caused a run on eggs. In September egg cards limited each person to two eggs per week, in December the maximum became one egg in two weeks. Vegetables, particularly cabbage and turnips, were plentiful enough to be of great help.

In Berlin the meat shortage became ,so acute in April, 1916, that for five days in the week preceding Easter most butchers' shops did not open their doors. This made it imperative that the city should extend the ticket rationing system to meat. The police issued cards to the residents of their districts, permitting them to purchase one-half pound of meat per week from a butcher to whom they were arbitrarily assigned in order to facilitate distribution. The butchers buy through the municipal authorities, who contract for the entire supply of the city. The tickets are in strips, each of which represents a week, and each strip is subdivided into five sections for the convenience of diners in restaurants.

Since the supply in each butcher's shop was seldom sufficient to let everybody be served in one day, the custom of posting in the windows or advertising in the local papers "Thursday, Nos. 1-500," and later, Saturday, Nos. 501-1000," was introduced. A few butchers went still further and announced at what hours certain numbers could be served, thus doing away with the long *queues.*

Most of the competent authorities with whom I discussed the matter agreed that the great flaw in the meat regulations was that, unlike those of bread, they were only local and thus there were great differences and correspondinng discontent all over Germany.

One factor which contributed to Germany's shortage of meat was the indiscriminate killing of the live-stock, especially pigs, when the price of fodder first rose in the last months of 1914. Most of this excess killing was done by the small owners. Our plates were heaped unnecessarily. Some of the dressing was done so hurriedly and carelessly that there were numerous cases of pork becoming so full of worms that it had to be destroyed.

The great agrarian junkers were not forced by lack of fodder to kill; consequently they own a still larger proportion of the live-stock than they did at the beginning of the war.

On October 1st, 1916, the regulation of meat was taken out of the hands of the local authorities so far as their power to regulate the amount for each person was concerned, and this amount was made practically the same throughout Germany.

First and foremost in the welfare of the people, whatever may be said by the vegetarians, is the vital question of the meat supply. Involved in the question of cattle is milk, leather, other products, and of course, meat itself.

One German statistician told me he believed that the conquest of Roumania would add between nine and ten months to Germany's capacity to hold out, during which time, no doubt, one or other of the Allies would succumb.

At the beginning of 1917 the actual number of cattle in Germany does not seem to be so greatly depreciated as one would expect. After a very thorough investigation I am convinced that there are in Germany to-day from three-fourths to four-fifths as many head of cattle as there were before the war.

In the spring and summer these cattle did very well, but with the passing of the grazing season new difficulties are arising. Cattle must be fed, and unless sufficient grain comes from Roumania to supply the bread for the people and the fodder for the cattle it is obvious that there must be a wholesale slaughtering, and consequent reduction of milk, butter, and cheese.

All these details may seem tiresome, but they directly concern the length of the war.

To add to the shortage, the present stock of cattle in Germany was, when I left, being largely drawn upon for the supply of the German armies in the occupied parts of France, Belgium, and Russia, and the winter prospect for Germany, therefore, is one of obviously increased privation, provided always that the blockade is drastic.

Cattle are, of course, not the only food supply. There is game. Venison is a much commoner food in Germany than in England, especially now there is much of it left. Hares, rabbits, partridges are in some parts of Germany much more numerous even than in England. A friend of mine recently arrived from Hungary told me that he had been present at a shoot over driven partridges at which, on three successive days, over 400 brace fell to the guns. Wherever I went in Germany, however, game was being netted.

Before the war, pork, ham, and bacon were the most popular German food, but owing to the mistake of killing pigs in what I heard called the "pork panic" the Germans are to-day facing a remarkable shortage of their favourite meat. I am convinced that they began 1917 with less than one-fourth as many pigs as they had before the war.

The Berlin stockyards slaughtered over 25,000 pigs weekly before August, 1914. During the first 10 months of the war the figure actually rose to 50,000 pigs per week in that one city alone. In one week in September last the figure had fallen to 350 pigs!

The great slaughter early in the war gave a false optimism not only to Germans, but also to visitors. If you have the curiosity to look back at newspapers of that time you will find that the great plenty of pork was dilated upon by travelling neutrals.

To-day the most tremendous efforts are being made to increase the number of pigs. You will not find much about this in the German newspapers—in fact what the German newspapers do not print is often more important than what they do print. In the rural districts you can learn much more of Germany's food secrets than in the newspapers.

In one small village which I went to I counted no fewer than thirty public notices on various topics. Here is one:—

FATTEN PIGS.

Fat is an essential for soldiers and hard workers.
Not to keep and fatten pigs

if you are able to do
so is treason to the
Fatherland.
No pen empty—every pen full.

These food notices may be necessary, but they are
bringing about intense class hatred in Germany. They
are directed at the small farmer, who in many cases has
killed all his pigs and most of his cows, because of his
difficulty in getting fodder. As I have said, the great
agrarian junkers, the wealthy landowners of Prussia,
have in many cases more cows, more pigs, more poultry
than before the war.

The facts of these great disparities of life are well
known, and if there were more individuality in the
German character they would lead to something more
serious than the very tame riots, at several of which I
have been present.

That the food question is the dominating topic in
Germany among all except the very rich, and that this
winter will add to the intensity of the conversations on
the subject, is not difficult to understand. Most of the
shopping of the world is done by women, and the German woman of the middle class, whose maidservant
has gone off to a munition factory, has to spend at least
half her day waiting in a long line for potatoes, butter,
or meat.

There is a curious belief in England and in the
United States in the perfection of German organisation.
My experience of their organisation is that it is absolutely marvellous—when there are no unexpected difficulties in the way. When the Germans first put the
nation on rations as to certain commodities, the outside

world said, "Ah, they are beginning to starve!" or "What wonderful organisers!"

As a matter of fact, they were not beginning to starve, and they were not wonderful organisers. The rationing was done about as badly as it could be done. It was arranged in such a fashion as to produce plenty in some places and dearth in others. It was done so that wealthy men made fortunes and poor men were made still poorer. The inordinate greed and lack of real patriotism on the part of influential parties in both Germany and Austria-Hungary have added to the bad state of affairs. As if to make matters worse, the whole vast machine of rationing by ticket was based on the expectation of a comparatively quick and decisive victory for Germany. This led to reckless consumption and a great rise in prices. The fight that is now going on between the masses in the towns and the wealthy land-owning farmers has been denounced in public by food dictator Batocki (pronounced Batoski), who, in words almost of despair, complained of the selfish landed proprietor, who would only disgorge to the suffering millions in the great manufacturing centres at a price greatly exceeding that fixed by the food authorities.

All manner of earnest public men are endeavouring to cope with the coming distress, and at this point I can do no better than quote from an interview given me by Dr. Südekum, Social Democratic member of the Reichstag for Nuremberg, Bavaria. He is a sincere patriot, and a prominent worker in food organisation.

"More than a year ago," he explained, "I worked out a plan for the distribution of food, which provided for uniform food-cards throughout the entire empire.

For example, everyone, whether he lived in a Bavarian village or in a Prussian city, would receive, say, half a pound of meat a week. I presented my plan to the Government, with whose approval it met. Nevertheless, they did not see fit to adopt it for three reasons. In the first place because they believed that the people might become unnecessarily alarmed. Secondly, because our enemies might make capital out of such measures. *Thirdly, because our leaders at that time believed that the war might be over before the end of 1915.*

"But the war dragged on, and we were somewhat extravagant with our supplies—I except bread, for which we introduced cards in February, 1915—and instead of the whole Empire husbanding the distribution of meat, for example, various sections here and there introduced purely local measures, with the inevitable resulting confusion.

"Hunger has been a cause of revolution in the past," Dr. Südekum continued thoughtfully. "We should take lessons from history, and do everything in our power to provide for the poor. I have worked hard in the development of the 'People's Kitchens' in Berlin. We started in the suburbs early in 1916, in some great central kitchens in which we cook a nourishing meat and vegetable stew. From these kitchens distributing vehicles—*Gulasch-kanonen* (stew cannons) as they are jocularly called—are sent through the city, and from them one may purchase enough for a meal at less than the cost of production. We have added a new central kitchen each week until we now have 30, each of which supplies 10,000 people a day with a meal, or, more correctly, a meal and a half. In July, however, the work assumed greater proportions, for the municipal authorities also created great central kitchens. Most of the dinners are taken to the homes and eaten there.

"The People's Kitchen idea is now spreading throughout Germany. But I believe in going further. I believe in putting *every German*—I make no exception—upon rations. That is what is done *in a besieged city,* and our position is sufficiently analogous to a besieged city to warrant the same measures. All our food would then be available for equal distribution, and each person would get his allowance."

This earnest Social Democrat's idea is, of course, perfect in theory. Even the able, hard-working Batocki, however, cannot make it practicable. Why not? *The Agrarian, the great Junker of Prussia,* not only will not make sacrifices, but stubbornly insists upon wringing every pfennig of misery money from the nation which has boasted to the world that its patriotism was unselfish and unrivalled.

The most important German crop of all at this juncture is potatoes, for potatoes are an integral part of German and Austrian bread. The handling of the crop, to which all Germany was looking forward so eagerly, exhibits in its most naked form the horrid profiteering to which the German poor are being subjected by the German rich.

It was a wet summer in Germany. Wherever I went in my rural excursions I heard that the potatoes were poor. The people in the towns knew little of this, and were told that the harvests were good.

An abominable deception was practised upon the public with the first potato supply. For many months tickets had been in use for this food, which is called the "German staff of life." Suddenly official notices appeared that potatoes could be had for a few days *without tickets,* and the unsuspecting public at once ordered great quantities.

The Agrarians thus got rid of all their bad potatoes to the mass of the people. In many cases they were rotting so fast that the purchaser had to bury them. It was found that they produced illness when given to swine.

What other people in the world than the Germans would stand that? But they did stand it. "These are only the early potattoes—the main crop will be all right," said the profiteers right and left, and gradually the masses began to echo them, as is usual in Germany.

Well, the main crop has been gathered, and Food Dictator von Batocki is, according to the latest reports I hear from Germany, unable to make the Agrarians put their potatoes upon the market even at the maximum price set by the Food Commission.

They are holding back their supplies until they have forced up the maximum price, just as a year ago many of them allowed their potatoes to rot rather than sell them to the millions in the cities at the price set by law.

Some Germans, mostly Social Democratic leaders, declare that since their country is in a state of siege, the Government should, beyond question, commandeer the supplies and distribute them, but just as the industrial classes have, until quite recently, resisted war taxes, so do the Prussian Junkers, by reason of their power in the Reichstag, snap their fingers at any suggested fair laws for food distribution.

The Burgomaster—usually a powerful person in Germany—is helpless. When on September 1 the great house-to-house inventory of food supplies was taken, burgomasters of the various sections of Greater Berlin took orders from the people for the whole winter supply of potatoes on special forms delivered at every house. Up to the time I left, the burgomasters were unable to deliver the potatoes.

Any dupes of German propaganda who imagine that there is much self-sacrifice among the wealthy class in Germany in this war should disabuse their minds of that theory at once. While the poor are being deprived of what they have, the purchases of pearls, diamonds, and other gems by the profiteers are on a scale never before known in Germany.

One of the paradoxes of the situation, both in Austria and in Germany, is the coincidence of the great gold hunt, which is clearing out the trinkets of the humblest, with the roaring trade in jewelry in Berlin and Vienna. As an instance I can vouch for the veracity of the following story:—

A Berlin woman went to Werner's, the well-known jewellers in the Unter den Linden, and asked to be shown some pearl necklaces. After very little examination she selected one that cost 40,000 marks (£2,000). The manager, who knew the purchaser as a regular customer for small articles of jewelry, ventured to express his surprise, remarking, "I well remember, madam, that you have been coming here for many years, and that you have never bought anything exceeding in value 100 marks. Naturally I am somewhat

surprised at the purchase of this necklace." "Oh, it
it very simple," she replied. "My husband is in the
leather business, and our war profits have made us rich
beyond our fondest hopes."

Throughout Austria and Germany in every village
and townlet are appearing notices to bring in gold.
The following notice is to be met with in all parts of
Germany:—

Let Every One Worthy of the Name of German do his Duty now.

Our enemies, after realising that they cannot defeat us on the field of battle, are striving to defeat
us economically. But here they will also fail.

Out with your Gold.

Out with your gold! What is the value of a trinket
to the life of the dear one that gave it? By giving
now you may save the life of a husband, brother, or
son.

Bring your gold to the places designated below.

If the value of the gold you bring exceeds five
marks, you will receive an iron memento of "Die
grosse Zeit."

Iron chains will be given for gold chains.

*Wedding rings of those still living will not be ac-
cepted.*

From rural pulpits is preached the wickedness of
retaining gold which might purchase food for the man
in the trenches.

The precedent of the historic great ladies of Prussia
who exchanged their golden wedding rings for rings
of iron is drummed into the smaller folk continuously.
The example is being followed by the exchange of gold
trinkets for trinkets made of iron, with the addition of

the price paid at the central collecting station—paid, of course, in paper, which is at a 30 per cent. discount in Germany and 47 per cent. discount in Austria. Every bringer of a trinket worth more than 5s. receives a small iron token of *"die grosse Zeit"* (the great epoch).

The gold hunt has revealed unexpected possessions in the hands of the German and Austrian lower classes. To me it was pathetic to see an old woman tremblingly handing over treasures that had come down probably for two or three generations—treasures that had never been worn except on high days and festivals, weddings, and perhaps on the day of the local fair. Particularly sad is this self-sacrifice in view of the gigantic profits of the food usurers and war profiteers. The matter is no secret in Germany or Austria. It is denounced by the small Socialist minority in the Reichstag, to whose impotence I have often referred. It is stoutly defended in good Prussian fashion by those openly making the profits.

There has arisen a one-sided Socialism which no one but Bismarck's famous "nation of lackeys" would tolerate. At the top is a narrow circle of agrarian and industrial profiteers, often belonging to the aristocratic classes. At the other end of the scale is, for example, the small farmer, who has now absolutely nothing to say concerning either the planting, the marketing, or the selling of his crops. Regulations are laid down as to what he should sow, where he should sell, and the price at which he should sell. Unlike the Junker, he has not a long purse. He *must sell*.

What state of mind does this produce among the people? I know that outside Germany there is an idea that every German is working at top speed with the spirit of the Fatherland flaming him on. That was the spirit I witnessed in the early days of the war, when Germany was winning and food was plentiful.

In certain rural districts as well as in centres of population there is an intense longing for peace—not merely for a German peace—but any peace, and a peace not merely for military reasons, but arising out of utter weariness of the rule of the profiteers and the casualties not revealed by the doctored lists—ingeniously issued lists, which, for example, have never revealed the loss of a submarine crew, though intelligent Hamburg shipping people, who are in close touch with German naval people, estimate the loss of German submarines as at least one hundred. I have heard the figure put higher, and also lower.

This kind of one-sided Socialism makes the people so apathetic that in some parts of Germany it has been very difficult to induce them to harvest their own crops, and in German Poland they have been forced to garner the fields at the point of the bayonet.

When a man has no interest in the planting, marketing, and selling price of his produce; when he knows that what he grows may be swept away from his district without being sure that it will be of any benfit to himself and his family; when, in addition, the father or sons of the households lie buried by the Yser, the Somme, the Meuse or the Drina, it is impossible for the authorities to inspire any enthusiasm for life, let alone war, even among so docile a people as those they deal with.

*   *   *   *   *   *   *

With regard to the other crops, rye is good; beets look good, but are believed to be deficient in sugar owing to the absence of South American fertilisers; wheat is fairly good; oats extremely good, and barley also excellent. The Germans have boasted to the neutral visitor that their artificial nitrates are just as good fertilisers as those imported from South America. It is true that they do very well for most crops when the weather is damp. But beets, strangely enough, require the genuine Chilean saltpetre to produce their maximum of sugar. The failure to get this, plus the use of sugar in munition making, accounts for the dearth of that commodity among the civilian population.

In order that nothing shall be wasted, the Government decreed this year that the public should be allowed to scavenge the fields after the harvest had been gathered, and this was a source of some benefit to those residing near the great centres of population.

Schoolmasters were also ordered to teach the children the need of gathering every sort of berry and nut.

Passing along an English hedgerow the other day, and seeing it still covered with withered blackberries, I compared them with the bare brambles which I saw in Germany from which all berries have gone to help the great jam-making business which is to eke out the gradually decreasing butter and margarine supply. Sickness and death have resulted from mistakes made, not only in gathering berries, but in gathering mushrooms and other fungi, which have been keenly sought.

It is safe to say that the Germans are leaving no stone unturned to avoid the starvation of the Seven Years' War. The ingenuity of the chemists in producing substitutes was never greater. One of the most disagreeable foods I have tasted was bread made of straw. Countless experiments have been made in the last year to adapt straw to the human stomach, but although something resembling bread has been produced, it contains almost no nourishment and results in illness.

People who reside in the cities and carefully shepherded visiting neutrals, who do not go into the country, have little notion of the terrific effort being put forward to make the fruits of Mother Earth defeat the blockade, and *above all* to extract any kind of *oil* from anything that grows.

Here is one notice:—

HOW THE CIVIL POPULATION CAN HELP IN THE WAR.

Our enemies are trying to exhaust us, but they
cannot succeed if every one
does his duty.
OIL *is a Necessity.*
You can help the Fatherland if you plant
poppies, castor plant, sunflowers.
In addition to doing important work for
the Fatherland you benefit yourself because the price for oil is high.

I may say that the populace have responded. Never have I seen such vast fields of poppies, sunflowers, rape plant, and other oleaginous crops. Oil has been extracted from plum-stones, cherry-stones, and walnuts.

The Government have not pleased the people even in this matter. One glorious summer day, after tramping alone the sandy roads of Southern Brandenburg, I came to a little red-brick village in the midst of its sea of waving rye and blaze of sunflowers and poppies. Taking my seat at the long table in front of the local *Gasthaus,* and ordering some imitation coffee—the only refreshment provided in the absence of a local bread ticket—I pointed out one of these notices to the only other person at the table, who was drinking some "extraordinarily weak beer," as he put it. "Have the people here planted much of these things I see on that notice?" I asked, pointing to one of the placards. "Yes," he said, "certainly. A great deal; but the Government is going to be false to us again. It will be commandeered at a price which they have already set." Then came the usual string of grumbles which one hears everywhere in the agricultural districts. I will not repeat them. They all have to do with the food shortage, profiteering, and discontent at the length of the war.

Though all Germans, with the exception of a few profiteers, are grumbling at the length of the war, it must not be supposed that they have lost hope. In fact their grumblings are punctuated frequently by very bright hopes. When Douaumont fell, food troubles were forgotten. The bells rang, the flags were unfurled, faces brightened, crowds gathered before the maps and discussed the early fall of Verdun and the collapse of France. Again I heard on every hand the echo of the boasts of the first year of the war.

The glorious manner in which France hurled back the assault was making itself felt in Germany with a consequent depression over food shortage when the greatest naval victory in history—so we gathered, at least, from the first German reports—raised the spirits and hopes of the people so high that they fully believed that the blockade had been smashed. On the third day of the celebration, Saturday, June 3rd, I rode in a tram from Wilmersdorf, a suburb of Berlin, to the heart of the city through miles of streets flaring with a solid mass of colour. From nearly every window and balcony hung pennants and flags; on every trolley pole fluttered a pennant of red, white and black. Even the ancient horse 'buses rattled through the streets with the flags of Germany and her allies on each corner of the roof. The newspapers screamed headlines of triumph, nobody could settle down to business, the faces one met were wreathed in smiles, complaining was forgotten, the assurance of final victory was in the very air.

Unter den Linden, the decorations on which were so thick that in many cases they screened the buildings from which they hung, was particularly happy. Knots of excited men stood discussing the defeat of the British Fleet. Two American friends and I went from the street of happy and confident talk into the Zollernhof Restaurant. With the din of the celebration over the "lifting of the blockade" ringing in our ears from the street, we looked on the bill of fare, and there, for the first time, we saw *Boiled Crow*.

Through the spring and early summer the people were officially buoyed up with the hope that the new harvest would make an end of their troubles. They had many reasons, it is true, to expect an improvement. The 1915 harvest in Germany had fallen below the average. Therefore, if the 1916 harvest would be better per acre, the additional supplies from the conquered regions of Russia would enable Germany to laugh at the efforts of her enemies to starve her out. Once more, however, official assurances and predictions were wrong, and the economic condition grew worse through every month of 1916.

CHAPTER XIII

A LAND OF SUBSTITUTES

T HE only food substitute which meets the casual eye of the visitor to England in war time is margarine for butter. Germany, on the contrary, is a land of substitutes.

Since the war, food exhibitions in various cities, but more especially in Berlin, have had as one of their most prominent features booths where you could sample substitutes for coffee, yeast, eggs, butter, olive oil, and the like. Undoubtedly many of these substitutes are destined to take their place in the future alongside some of the products for which they are rendering vicarious service. In fact, in a "Proclamation touching the Protection of Inventions, Designs, and Trade Marks in the Exhibition of Substitute-Materials in Berlin-Charlottenburg, 1916," it is provided that the substitutes to be exhibited shall enjoy the protection of the Law. Even before the war, substitutes like Kathreiner's malt coffee were household words, whilst the roasting of acorns for admixture with coffee was not only a usual practice on the part of some families in the lower middle class, but was so generally recognised among the humbler folk that the children of poor families were given special printed permissions by the police to gather acorns for the purpose on the sacred grass of the public parks.

To deal with meat which in other countries would

be regarded as unfit for human consumption there have
long been special appliances in regular use in peace
time. The so-called *Freibank* was a State or municipal
butcher's shop attached to the extensive municipal
abattoirs in Berlin, Munich, Cologne, and elsewhere.
Here tainted meat, or meat from animals locally
affected by disease, is specially treated by a steam process and other methods, so as to free it from all danger
to health. Meat so treated does not, of course, have the
nutritive value of ordinary fresh meat, but the Germans acted on the principle that anything was better
than nothing. Such meat was described as *bedingt
tauglich* (that is, fit for consumption under reserve).
It was sold before the war at very low rates to the poorer
population, who in times of scarcity came great distances and kept long vigils outside the *Freibank,* to be
near the head of the queue when the sale began. Thus
we see that many Germans long ago acquired the habit
of standing in line for food, which is such a characteristic of German city life to-day.

Horseflesh was consumed before the war in Germany,
as in Belgium and France. Its sale was carefully controlled by the police, and severe punishment fell upon
anyone who tried to disguise its character. An ordinary butcher might not sell it at all. He had to be
specially licensed, and to maintain a special establish-
ment or a special branch of his business for the purpose.
Thus, when wider circles of the population were driven
to resort to substitutes, there was already in existence
a State-organised system to control the output.

Since the war began, sausage has served as a German
stand-by from the time that beef and pork became diffi-

cult to obtain. In the late spring, however, the increased demand for sausage made that also more difficut to procure, and we often got a substitute full of breadcrumbs, which made the food-value of this particular *Wurst* considerably less than its size would indicate. It was frequently so soft that it was practically impossible to cut, and we had to spread it on our bread like butter.

The substitute of which the world has read the most is war bread. This differs in various localities, but it consists chiefly of a mixture of rye and potato with a little wheat flour. In Hungary, which is a great maize-growing country, maize is substituted for rye.

Imitation tea is made of plum and other leaves boiled in real tea and dried.

To turn to substitutes other than food, it will be recalled that Germany very early began to popularise the use of benzol as an alternative to petrol for motor engines. This was a natural outgrowth of her marvellously developed coal-tar industry, of which benzol is a product. Prizes for the most effective benzol-consuming engine, for benzol carburettors, etc., have been offered by various official departments in recent years, and I am told that during the war ingenious inventions for the more satisfactory employment of benzol have been adopted. Owing to the increased use of potatoes as food, the alcoholic extract from them, always a great German and Austro-Hungarian industry, has had to be restricted.

It is an ill wind that blows nobody good, as I learned from the owner of a little general shop in a Brandenburg village. He told me that about twenty-five years ago, when kerosene became widely used in the village for illuminating purposes, he was left with a tremendous supply of candles which he could never sell. The oil famine has caused the substitution of candle light for lamp light during the war, and has enabled him to sell out the whole stock at inflated prices. All oils are at a premium. The price of castor-oil has risen fivefold in Germany, chiefly owing to the fact that it is being extensively used for aeroplane and other lubrication purposes.

But it is oil from which explosives are derived that chiefly interests Germany. Almost any kind of fruit stone contains glycerine. That is why notices have been put on all trains which run through fruit districts, such as Werder, near Berlin, and Baden, advising the people to save their fruit stones and bring them to special depots for collection.

Five pounds of fat treated with caustic soda can be made to yield one pound of glycerine. This is one reason, in addition to the British blockade, which causes the great fat shortage among the civil population.

Glycerine united with ammonium nitrate is used in the manufacture of explosives. Deprived of nitrogenous material from South America, Germany has greatly developed the process for the manufacture of artificial nitrates. She spent £25,000,000 after the outbreak of war to enable her chemists and engineers to turn out a sufficient amount of nitric acid.

Toluol, a very important ingredient of explosives, is obtained from coal-tar, which Germany is naturally able to manufacture at present better than any other country in the world, since she had practically a monopoly in coal-tar products before hostilities commenced.

Evidently, however, substitutes to reinforce goods smuggled through the blockade have not sufficed to meet the chemical demands of the German Government, for great flaming placards were posted up all over the Empire announcing the commandeering of such commodities as sulphur, sulphuric acid, toluol, saltpetre, and the like.

Germany long ago claimed to have perfected woodpulp as a substitute for cotton in propulsive ammunition. She made this claim very early, however, for the (purpose of hoodwinking British blockade advocates. Her great need eventually led her to take steps to induce the United States to insist on the Entente Powers raising the blockade on cotton. She went to great trouble and expense to send samples by special means to her agents in America.

The cotton shortage began to be seriously felt early in 1916 in the manufacturing districts of Saxony, where so many operatives were suddenly thrown out of work that the Government had to set aside a special fund for their temporary relief, until they could be transferred to other war industries.

The success which Germany claimed for a cottoncloth substitute has been greatly exaggerated. When the Germans realised that Great Britain really meant business on the question of cotton they cultivated nettle and willow fibre, and made a cloth consisting for the most part of nettle or willow fibre with a small proportion of cotton or wool.

It was boasted in many quarters that the exclusion of cotton would make but little difference so far as clothing was concerned. Not only does the universal introduction of clothing tickets falsify this boast, but the cloth is found to be a mere makeshift when tested. Blouses and stockings wear out with discouraging rapidity when made of the substitute.

My personal investigations still lead me to believe in the motto of the Sunny South that: "Cotton is king."

Paper, although running short in Germany, is the substitute for cloth in many cases. Sacking, formerly used for making bags in which to ship potatoes and other vegetables, has given way to it. Paper-string is a good substitute widely used, although "no string" was the verbal substitute I often got when buying various articles, and it was necessary for me to hold the paper on to the parcel with my hands.

The craze for substitutes has spread so extensively that there have been some unpleasant results both for the purchaser and the producer, as was the case with several bakers, who were finally detected and convicted of a liberal use of sawdust in their cakes.

Germany has worked especially hard to find a substitute for indiarubber, though with only moderate success. I know that the Kaiser's Government is still sending men into contiguous neutral countries to buy up every scrap of rubber obtainable. In no other commodity has there been more relentless commandeering. When bicycle tyres were commandeered—the authorities deciding that three marks was the proper price to pay for a new pair of tyres which had cost ten—there was a great deal of complaining. Nevertheless, without an excellent reason, no German could secure the police pass necessary to allow him to ride a bicycle. Those who did obtain permission to ride to and from their work had to select the shortest route, and "joy-riding" was forbidden.

"Substitute rubber" heels for boots could be readily obtained until the late summer, but after that only with difficulty. They were practically worthless, as I know from personal experience, and were as hard as leather after one or two days' use.

Despite the rubber shortage, the Lower Saxon Rubber Company, of Hildersheim, does a thriving business in raincoats made from rubber substitutes. The factory is running almost full blast, all the work being done by women, and the finished product is a tribute to the skill of those in charge.

It is impossible to buy a real tennis ball in the German Empire to-day. A most hopeless makeshift ball has been put on the market, but after a few minutes' play it no longer keeps its shape or resiliency.

Germany has been very successful in the substitution of a sort of enamelled-iron for aluminium, brass, and copper. Some of the Rhenish-Westphalian iron industries have made enormous war profits, supplying iron chandeliers, stove doors, pots and pans, and other articles formerly made of brass to take the place of those commandeered for the purpose of supplying the Army with much-needed metals.

For copper used in electrical and other industries she claims to have devised substitutes before the war, and her experts now assert that a two-years' supply of copper and brass has been gathered from the kitchens and roofs of Germany. The copper quest has assumed such proportions that the roof of the historic, world-renowned Rathaus at Bremen has been stripped. Nearly half the church bells of Austria have found their way to the great Skoda Works.

Of course Germans never boast of the priceless ornaments they have stolen from Belgium and Northern France. They joyfully claim that every pound of copper made available at home diminishes the amount which they must import from abroad, and pay for with their cherished gold.

The authorities delight in telling the neutral visitors that they have found adequate substitutes for nickel, chromium, and vanadium for the hardening of steel. If that is really so, why does the *Deutschland's* cargo consist mainly of these three commodities?

CHAPTER XIV

THE GAGGING OF LIEBKNECHT

ALTHOUGH Bismarck gave the Germans a Constitution and a Parliament after the Franco-Prussian War as a sop for their sacrifices in that campaign, he never intended the Reichstag to be a Parliament in the sense in which the institution is understood in Great Britain.

What Bismarck gave the Germans was a debating society and a safety-valve. They needed a place to air their theories and ventilate their grievances. But the Chancellor of Iron was very careful, in drawing up the plans for the "debating society," to see that it conferred little more real power on the nation's "representatives" than is enjoyed by the stump-speakers near Marble Arch in London on Sundays.

Many people in England and the United States of America, I find, do not at all understand the meaninglessness of German Parliamentary proceedings. When they read about "stormy sittings" of the Reichstag and "bitter criticism" of the Chancellor, they judge such things as they judge similar events in the House of Commons or the American House of Representatives. Nothing could be more inaccurate. Governments do not fall in Germany in consequence of adverse Reichstag votes, as they do in England. They are not the people's Governments, but merely the Kaiser's creatures. They rise and fall by his grace alone.

Even this state of affairs needs to be qualified and explained to the citizens of free countries. The Government is not a Cabinet or a Ministry.

The *German Government is a one-man affair. It consists of the Imperial Chancellor.* He, and nobody else, is the "Government," subject only to the All-Highest will of the Emperor, whose bidding the Chancellor is required to do.

The Chancellor, in the name of the "Government," brings in Bills to be passed by the Reichstag. If the Reichstag does not like a Bill, which sometimes happens, it refuses to give it a majority. But the "Government" does not fall. It can simply, as it has done on numerous occasions, dissolve the Reichstag, order a General Election, *and keep on doing so indefinitely,* until it gets exactly the kind of "Parliament" it wants. Thus, though the Reichstag votes on financial matters, it can be made to vote as the "Government" wishes.

As I have said, the Reichstag was invented to be, and has always served the purpose hitherto of, a forum in which discontented Germany could blow off steam, but achieve little in the way of remedy or reform. *But during the war the Reichstag has even ceased to be a place where free speech is tolerated.* It has been gagged as effectually as the German Press. I was an eye-witness of one of the most drastic muzzling episodes which has occurred in the Reichstag during the war— or probably in the history of any modern Parliament— the suppression of Dr. Karl Liebknecht, member for Potsdam, during the debate on military affairs on January 17, 1916. That event will be of historic importance in establishing how public opinion in Germany during the war has been ruthlessly trampled under foot.

The Reichstag has practically nothing to do with the conduct of the war.

Up, practically, to the beginning of 1916 the sporadic Social Democratic opposition to the war, mainly by Dr. Liebknecht, was ignored by the Government. The war-machine was running so smoothly, and, from the German standpoint, so victoriously, that the Government thought it could safely let Liebknecht rant to his heart's content.

Dr. Liebknecht had long been a thorn in the War Party's side. He inherited an animosity to Prussian militarism from his late father, Dr. Wilhelm Lieb-knecht, who with August Bebel founded the modern German Social Democratic Party. Four or five years before the war Liebknecht, a lawyer by profession, campaigned so fiercely against militarism that he was sentenced to eighteen months' fortress imprisonment for "sedition." He served his sentence, and soon afterwards his political friends nominated him for the Reichstag for the Royal Division of Potsdam, of all places in the world, knowing that such a candidature would be as ironical a blow as could be dealt to the war aristocrats. He was elected by a big majority in 1912, the votes of the large working-class population of the division, including Spandau (the Prussian Woolwich), being more than enough to offset the military vote which the Kaiser's henchmen mobilised against him. Some time afterwards Liebknecht was also elected to represent a Berlin Labour constituency in the *Prussian Diet,* the Legislature which deals with the affairs in the Kingdom of Prussia, as distinct from the Reichstag (the *Imperial*

Diet), which concerns itself with Empire matters only.

Dr. Liebknecht is forty-four years old. Of medium build, he wears a shock of long, curly, upstanding hair, which rather accentuates his "agitator" type of countenance, and is a skilful and eloquent debater. A university graduate and well-read thinker and student, he turned out to be the one consistent Social Democratic politician in Germany on the question of the war. When the war began the Socialist Party was effectually and willingly tied to the Government's chariot—including, nominally, even Liebknecht. A few hours before making his notorious "Necessity-knows-no-law" speech in the Reichstag on August 4, 1914, Bethmann-Hollweg conferred with all the Parliamentary parties, and convinced them (including the Socialists) that Germany had been cruelly dragged into a war of defence. Later in the day, following other party leaders, Herr Haase, spokesman for the Socialists, got up in the House, voiced a few harmless platitudes about Socialist opposition to war on principle, and then pledged the party's 111 votes solidly to the War Credits for which the Government was asking. When the Chancellor afterwards made his celebrated speech it was cheered to the echo by the entire House, *including the Socialists*. I do not know whether Liebknecht was present, though he is almost certain to have been, but if so he made no noteworthy protest. How completely the Government befooled the Socialists about the war was proved a few days later when Dr. Franck, one of the Social Democracy's most shining lights and the man who was in line to be Bebel's successor, *volunteered* for military service. He was one of the first to fall fighting in September, somewhere in the West.

The authorities might have known that Liebknecht was a hard man to keep quiet if he ever decided to speak out. Fresh in the Government's mind was his bold exposure of the Krupp bribery scandals at the War Office (in 1913) and his disclosures about how the German munition trust for years systematically stirred up war fever abroad, in order to convince the German people of the necessity of speeding up their own huge armaments on land and sea. As soon as Liebknecht's Reichstag and Prussian Diet speeches began to show that he was tired of the muzzle, the Government called him up for military service. They stuck him into the uniform of an *Armierungssoldat* (Army Service Corps soldier). This meant that his public speeches in connection with the war had to be confined to the two Parliaments in which he held seats. Anything of an opposition character which he said or did *outside* would be "treason" or "sedition."

Liebknecht was put to work on A.S.C. jobs behind the fronts alternately in the East and West, I believe, but was given leaves of absence to attend to his Parliamentary duties from time to time. On these occasions he would appear in the Reichstag in the dull field-grey of an ordinary private—the only member so clad in a House of 397 Deputies, among whom are dozens of officers in uniform up to the rank of generals.

I was particularly fortunate to be able to secure a card of admission to the Strangers' Gallery of the Reichstag on January 17, the day set for discussion of military matters. I went to my place early—a few

minutes past the noon hour, as the Reichstag usually
convenes at 1 p.m. The floor was still quite empty,
though the galleries were filled with people anxious, like
myself, to see the show from start to finish.

The Reichstag's decorative scheme is panelled oak
and gilt-paint. The members' seating space spreads
fanlike round the floor, with individual seats and desks
exactly like those used by schoolboys, which is not an
inappropriate simile. On the extreme right are the
places of the Conservative-Junker—landowners—
Party; to their left sit, in succession, the Roman Catholic Clericals (who occupy the exact centre of the floor
and are thus known as the *Zentrum,* or Centre Party).
The "Centre" includes many priests, mostly Rhinelanders and Bavarians. Then come the National
Liberals, the violently anti-British and anti-American
Party, the Progressive People's Party, and the Social
Democrats. The latter are on the "extreme left." That
is why they are often so described in reports of Reichstag proceedings abroad. The Socialists comprise 111
out of 397 members of the House, so their segment of
the fan is the largest of all. Next in size is the Centre
Party, with eighty-five or ninety seats, the Conserva-
tives, National Liberals, and Progressives accounting
for the rest of the floor in more or less equal proportions.

The outstanding aspect of the Reichstag is the
tribune for speakers, which faces the floor and is ele-
vated above it some five or six feet. It is flanked on the
right by the Government "table," consisting of individual seats and desks for Ministers. In the centre of
the tribune the presiding officer, who is "President," not

Speaker, of the House, sits. On his left is a row of seats and desks, like the opposite Government "table," for the members of the *Federal Council*. The Federal Council, I may remind my readers, consists of the delegates of the various States of Germany. They are not elected by the people, but are appointed by the rulers of the several States. They constitute practically an Imperial Upper Chamber, and are the *real* legislative body of the Empire. Bills require the Federal Council's approval before submission to the Reichstag.

On so-called "big days" in the Reichstag a host of small fry from the Departments collects behind the Government and this dominent Federal Council. The Chancellor, whose place is at the corner of the Government "table" nearest the President, is always shepherded by his political aide-de-camp, Dr. Wahnschaffe. There is always a group of uniformed Army and Navy officers on the tribune, too, and to-day, of course, as the Army discussions were on the agenda, there was an unusually brave array of gold braid and brass buttons. Herr von Oldenburg, a prominent Junker M.P., once said if he were the Kaiser he would send a Prussian lieutenant and ten men to close up the Reichstag.

Liebknecht arrived early, a slight and unimpressive figure in somewhat worn field-grey, the German khaki. The "debate" having begun, I noticed how he listened eagerly to every word spoken, jotting down notes incessantly for the evident purpose of replying to the grandiloquent utterances about our "glorious army of *Kultur*-bearers" which were falling from the lips of "patriotic" party orators. Liebknecht had earned the displeasure of the House a few days before by asking some embarrassing questions about Turkish massacres in Armenia. He was jerred and laughed at hilariously when he went on to say that a "Black Chamber" was spying on his every movement, shadowing other members of the Reichstag, even eavesdropping on their telephone conversations and opening their private correspondence.

While a Socialist comrade, Herr Davidssohn, was speaking from the desk in the centre of the tribune, at which all members must stand when addressing the House, I now saw Liebknecht walking up the aisle leading from the Socialist seats to the President's chair as unobtrusively as possible. He was walking furtively and he cut the figure of a hunted animal which is conscious that it is surrounded by other animals anxious to pounce upon it and devour it if it dares to show itself in the open.

Liebknecht has now reached the President's side. The President, a long-whiskered septuagenarian, is popularly known as "Papa" Kaempf. I see Liebknecht whispering quietly in Kaempf's ear. He is asking for permission to speak, probably as soon as comrade Davidssohn has finished making his innocuous suggestions of minor reforms to relieve discomforts in the trenches. Kaempf is shaking his head negatively. As the official executor of the House's wishes, the old man understands perfectly well that Liebknecht must under no circumstances have a hearing. Davidssohn has now stopped talking. Liebknecht has meantime reached the bottom step of the stairway of five or six steps leading from the tribune to the level of the floor. He can be plainly seen from all sections of the House. I hear him start to say that he has a double right to be heard on the Army Bill, not only as a member of the House, but as a soldier. He gets no further. The Chamber is already filled with shouts and jeers. *"Maul halten!"* (shut your mouth!) bursts from a dozen places in the Conservative and National Liberal and Centre benches. *"'Raus mit ihm!"* (throw him out!) is another angry taunt which I can distinguish in the bedlam. Liebknecht has been howled down many times before under similar circumstances. He is not terrified to-day, though his face is pale with excitement and anger. He stands his ground. His right arm is extended, a finger levelled accusingly at the Right and Centre from which imprecations, unceasingly, are being snarled at him. But he cannot make himself heard amid the uproar.

A Socialist colleague intervenes, Ledebour, a thin, grey-haired, actor-like person, of ascetic mien and resonant voice. "Checking free speech is an evil custom of this House," declares Ledebour. "Papa" Kaempf clangs his big hand-bell. He rules out "such improper expressions as 'evil custom' in this high House." Ledebour is the Reichstag's master of repartee. He rejoins smilingly:—"Very well, not an 'evil custom,' but not altogether a pleasant custom." Now the House is howling Ledebour down. He, too, has weathered such storms before. He waits, impassive and undismayed, for a lull in the cyclone. It comes. "Wait, wait!" he thunders. "My friend Liebknecht and I, and others like us, have a great following. You grievously underestimate that following. Some day you will realise *that*. Wait——" Ledebour, like Liebknecht, can no longer

proceed. The House is now boiling, an indistinguish-
able and most undignified pandemonium. I can detect
that there is considerable ironical laughter mixed with
its indignation. Members are not taking Ledebour's
threat seriously.

Liebknecht has temporarily returned to his seat
under cover of the tornado provoked by Ledebour's in-
tervention, but now I see him stealthily crawling, dodg-
ing, almost panther-like, back to the steps of the tribune.
He is bent upon renewing the attempt to raise his voice
above the hostile din. The sight of him unchains the
House's fury afresh. The racket is increased by the
mad ding-donging of "Papa" Kaempf, trying hopelessly
to restore a semblance of quiet. It is useless. The
House will not subside until Liebknecht is driven from
the speakers' tribune. He is not to have even the chance
of the lull which enabled Ledebour to say a pertinent
thing or two. A score of embittered deputies advance
toward the tribune, red-faced and gesticulating in the
German way when excitement is the dominant passion.
Their fists are clenched. I say to myself that Liebknecht will this time be beaten down, if he is not content to be shouted down. He makes an unforgettable
figure, alone there, assailed, barked and snarled at from
every side, a private in the German Army bidding
defiance to a hundred men, also in uniform, but superior
officers. Mere *Kanonenfutter* (cannon fodder) defying
the majestic authority of its helmeted and epauletted
overlords! An unprecedented episode, as well as an unforgettable one. . .

Liebknecht insists upon tempting fate once more. He
is going to try to outshout the crazy chorus howling

at him. He succeeds, but only for an instant and to the extent of one biting phrase:—"Such treatment," I can hear him shrieking, "is *unverschaemt* (shameless) and *unerhoert* (unheard of)! It could take place in no other legislative body in the world!"

With that the one German Social Democrat of conviction, courage, and consistency retires, baffled and discomfited. Potsdam's representative in the Reichstag is at last effectually muzzled, but in the muzzling I have seen the German Government at work on a task almost as prodigious as the one it now faces on the Somme— the task of keeping the German people deaf, dumb, and blind.

Of what has meantime happened to Liebknecht the main facts are known. He was arrested on May 1 for alleged "incitement to public disorder during a state of war," tried, convicted, and sentenced to penal servitude. A couple of months previously (on March 13) he had delivered another bitter attack on the War Government in the Prussian Diet. He accused the German educational authorities of systematically teaching hate to school children and of distorting even contemporary history so as to poison their minds to the glorification of Prussian militarism. He said it was not the business of the schools to turn children into machines for the Moloch of militarism.

"Let us teach history correctly," declared Liebknecht, *"and tell the children that the crime of Sarajevo was looked upon by wide circles in Austria-Hungary and Germany as a gift from Heaven. Let us. . . . ."*

He got no farther, for the cyclone broke. He had dared to do what no other man in Germany had done.

He had publicly accused his Government of making the
war. From that moment his doom was certain.

This narrative should be instructive to those Brit-
ishers and Americans who think it possible that German
Socialists may one day have the power to end the war.
There are two effective replies to this curious Anglo-
Saxon misunderstanding of Germany. The first is that
Liebknecht had not, and has not, the support of his own
party; the second, that were that party twice as numer-
ous as it is its votes would be worthless in view of the
power wielded by the Kaiser's representative, von
Bethmann-Hollweg, backed up by the Federal Council.
It is difficult to drive this fact into the heads of
British and American people, who are both prone to
judge German institutions by their own.

For, remember always that behind the dominant
Imperial Chancellor, von Bethmann-Hollweg, stands
the All-Highest War Lord, and behind him, what is still,
if damaged, the mightiest military machine in the world
—the German Army. Opposed to that there is at
present a slowly increasing Socialist vote—the two have
grown to about twenty.

CHAPTER XV

I<small>N</small> the beginning of the war, when all seemed to be going well, there was no disunity in Germany. When Germany was winning victory after victory, practically no censorship was needed in the newspapers; the police were tolerant; every German smiled upon every other German; soldiers went forth singing and their trains were gaily decorated with oak leaves; social democracy praised militarism.

All that has changed and the hosts who went singing on their way in the belief that they would be home in six weeks, have left behind homes many of them bereaved by the immense casualties, and most of them suffering from the increased food shortage.

Class feeling soon increased. The poor began to call the rich agrarians "usurers." The Government forbade socialistic papers such as the *Vorwaerts* to use the word "usurer" any more, because it was applied to the powerful junkers. Such papers as the *Tägliche Rundschau* and the *Tageszeitung* could continue to use it, however, for they applied it to the small shopkeeper who exceeded the maximum price by a fraction of a penny.

As the rigour of the blockade increased, the discontent of the small minority who were beginning to hate their own Government almost as much as, and in many cases more, than they hated enemies of Germany, assumed more threatening forms than mere discussion. Their disillusionment regarding Germany's invincibility opened their eyes to faults at home. Some of the extreme Social Democrats were secretly spreading the treasonable doctrine that the German Government was not entirely blameless in the causes of the war. It has been my custom to converse with all classes of society, and I was amazed at the increasing number of disgruntled citizens.

But the German Government is still determined to have unity. They had enlisted the services of editors, reporters, professors, parsons and cinema operators to create it; they are now giving the police an increasingly important rôle to maintain it.

As the German Parliament in no way resembles the British Parliament, so do the German police in no way resemble the British police. The German police, mounted or unmounted, are armed with a revolver, a sword, and not infrequently provided with a machine-gun. They have powers of search and arrest without warrant. They are allowed at their discretion to strike or otherwise maltreat not only civilians, but soldiers. Always armed with extraordinary power, their position during the past few months has risen to such an extent that the words used in the Reichstag, "The Reign of Terror," are not an exaggeration.

Aided and even abetted by a myriad of spies and *agents-provocateurs,* they have placed under what is known as "preventive arrest" throughout the German Empire and Austria so great a number of civilians that the German prisons, as has been admitted, are filled to repletion.

With the Reichstag shut up, and the hold on the newspapers tightening, what opportunity remains by which independent thought can be disseminated?

In Poland meetings to consider what they call "Church affairs," but which were really revolutionary gatherings, afforded opportunity for discussion. These have been ruled out of order.

The lectures taking place in their thousands all over Germany might afford a chance of expression of opinion, but the professors, like the pastors, are, as I have said, so absolutely dependent upon the Government for their position and promotion, that I have only heard of one of them who had the temerity to make any speech other than those of the "God-punish-England" and "We-must-hold-out" type. His resignation from the University of Munich was immediately demanded, and any number of sycophants were ready to take his place.

Clubs are illegal in Germany, and the humblest working-men's *cafés* are attended by spies. In my researches in the Berlin East-end I often visited these places and shared my adulterated beer and war bread with the working folk—all of them over or under military age.

One evening a shabby old man said rather more loudly than was necessary to a number of those round him:—"I am tired of reading in the newspapers how nice the war is. Even the *Vorwaerts* (then a Socialist paper) lies to us. I am tired of walking home night after night and finding restaurants turned into hospitals for the wounded."

He was referring in particular to the great *Schult-heiss* working-men's restaurants in Hasenheide. His remarks were received with obvious sympathy.

A couple of nights later I went into this same place and took my seat, but it was obvious that my visit was unwelcome. I was looked at suspiciously. I did not think very much of the incident, but ten days later in passing I called again, when a lusty young fellow of eighteen, to whom I had spoken on my first visit, came forward and said to me, almost threateningly, "You are a stranger here. May I ask what you are doing?"

I said: "I am an American newspaper correspondent, and am trying to find out what I can about the ways of German working folk."

He could tell by my accent that I was a foreigner, and said: "We thought that you had told the Government about that little free speaking we had here a few days ago. You know that the little old man who was complaining about the restaurants being turned into hospitals has been arrested?"

This form of arrest, by which hundreds of people are mysteriously disappearing, is one of the burning grievances of Germany to-day. In its application it resembles what we used to read about Russian police. It has created a condition beneath the surface in Germany resembling the terrorism of the French Revolution. In the absence of a Habeas Corpus Act, the victim lies in gaol indefinitely, while the police are, nominally, collecting the evidence against him. One cannot move about very long without coming across instances of this growing form of tyranny, but I will merely give one other.

A German family, resident in Sweden, were in correspondence with a woman resident in Prussia. In one of her letters she incautiously remarked, "What a pity that the two Emperors cannot be taught what war really means to the German peoples." She had lost two sons, and her expression of bitterness was just a feminine outburst, which in any other country, would have been passed by. She was placed under preventive arrest, and is still in gaol.

The police are armed with the censorship of the internal postal correspondence, telegrams and telephones. One of the complaints of the Social Democrat members of the Reichstag is that every movement is spied upon, and their communications tampered with by what they call the "Black Chamber."

There is no reason to suppose that the debates in the closing session of the Reichstag in 1916 on police tyranny, the Press censorship, the suppression of public opinion, will lead to any result other than the familiar expressions of mild indignation—such as that which came from the National Liberal and Pan-German leader, Dr. Paasche—and perhaps a little innocent legislation. But the reports of the detailed charges against the Government constitute, even as passed by the German censorship for publication, a remarkable revelation. It should be remembered in reading the following quotations that the whole subject has been discussed in the secrecy of the Reichstag Committee, and that what is now disclosed is in the main only what the Government has been unable to hush up or hide.

In his famous speech on "preventive arrest" the Social Democratic Deputy, Herr Dittmann said:—

"Last May I remarked that the system of preventive arrest was producing a real reign of terror, and since then things have got steadily worse. The law as it was before 1848 and the Socialist Law, of scandalous memory, are celebrating their resurrection. The system of denunciation and of *agents-provocateurs* is in full bloom, and it is all being done under the mask of patriotism and the saving of the country. Anybody who for personal or other reasons is regarded by the professional *agents-provocateurs* as unsatisfactory or inconvenient is put under suspicion of espionage, or treason, or other crime. And such vague denunciations are then sufficient to deprive the victim of his freedom, without any possibility of defence being given him. In many cases such arrest has been maintained by the year without any lawful foundation for it. Treachery and low cunning are now enjoying real orgies. A criminal is duly convicted and knows his fate. The man under preventive arrest is overburdened by the uncertainty of despair, and is simply buried alive. The members of the Government do not seem to have a spark of understanding for this situation, the mental and material effects of which are equally terrible.

"Dr. Helfferich said in the Budget Committee in the case of Dr. Franz Mehring that it is better that he should be under detention than that he should be at large and do something for which he would have to be punished. According to this reasoning the best thing would be to lock up everybody and keep them from breaking the law. The ideal of Dr. Helfferich seems to be the German National Prison of which Heine spoke. The case of Mehring is classical proof of the fact that we are no longer far removed from the Helf-ferich ideal."

Herr Dittmann went on to say that Herr Mehring's only offence was that in a letter seized by the police he wrote to a Reichstag deputy named Herzfeld in favour of a peace demonstration in Berlin, and offered to write a fly-sheet inviting attendance at such a meeting. Mehring, who is over 70 years of age, was then locked up. Herr Dittmann continued :—

"How much longer will it be before even thoughts become criminal in Germany? Mehring is one of the most brilliant historians and writers, and one of the first representatives of German intellectual life—known as such far beyond the German frontiers. When it is now known abroad that such a man has been put under a sort of preventive arrest merely in order to cut him off from the public for political reasons, one really cannot be astonished at the low reputation enjoyed by the German Government both at home and abroad. How evil must be the state of a Government which has to lock up the first minds of the country in order to choke their opposition!"

Herr Dittmann's second case was that of Frau Rosa Luxemburg. He said that she was put under arrest many months ago, without any charge being made against her, and merely out of fear of her intellectual influence upon the working classes. All the Socialist women of Germany were deeply indignant, and he invited the Government to consider that such things must make it the positive duty of Socialists in France, England, Italy and Russia "to fight against a Government which imprisons without any reason the best-known champions of the International proletariat." The treatment of both Mehring and Frau Luxemburg had been terrible. The former, old and ill, had had the greatest difficulty in getting admission to a prison infirmary. Frau Luxemburg a month ago was taken from her prison bed in the middle of the night, removed to the police headquarters, and put in a cell which was reserved for prostitutes. She had not been allowed a doctor, and had been given food which she could not eat. Just before the Reichstag debate she had been taken away from Berlin to Wronke, in the Province of Posen.

Herr Dittmann then gave a terrible account, some of it unfit for reproduction, of the treatment in prison of two girls of eighteen whose offence was that on June 27th they had distributed invitations to working women to attend a meeting of protest against the procedure in the case of Herr Liebknecht. He observed that they owed it entirely to themselves and to their training if they had not been ruined physically and morally in their "royal Prussian prison." When they were at last released they were informed that they would be imprisoned for the rest of the war if they attended any public meeting. Herr Dittmann proceeded:—

"Here we have police brutality in all its purity. This is how a working-class child who is trying to make her way up to knowledge and *Kultur* is treated in the country of the promised 'new orientation,' in which (according to the Imperial Chancellor) 'the road is to be opened for all who are efficient.' These are the methods by which the spirit of independence is syste-

matically to be killed. That is the reason for the arrests
of members of the Socialist party who stand on the side
of determined opposition. You imagine that by isolat-
ing the leading elements of the opposition you can crush
the head of the snake."

Herr Dittmann's next case was that of Dr. Meyer,
one of the editors of *Vorwaerts,* who was arrested many
months ago. He is suffering from tuberculosis, but is
not allowed to go to a sanatorium. Another Socialist
journalist named Regge, father of six children, has
been under arrest since August, his only offence being
that he has agitated against the militarist majority.
Herr Dittmann then dealt at lenght with the Socialist
journalist named Klühs, who has been in prison for
eight months, also for his activity on behalf of the Socialist minority against the majority, and was prevented from communicating with his dying wife or attending her funeral.

Herr Dittmann gave the details of three cases at
Düsseldorf and one at Brunswick, and then explained
how the military authorities in many parts of Germany
are deliberately offering Socialists the choice between
silence and military service. A well-known trade union
official at Elberfeld, named Sauerbrey, who had been
declared totally unfit for military service because he
had lost several fingers on his left hand, was arrested
and charged with treason. He was acquitted, but instead of obtaining his freedom he was immediately
called up and is now in training for the front. Herr
Dittmann said that this case had caused intense bitterness, and added:—

"The Military Command at Münster is surprised

that the feeling in the whole Wupper Valley is becoming more and more discontented, and the military are now hatching new measures of violence in order to be able to master this discontent. One would think that such things came from the madhouse. In reality they represent conditions under martial law, and this case is only one of very many."

Herr Dittmann gave several instances of men declared unfit for service who had been called up for political reasons, and he ended his speech as follows:—

"In regard to all this persecution of peaceful citizens there is a regular apparatus of *agents-provocateurs,* provided by officials of all kinds, and the apparatus is growing every day. If these persecutions were stopped a great number of these agents and officials could be released for military service. In most cases they are mere shirkers, and that is why they cling to their posts and *seek every day to prove themselves indispensable by discovering all sorts of crimes.* Because they do not want to go to the trenches other people must go to prison. Put an end to the state of martial law, and help us to root up a state of things which disgraces the German name."

The Alsatian deputy, Herr Haus, said that Alsace-Lorraine is suffering more than any other part of the country, and that more than 1,000 persons have been arrested without any charge being brought against them. Herr Seyda, for the Poles, said that the Polish population of Germany suffers especially from the system of preventive arrest.

In his contemptuous reply, which showed that the Government was confident that it had nothing to fear from the majority in the Reichstag, Herr Helfferich said:—

"The institution of the dictator comes from ancient Rome, from the classical Republic of antiquity. (Laughter.) When the State was fighting for its existence it was found necessary to place supreme power in the hands of a single man, and to give this Roman dictator authority which was much greater than the authority belonging to preventive arrest and martial law. The whole development proceeds by way of compromise between the needs of the State and the needs of protection for the individual. The results vary according to the particular level of civilisation reached by the particular State. (Socialist cries of 'Very true.') We are not at the lowest level. When one considers the state of things in Germany in peace time we can be proud. (Socialist interruptions.) I am proud of Germany. I think that our constitutional system before the outbreak of war and our level of *Kultur* were such as every German could be proud of. ('No, no.') I hope that we shall soon be able to revert to those conditions."

Herr Helfferich went on to argue that repression in Germany is really much milder than in France, England, or Italy; and for the debate on the censorship, which followed the debate on preventive arrest, he came armed with an account of the Defence of the Realm Acts. When he enlarged upon the powers of the British Government he was interrupted by cries of "It is a question not of theory but of practice," and the Socialist leader Herr Stadthagen made a scathing reply. He said:—

"Even if everything in England is as Herr Helfferich described it, the state of things is much better there than in Germany. Herr Helfferich stated the cases in which arrest and search of dwellings may take place, but those are cases in which similar action can be taken in Germany in time of peace under the ordinary criminal law. The Englishman has quite other rights. He has the right to his personality, and, above all, the officials in England, unlike Germany, are personally responsible. When we make a law, that law is repealed by the Administration. That is the whole point, but Herr Helfferich does not see it, and he does not see that we live in a Police State and under a police system. Did it ever occur to anybody in England to dispute the right of immunity of members of parliament? Did it ever occur to anybody in England to go to members of the Opposition in Parliament and demand that they should resign their seats on pain of arrest? Or has anybody in England been threatened with arrest if he does not withdraw a declaration against the committee of his party? Two newspapers have been suppressed in England because they opposed munitions work. I regret this check upon free criticism in England, but what would have happened in Germany? In Germany there would undoubtedly have been a prosecution for high treason. In England, moreover, the newspapers are allowed to reappear, and that without giving any guarantees. In Germany we are required to give guarantees that the papers shall be conducted by a person approved of by the political police. Herr Helfferich employs inappropriate comparisons. I will give him one which applies. The political police in Germany is precisely what the State Inquisition was in Venice."

An interesting point in the censorship debate was the disclosure of the fact that the local censors do what they please. Herr Seyda protested against the peculiar persecution of the Poles. He remarked that at Gnesen no Polish paper has been allowed to appear for the past two years.

But as significant as anything was Herr Stadthagen's account of the recruiting for the political police. He said that the police freely offer both money and exemption from military service to boys who are about to become liable for service. He gave a typical case of a boy of seventeen. The police called at his home and inquired whether he belonged to any Socialist organisation and whether he had been medically examined for the Army. A police official then waylaid the boy as he was leaving work and promised him that, if he would give information of what went on in his Socialist association, he could earn from £4 to £4 10s. a month and be exempt from military service.

There is a peculiar connection between censorship and police. The evil effect of the censorship of their own Press by the German Government is to hypnotise the thousands of Government bureaucrats into the belief that that which they read in their own controlled Press is true.

No people are more ready to believe what they want to believe than the governing class in Germany. They wanted to believe that Great Britain would not come into the war. They had got into their heads, too, that Japan was going to be an ally of theirs. They wrote

themselves into the belief that France was defeated and
would collapse.

Regarding the Press, as they do, as all-important,
they picked from the British Press any articles or
fragments of articles suitable for their purpose and
quoted them.   They are adepts in the art of dissecting
a paragraph so that the sense is quite contrary to that
meant by the writer.

But the German Government goes further than that.
It is quite content to quote to-day expressions of Greek
opinion from Athens organs well known to be subsidised
by Germany.   Certain bribed papers in Zurich and
Stockholm, and one notorious American paper, are used
for this process of self-hypnotism.   The object is two-
fold.   First, to influence public opinion in the foreign
country, and, secondly, by requoting the opinion, to influence their own people into believing that this is the
opinion held in the country from which it emanates.
Thus, when I told Germans that large numbers of the
Dutch people are pro-Ally, they point to an extract
from an article in *De Toekomst* and controvert me.

These methods go to strengthen the hands of the police when they declare that in acting severely they are
only acting against anarchistic opinions likely to create
the impression abroad that there is disunity within the
Empire.

Never, so far as I can gather, in the world's history
was there so complete a machine for the suppression of
individual opinion as the German police.

The anti-war demonstrations in Germany range all
the way from the smashing of a few food-shop windows

to the complete preparations for a serious crippling of the armies in the field by a general munition strike.

Half-way between were the so-called "Liebknecht riots" in Berlin. The notices summoning these semi-revolutionary meetings were whispered through factories, and from mouth to mouth by women standing in the food lines waiting for their potatoes, morning bread, meat, sugar, cheese, and other supplies. Liebknecht was brought to secret trial on June 27th, on the evening of which demonstrations took place throughout the city. I was present at the one near the Rathaus, which was dispersed towards midnight when the police actually drew their revolvers and charged the crowd.

The following evening I was at an early hour in the Potsdamer Platz, where a great demonstration was to take place. It was the second anniversary of the murder at Sarajevo. The city was clearly restless, agitated; people were on the watch for something to happen. The Potsdamer Platz is the centre through which the great arteries of traffic flow westward after the work of the day is done. The people who stream through it do not belong to the poorer classes, for these live in the east and the north. But on this mild June evening there was a noticeably large number of working men in the streets leading into the Platz. I was standing near a group of these when the evening editions appeared with the news that Liebknecht had been sentenced. A low murmur among the workmen, mutterings of suppressed rage when they realised the significance of the short trial of two days, and a determined movement toward the place of demonstration.

I hurried to the Potsdamer Platz. The number of

police stationed in the streets leading into it increased.
The Platz itself was blue with them, for they stood
together in groups of six, ten and twelve. I went along
the Budapester Strasse to the Brandenburger Tor,
through which workmen from Moabit had streamed at
noon declaring that they would strike. They had been
charged by the mounted police, who drove them back
across the Spree. There was a blue patrol along the
Unter den Linden now. A whole army corps of police
were on the alert in the German capital.

I returned to the Potsdamer Platz. It was thick
with people now—curious onlookers. There were
crowds of workmen in the adjacent streets, but they
were not allowed to approach too near. Again and
again they tried, but, unarmed, they were powerless
when the horses were driven into them. I saw a few
of the most obstinate struck with the flat of sabres, and
on others were rained blows from the police on foot.
Nobody hit back, or even defended himself.

There was practically no violence such as one expects
from a mob. It was something else which impressed
me. It impressed my police-lieutenant friend, also.
That was the dangerous ugliness in the workmen. Hate
was written in their faces, and the low growl in the
crowd told all too plainly the growing feeling against
the war.

The Government realised this. They had already
seen that the unity they had so artificially created could
only be held by force. They had used force in the muzzling of Liebknecht, and quietly they were employing
a most potent force every day, the force of preventive
arrest.

In July there was agitation for the great munition strike which was to have taken place on the day of the second anniversary of the war. The dimensions of the proposed rising were effectually concealed by the censorship. The ugly feeling in the Potsdamer Platz had taught the Government a lesson.

No detail was neglected in the preparations against the strike. There was a significant movement of machine-guns to all points of danger, such as the Moabit district of Berlin, and Spandau, together with countless warnings against so-called "anarchists." Any workman who showed the slightest tendency to be a leader in a factory group was taken away. The expressions of intention not to work the first four days of August became so strong that the Press issued a warning that any man refusing to work would be put into a uniform, and he would receive not eight or more marks a day as in munition work, but three marks in ten days. Even the Kaiser supplemented his regular anniversary manifestoes to the armed forces of the Empire and the civilian population with a special appeal to the workmen.

I was up and ready at an early hour on the morning of August 1st. Again the city was blue with police. But this time they were reinforced. As I walked through streets lined with soldiers in the workingmen's quarters, I realised the futility of any further anti-war demonstrations in the Fatherland.

I stood in the immense square before the Royal Palace, and reflected that two years ago it was packed with a crowd wild with joy at the opportunity of going to war. There was unity. I stood on the very spot where the old man was jeered because he had said, "War is a serious business, young fellow."

On August 1st, 1916, there were more police in the square than civilians. On Unter den Linden paced the blue patrol. There was still unity in Germany, but a unity maintained by revolver, sword and machine-gun.

CHAPTER XVI

POLICE RULE IN BOHEMIA

In his speech to the Senate President Wilson said: "No peace can last, or ought to last, which does not recognise and accept the principle that Governments derive all their just powers from the consent of the governed. . . . No nation should seek to extend its polity over any other nation or people, but every people should be left free to determine its own policy, its own way of development, unhindered, unthreatened, unafraid, the little along with the great and powerful."

The realisation of these admirable sentiments presents infinite problems in various sections of Europe, but nowhere, perhaps, more than in Austria-Hungary. In his heterogeneous collection of peoples, the old Emperor had to make a choice between two courses in order to hold his thirteen distinct races together in one Empire. He could have tried to make them politically contented through freedom to manage their own affairs while owing allegiance to the Empire as a whole, or he could suppress the individual people to such an extent that he would have unity by force.

He chose the second course. With the Germans dominant in Austria and the Magyars in Hungary, other nations have been scientifically subjugated. As in the case of the procedure of "Preventive Arrest" in Germany, the authorities seek to work smoothly and silently, with the result that only an occasional echo reaches the outside world.

The description of the relations of the various peoples and the "Unity-Machine" employed would fill a large book. Control of public opinion has been the first action of the rulers of the Dual Monarchy. In peace time, not only were the suppressed nations, such as the Czechs, Slovaks, Rumanians, Luthenians, Poles, Slovenes, Italians, but all the citizens of Austria-Hungary, denied the right of free speech and freedom of the Press. Some of the regulations by which the Government held absolute sway over its subjects are:

(1) No newspaper or other printing business could be established until a heavy deposit was made with the police for the payment of fines, such fines to be arbitrarily imposed by the police—in whom is vested extraordinary power—when anything political was written which did not please them. They are difficult to please, I may add.

(2) A complete copy of each edition must be sent to the police before it was put on sale. "Good" editors whose inspiration was of a nature to enable them to interpret the wishes of the Government, sometimes received a dispensation from this formality.

(3) No club might hold a private meeting. A representative of the police must be present. This rule was often extended even to friendly gatherings in private homes in such places as Bohemia.

(4) No political meeting might be held without a permit, and a representative of the police must be present. Often he sat on the platform. It is amusing for the visitor from a free country to attend a political

meeting where the chairman, speaker and policeman file up on the stage to occupy the three chairs reserved for them. The policeman may be heard by those in the front rows continually cautioning the speaker. If he thinks the speaker is talking too freely he either intervenes through the chairman and asks him to be moderate or dismisses the meeting.

These regulations, I again remind the reader, were in force in peace time. It is easy to see how an extension of them effectually checks attempts of the Czechs (Bohemians) and other peoples to legislate themselves into a little freedom.

When I came to England early in the war from Austria-Hungary and Germany I heard many expressions of hope that the discontented races in the Empire of Francis Joseph would rebel, and later expressions of surprise that they did not. Englishmen held the opinion that such races would be decidedly averse from fighting for the Hapsburgs. The opinion was correct, and nobody knew this better than the Hapsburgs themselves.

Like the German Government in the matter of Alsace-Lorraine, the Austrian Government has endeavoured to mislead public opinion in foreign countries as to the state of mind of the Czechs by false information and to conceal the true military and political situation from the population at home. Austria's first problem at the outbreak of war—a problem which has been worked out to the last detail—was rapidly to move the soldiers of the subjugated races from their native lands. Since the Bosnians, for example, are of the Serbian race, they were mobilised secretly in the middle of July and sent out of Bosnia. I saw 30,000 moved through Trieste several days before war was declared on Serbia. A German acquaintance, with great shipping interests, enthusiastically indiscreet at sight of them, exclaimed to the little group of which I was one: "A wonderful system—a wonderful system! The Bosnians could not be trusted to fight the Serbs. But we Germans can use them if they prove troublesome to Austria," he continued excitedly. "We can send them against the French. We will tell them that if they do not shoot the French, we will shoot *them*." I thought this a rather curious conversation for July 25th, 1914.

Less than fortnight later I saw two Bohemian regiments arrive at Prasso, Transylvania, the province farthest removed from their homes, to be garrisoned in a region, the population of which is Rumanian, Hungarian and Saxon. I was told later that the Rumanians who had left the garrisons at Brasso had gone to Bohemia. As I observed these initial steps in the great smooth-running Austro-Hungarian military machine, I was impressed with the impossibility of revolution. With the soldier element scientifically broken up and scattered all over the country, who could revolt—the women and children?

The Slav soldiers of Austria-Hungary desert to Russia at every opportunity. The fact that she now has upwards of 1,200,000 Austro-Hungarian prisoners is sufficient refutation of the sugar-coated propaganda describing how all the peoples who make up Austria-Hungary rushed loyally and enthusiastically to arms to the defence of their Emperor and common country. This is perfectly true of the politically dominant races, the Germans and the Magyars, but the "enthusiasm" I witnessed among the subjugated races consisted chiefly of sad-faced soldiers and weeping women.

The Bohemians have given most trouble. One German officer who was sent to Austria to help bolster up her army told me that he didn't worry over the desertion of Bohemians singly and in small groups. He expected that. But he did take serious exception to the increasingly popular custom of whole battalions with their officers and equipment passing over to the Russian lines intact.

The story of the Bohemian regiment trapped in the Army of Leopold of Bavaria is generally known in Austria. When the staff learned that this regiment planned to cross to the Russians on a certain night, three Bavarian regiments, well equipped with machine-guns, were set to trap it. Contrary to usual procedure, the Bohemians were induced by the men impersonating the Russians to lay down their arms as an evidence of good faith before crossing. The whole regiment was then rounded up and marched to the rear, where a public example was made of it. The officers were shot. Then every tenth man was shot. The Government, in order to circumvent any unfavourable impression which this act might make in Bohemia, caused to be read each day for three days in the schools a decree of the Emperor, condemning the treachery of this regiment, the number of which was ordered for ever to be struck from the military rolls of the Empire.

During the terrific fighting at Baranowitchi in the great Russian offensive last summer, at a time when the Russians repeatedly but unsuccessfully stormed that important railway junction, some Prussian units found their right flank unsupported one morning at dawn, because two Bohemian battalions had changed flags during the night. The next Russian attack caused the Prussians to lose 48 per cent. of their men.

This was the final straw for the Staff of Leopold's Army. An Order was issued explaining to the troops that henceforth no more Czechs would have the honour of doing first line duty, since their courage was not of as high a degree as that of the others. I found that the Prussians, despite their depleted state, actually believed this explanation, which filled them with pride in themselves and contempt for the Czechs.

But the German officers in charge of reorganising the Austro-Hungarian Army were not content to let Bohemians perform safe duties in the rear. Consequently, they diluted them until no regiment contained more than 20 per cent.

The authorities have been no less thorough with the civilian population. From the day of mobilisation all political life was suspended. The three parties of the Opposition, the Radicals, the National-Socialists, and the Progressives, were annihilated and their newspapers suppressed. Their leaders, such men as Kramarzh, Rasin, Klofatch, Scheiner, Mazaryk, Durich, the men who served as guides to the nation, were imprisoned or exiled. This is surely a violation of the principle that Governments derive their just powers from the consent of the governed, for all these men were the true representatives of the people. The fact that the Government was obliged to get rid of the leaders of the nation shows what the real situation in Bohemia is.

The Czech deputies who were considered dangerous, numbering forty, were mobilised. They were not all sent to the front; some were allowed temporary exemption; but the Government gave them to understand that the slightest act of hostility towards the Monarchy on their part would result in their being called up immediately and sent to the front.

The fetters of the Press were drawn more tightly. Even the German papers were not allowed into Bohemia. For some months, two or three enterprising editors used to send a representative to Dresden to read the German and English papers there. At present three-quarters of the Czech papers and all the Slovak newspapers have been suppressed. The columns of those which are still allowed to appear in Bohemia and Moravia are congested by mandates of the police and the military authorities, which the editors are compelled to insert. Recently the Government censorship has been particularly active against books, collections of national songs, and post-cards. It has even gone so far as to confiscate scientific works dealing with Slav questions, Dostoyevski's novels, the books of Tolstoi and Millioukoff, and collections of purely scientific Slav study and histories.

The Government, however, have had to proceed to far greater lengths. By May, 1916, the death sentences of civilians pronounced in Austria since the beginning of the war exceeded 4,000. Of these, 965 were Czechs. A large proportion of the condemned were women. The total of soldiers executed amounts to several thousands.

Is it not peculiar that among people which the

Viennese propaganda represents as loyal, hostages are taken in Bohemia, and condemned to death, under the threat of execution if a popular movement takes place? The people are told of this and are given to understand that the hostages have hopes for mercy if all is quiet.

Not only have the authorities confiscated the property of all persons convicted of political offences and of all Czechs who have fled from Austria-Hungary, but a system has been established by which the property of Czech soldiers who are prisoners in Russia is confiscated. The State profits doubly by this measure, for it futher suppresses the allowances made to the families of these soldiers. In order to terrorise its adversaries through such measures, the Government instructs the Austrian newspapers to publish long lists of confiscations and other penalties.

After a time, however, the Austrian Government practically abdicated in favour of the Prussians and now undertake to carry out the measures of Germanisation dictated by Berlin. The rights in connection with the use of the Czech language in administration, in the Law Courts and on the railways, rights which were won by the desperate efforts of two generations of Czech politicians, have been abrogated. The management of the railways has been placed in the hands of Prussian military officials; the use of the Czech language has been suppressed in the administration, where it had formerly been lawful. The Czechs have been denied access to the Magistrature and to public offices where they had occasionally succeeded in directing the affairs in their own country.

CHAPTER XVII

SPIES AND SEMI-SPIES

A COMPREHENSIVE account of the German system of espionage would need something resembling the dimensions of a general encyclopædia, but for the present I must endeavour to summarise the subject in the course of a chapter.

Spying is just as essential an ingredient of Prussian character as conceit, indifference to the feelings of others, jealousy, envy, self-satisfaction, conceit, industry, inquisitiveness, veneration for officialdom, imitativeness, materialism, and the other national attributes that will occur to those who know Prussia, as distinct from the other German States.

Prussian men and women hardly know the meaning of the word "private," and, as they have Prussianised to a great or less degree all the other States of the Empire, they have inured the German to publicity from childhood upwards.

In the enforcement of food regulations the hands of the Government in Germany are strengthened by certain elements in the German character, one of which is the tendency of people to spy upon each other. Here is a case. Last Easter the customary baking of cakes—a time-honoured ceremony in Germany—was forbidden all over Prussia from April 1 to 26. A certain good woman of Stettin, whose husband was coming home

from the trenches, thought that she would welcome her
soldier with one of the cakes of which German men and
women are so fond. She foolishly displayed her treasure
to a neighbour, who had dropped in for gossip. The
neighbour cut short the interview, went home to her
telephone, called up the police and, as she put it, did
her duty. I suppose from the German point of view it
is the duty of people to spy in each other's houses.
From an Anglo-Saxon point of view it is something
rather like sneaking at school.

With these elements in their character, it is natural
that the Germans should be past masters in the art of
espionage. It does not follow that they are equally
successful in the deductions formed from their investigations in foreign matters, but they are so egoistical and
so literal, so fond of making reports, so fond of seeing
things only from their own point of view, that, while
they may be successful in obtaining possession by spying, purchase, or theft, of the plans, say, of a new bat-
tleship, they are not able to form an accurate estimate
of the character and intentions of the people among
whom they may be spying.

Their military spying is believed to be as perfect as
such work can be, marred occasionally by the contempt
they feel for other nations in military matters. I presume that there is not much difference in the systems
of various nations except that the German military spying is probably more thorough.

It is also true that Germans of social distinction will
often take positions far beneath their rank in order to
gather valuable information for their Government.
The case of the hall porter in the *Hotel des Indes,* the

most fashionable hotel in The Hague, is a notorious example. He is of gentle birth, a brother of Baron von Wangenheim, late German Ambassador to Constantinople.

In one of the most luxurious dining-saloons on one of the most luxurious of the great German liners—I promised my trustworthy informant not to be more definite—the man who was head-waiter during the year preceding the war impressed those under him with being much more interested in some mysterious business ashore than in his duties aboard ship. He threw most of his work on subordinates, who complained, though unsuccessfully, to the management. Unlike other head-waiters and chief stewards, he was never aboard the ship when it was in port. He was the only German in the dining-saloon, and he seemed to have great influence. He conversed freely with influential passengers of various nationalities.

The liner was in the English Channel eastward bound when news came that Germany had declared war upon Russia. What little interest he had previously displayed in his duties now vanished completely, and he paced the deck more and more impatiently as the vessel neared Cuxhaven. He was one of the first to go ashore, but before leaving he turned to two of the stewards and exclaimed, "Good-bye. I am going to Wilhelmshaven to take command of my cruiser."

In general, the work of military *attachés* of all countries is added to by more or less formal reports by officers who may be travelling on leave. But German military spying goes much farther than this, for inasmuch as most Germans have been soldiers, the majority of Germans travelling or resident in a foreign country are trained observers of military matters and often act as semi-spies.

The system of "sowing" Germans in foreign countries, as I have heard it called in Germany, and getting them naturalised, was begun by Prussia before the war of 1866 against Austria. It was so successful under the indirect auspices of the Triumvirate—Moltke, Roon, and Bismarck—that it was developed in other countries. Thus it is that, while there are comparatively few Frenchmen, for example, naturalised in England, many German residents go through this more or less meaningless form just as suits their particular business or the German Government, double nationality being regarded as a patriotic duty to the Fatherland.

There are, as a rule, three schools of German espionage in other countries—the Embassy, the Consulates, and the individual spies, who have no connection with either and who forward their reports direct to Germany.

There is a fourth class of fairly well-paid professional spies, men and women, of all classes, who visit foreign countries with letters of introduction, who attend working-men's conventions, scientific, military, and other industrial congresses, receiving from £40 to £100 monthly by way of pay. The case of Lody, whom the British caught and executed, was a type of the patriotic officer spy. But his execution caused no real regret in Germany, for he was regarded as a clumsy fellow, who roused the vigilance of the British authorities, with the result, I was informed in Germany, of the arrest and execution of several others, mostly, it is said, Dutch, South American and other neutrals.

The atmosphere of spying in business is a subtle and comparatively modern form of German espionage, and has developed with the remarkable rise of German industry in the last quarter of a century. It fits in admirably with the Consular spy system, and links up Germans, naturalised and otherwise, in a chain which binds them together in a solidarity of workers for the cause. The Deutsche Bank and the Hamburg-Amerika Line were very potent engines of espionage.

Nor does the "Viktoria Insurance Company of Berlin" limit its activities to the kind of business suggested by the sign over the door. A "Special Bureau" in the Avenue de l'Opéra, Paris, consisted of German Reserve officers who spent a half-year or more in France. As soon as one of these "finished his education" he was replaced by another Reserve officer. Their duties took them on long motor-trips through eastern France, strangely enough to localities which might be of strategic importance in the event of war. It is not without significance that all the clerks of the "Special Bureau" left for Germany the day of mobilisation.

Many of the semi-spies of the German commercial, musical, and theatrical world are, from their point of view, honest workers and enthusiastic for German *Kultur*. They recently fastened upon England, because the Germans for many years have been taught to regard this country as their next opponent.

They are now as industrious in the United States as they were in England before the war, because those Germans who think they have won the war believe that the United States is their next enemy. How active they have been in my country may be gathered from the revelations concerning Bernstorff, von Papen, Boyed, Dumba, the officials of the Hamburg-Amerika Line, and many others, whose machinations have been revealed by the *New York World* and other journals.

It is the duty of the German Minister and his staff in any foreign conutry, and particularly in countries likely to become hostile, to get as close as possible to members of Governments, members of Legislatures, leaders of thought and society, and members of the Press, especially the first and the last in this category. Count Bernstorff in the United States did exactly what Prince Lichnowsky did in Britain before the war, and, if I may say so, did it a great deal more successfully, though it is the plea of the Prince's defenders that he succeeded in making very powerful and permanent connections in Great Britain.

Our American Ambassadors, on the other hand, confine their attention to strictly ambassadorial work, attend to the needs of travelling Americans, and communicate with their Government on matters vital to American interests.

The excellent German Consular system, which has done so much to help German trade invaders in foreign countries, is openly a spy bureau, and is provided in almost every important centre with its own secret service fund. Attached to it are spies and semi-spies, hotel-keepers, hairdressers, tutors, governesses, and employees in Government establishments, such as ship-building yards and armament factories. It is a mistake to suppose that all these are Germans. Some, I regret to say, are natives of the land in which the Germans are spying, mostly people who have got into trouble and with whom the German agents have got into touch. Such men, especially those who have suffered imprisonment, have often a grudge against their own country and are easily caught in the spy net.

Part of the system in England before the war was a commercial information bureau resembling the American Bradstreets and the English Stubbs, by which, on payment of a small sum, the commercial standing of any firm or individual can be obtained. This bureau, which had its branches also in France and Belgium, closed its activities immediately prior to the war, the whole of the card-indexes being removed to Berlin.

It is the German boast, and I believe a legitimate one, that they know England better than do the English. *Their error is in believing that in knowing England they know the English themselves.*

At the outset of the war, when the Germans were winning, Herr Albert Ulrich, of the Deutsche Bank, and chief of their Oil Development Department, speaking in perfect English, told me in a rather heated altercation we had in regard to my country that he knew the United States and Great Britain very thoroughly indeed, and boasted that the American submarines, building at Fore River, of which the Germans had secured the designs, would be of little value in the case of hostilities between Germany and the United States, which he then thought imminent.

It is typical of German mentality that when I met him in Berlin, fifteen months later, he had completely altered his tune as to the war, and his tone was, "When is this dreadful war going to end?" This, however, is by the way. Herr Ulrich is only an instance of the solidarity of Pan-Germanism. An English or American banker visting a foreign country attends to his affairs and departs. A German in a similar position is a sort of human ferret. An hotel with us is a place of residence for transient strangers. The Hotel Adlon and others in Berlin are excellent hotels as such, but mixed up with spying upon strangers; Herr Adlon, senior, a friend of the Kaiser's, assists the Government spies when any important or suspicious visitor registers. The hotel telephones or any other telephones are systematically tapped. German soldiers are granted special leave for hotel service—that is to say, hotel spying.

When Belgium and France were invaded, German officers led their men through particular districts to particular houses with certainty, with knowledge gained by previous residence and spying. I know an officer with von Kluck's army who received the Iron Cross, First Class, for special information he had given to von Kluck which facilitated his progress through Belgium.

Any German spies who may be working in England to-day have no great difficulty in communicating with Germany, though communication is slow and expensive. They can do so by many routes and many means. As it is impossible to isolate Great Britain from Europe, it is equally impossible to prevent the conveyance of information to the enemy with more or less rapidity. Agents of the various belligerent Powers are plentiful in Switzerland, Holland, Denmark, Norway and Sweden, and the United States. So far as the maritime

countries are concerned, ships leave and enter daily.
It is quite impossible to control the movements of neutral sailors and others engaged in these vessels. To
watch all the movements of all those men would require
a detective force of impossible dimensions. That information comes and goes freely by these channels is
notorious. That all the sailors are legitimate sailors
I do not believe, and as a matter of fact I know that
they are not.

The transmission of documents *via* Switzerland,
Holland, Denmark, Sweden, and Norway has been
rendered difficult, but not always impossible. Cabling
and telegraphing have been made very risky.

Judging by the impatience manifested in certain
quarters in Berlin at delay in getting news of Zeppelin
raids, for example, I believe that the steps taken to
delay communication between England and Germany
have been effective, and delay in spy work is very often
fatal to its efficiency. The various tentacles of the
German spy system, its checks and counter-checks,
whereby one spy watches another; whereby the naval
spy system has no connection with the military spy
system, and the political with neither, greatly mars its
utility.

Take one great question—the question that was all-
important to Germany as to whether Great Britain
would or would not enter the war in the event of an
invasion of Belgium or declaration of war against
France. I was informed on good Berlin authority
that from every part of Great Britain and Ireland
came different reports. So far as London was concerned, Prince Lichnowsky said "No." Baron von

Kühlmann was non-committal. As a result Lichnowsky was disgraced and von Kühlmann continued in favour.

It is common knowledge in Berlin, and may be elsewhere, that the most surprised person in Germany at Great Britain's action was the Kaiser, whose violent and continual denunciations of Great Britain's Government, of King Edward, and King George, are repeated from mouth to mouth in official circles with a sameness that indicates accuracy.

All the ignorance of Great Britain's intentions in 1914 is to me the best proof that the German minute system of working does not always produce the result desired.

As one with Irish blood in my veins, I found that Germany's Irish spy system (largely conducted by hotel waiters and active for more than five and twenty years) had resulted in hopeless misunderstanding of Irish affairs and Irish character, North and South.

German spies are as a rule badly paid. The semi-spies, such as waiters, were usually "helped" by the German Government through waiters' friendly societies. It was the duty of these men to communicate either in writing or verbally with the Consul, or with certain headquarters either in Brussels or Berlin, and it is only in accordance with human nature that spies of that class, in order to gain a reputation for acumen and consequent increase of pay, provided the kind of information that pleased the paymaster. That, indeed, was one of the causes of the breakdown of the German political spy system. A spy waiter or governess in the County of Cork, for instance, who assiduously reported that a revolution throughout the whole of Ireland would immediately follow Great Britain's entry into the war, received much more attention than the spy waiter in Belfast who told the authorities that if Germany went to war many Irishmen would join England. Ireland, I admit, is very difficult and puzzling ground for spy work, but it was ground thoroughly covered by the Germans according to their methods.

The military party in Germany, who are flaying von Bethmann-Hollweg for his ignorance of the intentions of Britain's Dominions and of Ireland, never cease to throw in his teeth the fact that he had millions of pounds (not marks) at his back to make the necessary investigations, and that he failed. That and his lack of the use of ruthlessness, his alleged three days' delay to mobilise in 1914, are the principal charges against him—charges which, in my opinion, may eventually result in his downfall.

The great mob of semi-spies do not derive their whole income from Germany, nor are they, I believe, all actually paid at regular intervals. The struggling German shopkeeper in England was helped, and I have no doubt is still helped, by occasional sums received for business development—sums nominally in the nature of donations or loans from other Germans. The army of German clerks, who came to England and worked without salary between 1875 and 1900, received, as a rule, their travelling money and an allowance paid direct from Germany, or, when in urgent need, from the Consul in London or elsewhere. Their spying was largely commercial, although many of them formed connections here which became valuable as Germany began to prepare directly for war with Britain. They also helped to spread the knowledge of the English language which has enabled Germany to analyse the country by means of its books, Blue-books, statistical publications, and newspapers. They also brought back with them topographical and local knowledge that supplemented the military spy work later achieved by the German officers who came to live here for spying purposes, and the great army of *trained* spy waiters, who are not to be confused with the semi-spies in hotels, who drew small sums from Consuls.

One of the finest pieces of spy work achieved by Germany was the obtaining by a German professor of a unique set of photographs of the whole of the Scottish coast, from north to south. Those photographs showing every inlet and harbour, are now at the Reichs-Marine-Amt (Admiralty) in the Leipsigerplatz. They have been reproduced for the use of the Navy. I do not know how they were obtained. I *know* they are in existence, and they were taken for geological purposes.

Thefts of documents from British Government Departments are not always successfully accomplished by German agents, I was told. Some of the more astute officials are alleged, especially by the Naval Department, to have laid traps and supplied the spies with purposely misleading designs and codes.

Assiduous fishing in the troubled waters around the Wilhelmstrasse—waters that will become more and more troubled as the siege of Germany proceeds—renders the gathering of information not so difficult as it might appear.

By sympathising with the critics of the German Foreign Office in the violent attacks upon the Government by the non-official Social Democrats, a sympathetic listener can learn a great deal.

One thing I learned is that, beyond question, the German spy system, in that misty period called "after the war," will be very completely revised. The huge sums of money mentioned in the Reichstag as having been expended on secret service have, so far as England is concerned, proved of no political value, and the topographical and personal knowledge gained would only be of service in case of actual invasion and the consequent exactions of ransoms from individuals, cities, and districts.

CHAPTER XVIII

THE IRON HAND IN ALSACE-LORRAINE

THE state of affairs in Alsace-Lorraine is one of Germany's most carefully hidden secrets.

In the first months of the war I heard so much talk in Germany—talk based upon articles in the Press—of how the Alsatians, like the rest of the Kaiser's subjects, "rushed to the defence of the Fatherland," that I was filled with curiosity to go and see for myself if they had suddenly changed. I could hardly believe that they had, for I had studied conditions in the "lost provinces" before the war.

Still, the Wilhelmstrasse propaganda was convincing millions that the Alsations received the French very coldly when they invaded the province to Mulhouse, and that they greeted the German troops most heartily when they drove back the invader. Indeed, Alsatian fathers were depicted as rushing into the streets to cheer the German colours, while their wives and daughters "were so beside themselves with joy that they hung upon the necks of the brave German Michaels, hailing them as saviours."

A pretty picture of the appreciation of the blessings of German rule, but was it true?

Some months later in Paris, when I stood in the Place de la Concorde before the Monument of Strassburg, covered with new mourning wreaths and a British flag now added, I felt an irresistible yearning to visit the closely guarded region of secrecy and mystery.

On my subsequent trip to Germany I planned and planned day after day how I could get into Alsace and go about studying actual conditions there. When I told one American consul that I wished to go to Strassburg to see things for myself, he threw up his hands with a gesture of despair and reminded me that not an American or other consulate was allowed in Alsace-Lorraine, even in peace time. When I replied that I was determined to go he looked grave, and said earnestly: "Remember that you are going into a damn bad country, and you go at your own risk."

It is extremely difficult for Germans, to say nothing of foreigners, to enter the fortress-city of Strassburg. Business must be exceedingly urgent, and a military pass is required. A special pass is necessary to remain over night.

How did I get into Strassburg in war-time?

That is my own story, quite a simple one, but I do not propose to tell it now except by analogy, in order not to get anybody into trouble.

During my last voyage across the ocean, which was on the Dutch liner *Rotterdam,* I went into the fo'castle one day to talk to a stowaway, a simple young East Prussian lad, who had gone to sea and had found himself in the United States at the outbreak of war.

"How on earth did you manage to pass through the iron-clad regulations at the docks of Hoboken (New York) without a permit, and why did you do it?" I asked.

"I was home-sick," he answered, "and I wanted to

go back to Germany to see my mother. I got on board quite easily. I noticed a gentleman carrying his own baggage, and I said to him, 'Can I carry your suit-cases on board, sir?'"

Once on board his knowledge of ships told him how to hide.

Having myself stood for more than two hours on the quay in a long and growling queue of passengers, I could not but be amused by the simple device by which this country youth had outwitted the stringent war embarkation regulations of war-time New York. He was in due course taken off by the British authorities at Falmouth, and is now probably enjoying the sumptuous diet provided at the Alexandra Palace or the Isle of Man.

Well, that is not exactly how I got into Strassburg, but I got in.

Night had fallen when I crossed the Rhine from Baden. I was conscious of an indescribable thrill when my feet touched the soil so sacred to all Frenchmen, and I somehow felt as if I were walking in fairyland as I pushed on in the dark. I had good fortune, arising from the fact that a great troop movement was taking place, with consequent confusion and crowding.

On all sides from the surrounding girdle of forts the searchlights swept the sky, and columns of weary soldiers tramped past me on that four-mile road that led into Strassburg. I kept as close to them as possible with some other pedestrians, labourers returning from the great electric power plant.

Presently I was alone on the road when suddenly a

soldier lurched from the shadows and accosted me. I let him do the talking. But there was no need to be alarmed; he was only a drunken straggler who had got separated from his company and wanted to know whether any more troops were coming on.

I had already passed through two cordons of functionaries outside, and felt little fear in Strassburg itself, so long as I was duly cautious. I had thought out my project carefully. I realised that I must sleep in the open; for, unprovided with a pass it was impossible for me to go to an hotel. Thankful that I was familiar with my surroundings I wended my way to the beautiful park, the Orangerie, where I made myself comfortable in a clump of bushes and watched the unceasing flash of searchlights criss-cross in the sky until I fell asleep.

Next day I continued my investigations, but in Alsace as elsewhere my personal adventures are of no importance to the world unless, as in some instances, they throw light on conditions or are necessary to support statements made, whereas the facts set down belong to the history of the war. Therefore I shall here summarise what I found in the old French province.

The Germans have treated Alsace-Lorraine ruthlessly since the outbreak of war. In no part of the Empire is the iron hand so evident. In Strassburg itself all signs of the French have disappeared. Readers who know the place well will remark that they were vanishing before the war. Externally they have now gone altogether, but the hearts and spirit of the people are as before.

What I saw reminded me of the words of a Social

Democrat friend in Berlin, who told me that the Prussian Government determined at the beginning of the war that they would have no more Alsace-Lorraine problem in the future.

They have, therefore, sent the soldiers from these two provinces to the most dangerous places at the various fronts. One Alsace regiment was hurled again and again at the old British Army on the Yser in November, 1914, until at the end of a week only three officers and six men were left alive. Some of the most perilous work at Verdun was forced upon the Alsatians.

The Prussian authorities deliberately retain with the colours Alsatians and Lorrainers unfit for military service, and wounded men are not allowed to return to their homes.

In the little circle to which I was introduced in Strassburg I talked with one sorrowing woman, who said that her son, obviously in an advanced state of tuberculosis, had been called up in spite of protests. He died within three weeks. Another young man, suffering from hæmorrhage of the lungs, was called up. He was forced to stand for punishment all one winter's day in the snow. In less than two months a merciful death in a military hospital released him from the Prussian clutch.

The town of Strassburg is a vast hospital. I do not think I have ever seen so many Red Cross flags before. They waved from the Imperial Palace, the public library, the large and excellent military hospitals, the schoolhouses, hotels, and private residences. The Orangerie is thronged with convalescent wounded, and when hunger directed my steps to the extensive Park

Restaurant I found it, too, converted into a hospital. Even the large concert room was crowded with cots.

The glorious old sandstone Cathedral, with its gorgeous façade and lace-like spire, had a Red Cross flag waving over the nave while a wireless apparatus was installed on the spire. Sentries paced backwards and forwards on the uncompleted tower, which dominates the region to the Vosges.

The whole object of Prussia is to eliminate every vestige of French influence in the two provinces. The use of the French language, whether in speech or writing, is strictly forbidden. To print, sell, offer for sale, or purchase anything in French is to commit a crime. Detectives are everywhere on the alert to discover violations of the law. All French trade names have been changed to their German equivalents. For example, the sign *Guillaume Rondée, Tailleur,* has come down, and if the tradesman wants to continue in his business *Wilhelm Rondee, Schneider,* must go up. He may have a quantity of valuable business forms or letter-heads in French—even if they contain only one French word they must be destroyed. And those intimate friends who are accustomed to address him by his first name must bear in mind that it is *Wilhelm.*

Eloïse was a milliner at the outbreak of the war. To-day, if she desires to continue her business, she is obliged to remove the final "e" and thus Germanise her name.

After having been fed in Berlin on stories of Alsatian loyalty to the Kaiser, I was naturally puzzled by these things. If Guillaume had rushed into the street to cheer the German colours when the French were driven back, and Eloïse had hung upon the neck of the German Michael, was it not rather ungrateful of the Prussians subsequently to persecute them even to the stamping out of their names? Not only that, but to be so efficient in hate that even inscriptions on tombstones may no longer be written in French?

Alsace-Lorraine is to be literally *Elsass-Lothringen* to the last detail.

The truth of the matter is that the Alsatians greeted the French as deliverers and were depressed when they fell back. This, as might be expected, exasperated Prussia, for it was a slap in the face for her system of government by oppression. Thus, at the very time that the *Nachrichtendienst* (News Service) connected with the Wilhelmstrasse was instructing Germans and neutrals that the Alsatians' enthusiastic reception of German troops was evidence of their approval of German rule, the military authorities were posting quite a different kind of notice in Alsace, a notice which reveals the true story.

"During the transport of French prisoners of war a portion of the populace has given expression to a feeling of sympathy for these prisoners and for France. This is to inform all whom it may concern that such expressions of sympathy are criminal and punishable, and that, should they again take place, the persons taking part in them will be proceeded against by court-martial, and the rest of the inhabitants will be summarily deprived of the privileges they now enjoy.

"All crowding around prisoners of war, conversations with them, cries of welcome and demonstrations of sympathy of all kinds, as well as the supply of gifts, is strictly prohibited. It is also forbidden to remain standing while prisoners are being conducted or to follow the transport."

The result of the persecution of the French-speaking portion of the population has been a boomerang for Prussia. The Germans of the region, most of whom never cared much for Prussia, are now bitterly hostile to her, and thus it is that all citizens of Alsace, whether French or German, who go into other parts of Germany are under the same police regulations as alien enemies.

In order to permit military relentlessness to proceed smoothly without any opposition, the very members of the local Parliament, the Strassburg Diet, are absolutely muzzled. They have been compelled to promise not to criticise at any time, or in any way, the military control; otherwise their Parliament will be closed. As for the Local Councils, they are not allowed to discuss any political questions whatsoever. A representative of the police is present at every meeting to enforce this rule to the letter.

The people do not even get the sugared Reichstag reports, as does the rest of Germany. These are specially re-censored at Mulhouse. The official reports of the General Staff are often days late, and sometimes do not appear at all. In no part of the war zone is there so much ignorance about what is happening at the various fronts as in the two "lost provinces."

Those who do not sympathise with Germany in her career of conquest upon which she so joyfully and ruthlessly embarked in August, 1914, may well point to Alsace-Lorraine as an argument against the probability of other peoples delighting in the rule which she would force upon them.

She has become more intolerant, not less, in the old French provinces. It will be recalled that by the Treaty of Frankfurt, signed in March, 1871, they became a "Reichsland," that is, an Imperial Land, not a self-governing State like Bavaria, Saxony, or Württemberg. As Bismarck bluntly and truly said to the Alsatian deputies in the Reichstag: "It is not for *your* sakes nor in *your* interests that we conquered you, but in the interests of the Empire."

For more than forty years Prussia has employed every means but kindness to Germanise the conquered territory. But though she has hushed every syllable of French in the elementary schools and forced the children to learn the German language and history only; though freedom of speech, liberty of the Press, rights of public meeting, have been things unknown; though even the little children playing at sand castles have been arrested and fined if in their enthusiasm they raised a tiny French flag, or in the excitement of their mock contest cried "Vive la France!"; though men and women have been fined and thrown into prison for the most trifling manifestations that they had not become enthusiastic for their rulers across the Rhine; and though most of the men filling Government positions— and they are legion—are Prussians, the Alsatians preserve their individuality and remain uncowed.

Having failed in two score of years to absorb them by force, Prussia during the war has sought by scientific methods carried to any extreme to blot out for ever themselves and their spirit.

To do the German credit, I believe that he is sincere when he believes that his rule would be a benefit to others and that he is genuinely perplexed when he discovers that other people do not like his regulations. The attitude which I have found in Germany towards other nationalities was expressed by Treitschke when he said, "We Germans know better what is good for Alsace than the unhappy people themselves."

The German idea of how she should govern other people is an anachronism. This idea, which I have heard voiced all over Germany, was aptly set forth before the war by a speaker on "The Decadence of the British Empire," when he sought to prove such decadence by citing the fact that there was only one British soldier to every 4,000 of the people of India. "Why," he concluded, "Germany has more soldiers in Alsace-Lorraine alone than Great Britain has in all India."

That is a bad spirit for the world, and it is a bad spirit for Germany. She herself will receive one great blessing from the war if it is hammered out of her.

CHAPTER XIX

THE WOMAN IN THE SHADOW

THE handling of the always difficult question of the eternal feminine was firmly tackled by the German Government almost immediately after the outbreak of war.

To understand the differences between the situation here and in Germany it is necessary first to have a little understanding of the German woman and her status. With us, woman is treated as something apart, something on a pedestal. In Germany and in Austria the situation is reversed. The German man uses his home as a place to eat and sleep in, and be waited upon. The attitude of the German woman towards the man is nearly always that of the obedient humble servant to command. If a husband and wife are out shopping it is often enough the wife who carries the parcels. In entering any public place the middle-class man walks first and the wife dutifully follows. When leaving, it is the custom for the man to be helped with his coat before the woman. Indeed, she is generally left to shift for herself.

Woman is the under sex, the very much under sex, in Germany, regarded by the man as his plaything or as his cook-wife and nurse of his children; and she will continue to be the under sex until she develops pride enough to assert herself. She accepts her inferiority without murmur; indeed, she often impresses one as delighting in it.

It is no dishonour for a girl of the middle or lower class to have a *liaison* with some admirer, particularly if he is a student or a young officer; in fact, it is quite the proper thing for him to be welcomed by her parents, although it is perfectly well understood that he has not the slightest idea of marrying her. The girls are doing their part to help along the doctrine of free love, the preaching and practice of which are so greatly increasing in the modern German State.

After marriage the woman's influence in the world is nearly zero. The idolatry of titles is carried to an extreme in Germany which goes from the pathetic to the ludicrous. One does not address a German lady by her surname, as Frau Schmidt, but by her husband's title or position, as Frau Hauptmann (Mrs. Captain), Frau Doktor, Frau Professor, Frau Bäckermeister (Mrs. Bakershopowner), or even Frau Schornstein-fegermeister (Mrs. Master Chimneysweep), although her husband may be master over only some occasional juvenile assistant. In military social functions, and they are of daily occurrence in garrison towns, Mrs. Colonel naturally takes precedence in all matters over the wives and daughters of other members of the regiment. Contemplate the joyful existence of a vivacious American or British girl, accustomed to the respectful consideration of the other sex, married to a young lieutenant and ruled over by all the wives of his superior officers!

To try to marry money is considered praiseworthy and correct in German military circles. In Prussia a lieutenant in peace times receives for the first three years £60 a year, from the fourth to the sixth year £85, from the seventh to the ninth year £99, from the tenth to the twelfth year £110, and after the twelfth year £120 a year. A captain receives from the first to the fourth year £170, from the fifth to the eighth year £230, and 'the ninth year and after £255.

Thus it is that no young lady, however ugly, need be without an officer husband if she has money enough to buy one. If he has not a private income, the Government forbids him to marry until his pay is sufficient. That point is seldom reached before he is thirty-five years of age. Marriage helps him out of the difficulty, and since the army is so deified in the Fatherland that the highest ambition of nearly every girl is to marry an officer, his opportunity of trading shoulder-knots for a dowry is excellent.

The efforts of some women to increase their fortune sufficiently to enable them to invest in a military better-half are pathetic from an Anglo-Saxon point of view. One woman who requested an interview with me said that as I was an American correspondent I might be able to advise her how she could dispose of a collection of autographs to some American millionaire. She explained that her financial condition was not so good as formerly, but she was desperate to better it as she was in love with an officer, who, although he loved her, would have to marry another if she could not increase her income. The autographs she showed me were from Prince Henry of Prussia, Prince Bülow and other notables, and most of them were signed to private letters.

Take the story of Marie and Fritz, both of whom I

knew in a garrison city in eastern Germany. Nothing could illustrate better the difference between the German attitude and our own on certain matters. She was a charming, lovable girl of nineteen engaged to an impecunious young lieutenant a few years older. They moved in the best circle in the *Garnisonstadt*.

Two years after their engagement her father lost heavily in business and could no longer afford to settle £5,000 on her to enable them to marry.

It mattered not; theirs was true love, and they would wait until his pay was sufficient.

All went well until another girl, as unattractive as Marie was charming, decided that she would try to buy Fritz as a husband. After four months of her acquaintance he found time at the end of a day's drill to write a few lines informing the young lady, nine years of whose life he had monopolised, of his intention to marry the new rival. Life became black for Marie, the more as she realised that she and Fritz had only to wait a little longer and his pay would be sufficient.

How would Fritz be regarded in this country, and how was he regarded according to German standards? That is what makes the story worth telling. With us such a man as Fritz would have been cut socially and there would have been great sympathy for the sweet girl whose years had been wasted. But on the other side of the Rhine women exist solely for the comfort of men. In militaristic Germany Fritz lost not an iota of the esteem of his friends of either sex; as for Marie, she had failed in a fair game, that was all. The girl's mother even excused his conduct by saying that he was ambitious to get ahead in the army. Like most of her

sex in Germany she has been reared to venerate the
uniform so much that anything done by the man who
wears it is quite excusable. Indeed, Marie's mother
still listens with respectful approval at *Kaffeeklatsch*
to Fritz's mother when she boasts of what her son is
doing as a major over Turkish troops.

German women have many estimable qualities, but a
proper amount of independence and pride is noticeably
foreign to their natures. Is it surprising that the American girl of German parents requires only a very brief
visit to the Fatherland to convince her that the career
of the *Hausfrau* is not attractive.

On the whole, the efforts of the German woman have
almost doubled the national output of war energy. Except in Berlin few are idle, and these only among the
newly-rich class. The women of the upper classes, both
in Germany and Austria, are either in hospitals or are
making comforts for the troops. Women have always
worked harder in Germany and at more kinds of work
than in Britain or the States, and what, judging by
London illustrated papers, seems to be a novelty—the
engagement of women in agricultural and other pursuits—is just the natural way of things in Germany.
It should always be remembered, when estimating German man-power and German ability to hold out, that
the bulk of the work of civil life is being done by *prisoners* and women. A German woman and a prisoner
of war, usually a Russian, working side by side in the
fields is a common sight throughout Germany.

It is the boast of the Germans that their building
constructions are going on as usual. I have myself

seen plenty of evidence of this, such as the grading of the Isar at Munich, the completion of the colossal railway station at Leipzig, the largest in Germany, the construction of the new railway station at Görlitz, the complete building since the war of the palatial Hotel Astoria at Leipzig, also two gigantic new steel and concrete palaces in the same city for the semi-annual fair, the erection of a new Hamburg-America Line office building adjacent to the old one and dwarfing it. The slaughter-house annexes, contracted for in days of peace, continue their slow growth, although Berlin has no present need for such extension in these half-pound-of-meat-a-week times.

The construction of the Nord-Süd Bahn of the underground railway, for linking up the north and south sections of Berlin has proceeded right along, the women down in the pit with picks and shovels doing the heavy work of navvies. That department of the German Government whose duty it is to enlighten Neutrals is not too proud of the fact, surprisingly enough. An American kinematograph operator, Mr. Edwards, of Mr. Hearst's papers, was desirous of taking a film of these women navvies—heavy, sad creatures they are. The Government stepped in and suggested that, although they had no objection to a personally conducted and posed picture—in which the women would no doubt smile to order—they could not permit the realities of this unwomanly task to be shown in the form of a truth-telling moving picture.

German authorities are utilising every kind of woman. The social evil, against which the Bishop of London and others are agitating in England, was effectively dealt with by the German authorities, not only for the sake of the health of the troops, but in the interests of munitions. Women of doubtful character were first told that if found in the neighbourhood of barracks or in cafés they were liable to be arrested, and when so found were immediately removed to their native places, and put into the nearest cartridge filling or other shop. The double effect has been an increased output of munitions for the army and increased health for the soldier, and such scenes as one may witness in Piccadilly or other London streets at night have been effectively squelched by the strong Prussian hand, with benefit to all concerned.

I am not speaking of German morals in general, which are notorious. I merely state the practical way the Germans turn the women of the street into useful munition makers.

The lot of the German woman has been much more difficult than the lot of her sister in the Allied countries, for upon her has fallen the great and increasing burden of the struggle to get enough to eat for her household. In practically all classes of Germany it has been the custom of the man to come home from his work, whether in a Government office, bank, or factory, for his midday meal, usually followed by an hour's sleep.

The German man is often a greedy fellow as regards meals. For him special food is always provided, and the wife and children sit round patiently watching him eat it. He expects special food to-day. The soldier, of course, is getting it, and properly, but the stay-at-homes, who are men over forty-five or lads under nineteen, still get the best of such food as can be got. Ex-

ceptions to the nineteen to forty-five rule are very few
indeed. National work in Germany means war work
pure and simple, and now the women are treated exactly as the men in this respect, except that they will
not be sent to the front.

In January, 1917, Germany at length began formally
to organise the women of the country to help in the
war. Each of the six chief army "commands" throughout the Empire now has a woman attached to it as
Directress of the "Division for Women's Service."
Hitherto, as in England, war work by women has been
entirely voluntary. The Patriotic Auxiliary Service
(Mass Levy) Law is not compulsory so far as female
labour is concerned. German women, however, having
proclaimed that they regard themselves liable for
national service under the spirit if not the letter
of the law, it has finally been decided to mobilise
their services on a more systematic basis than in the
past.

None of the countless revolutions in German life
produced by the war outstrips in historical importance
this official linking up of women with the military machine. Equally striking is the fact that the directresses
of Women's Service, who hold office in Berlin, Breslau,
Magdeburg, Coblenz, Königsberg, and Karlsruhe, are
all feminist leaders and promoters of the women's eman-
cipation movement. The directress for the Mark of
Brandenburg (the Berlin-Potsdam district) is an able
Jewess named Dr. Alice Salomon, who is one of the
pioneers of the German women's movement. The main
object of the "Women's Service" Department is to organise female labour for munitions and other work

from which men can be liberated for the fighting line.

I have nothing but praise and admiration for the way in which the German women have thrown themselves into this struggle. Believing implicitly as they have been told—and with the exception of the lower classes, after more than two years of war, they believe everything the Government tells them—that this war was carefully prepared by "Sir Grey" (Lord Grey of Fallodon), "the man without a conscience," as he is called in Germany, they feel that they are helping to fight a war for the defence of their homes and their children, and the cynics at the German Foreign Office, who manufacture their opinions for them, rub this in in sermons from the pastors, novels, newspaper articles, faked cinema films, garbled extracts from Allied newspapers, books, and bogus photographs, Reichstag orations by Bethmann-Hollweg, and the rest of it, not forgetting the all-important lectures by the professors, who are unceasing in their efforts all over Germany.

To show how little the truth of the war is understood by the German women, I may mention an incident that occurred at the house of people of the official class at which I was visiting one day. The eldest son, who was just back from the Somme trenches, suffering from slight shell-shock, brought home a copy of a London illustrated paper, which had been thrown across the trenches by the English. In this photograph there was a picture of a long procession of German prisoners captured by the English. The daughter of the house, a well-read girl of nineteen, blazed up at the sight of this photograph, and showed it to her mother, who was equally surprised. The son of the house remarked, "Surely you know the English have taken a great many prisoners ?"

His mother, realising her mistake, looked confused, and simply said, "I didn't think." In other words, the obvious fact that Germans were sometimes captured had never been pointed out to her by the Government, and most Germans are accustomed to think only what they are officially told to think.

While there are an increasing number of doubters among the German males as to the accuracy of statements issued by the Government, in the class with which I mostly came into contact in Germany, the women are blindfold and believe all they are told. So strong, too, is the influence of Government propaganda on the people in Germany that in a town where I met two English ladies married to Germans, they believed that Germany had Verdun in her grasp, had annihilated the British troops (mainly black) on the Somme, had defeated the British Fleet in the battle of Skagerrak (Jutland), and reduced the greater part of the fortifications, docks, and munition factories of London to ruins by Zeppelins.

Their anguish for the fate of their English relations was sincere, and they were intensely hopeful that Britain would accept any sort of terms of peace in order to prevent the invasion which some people in Germany still believe possible.

At the beginning of the war the click of the knitting needle was heard everywhere; shop-girls knitted while waiting for customers, women knitted in trams and trains, at theatres, in churches, and, of course, in the home. The knitting is ceasing now for the very practical reason that the military authorities have commandeered all the wool for the clothing of the soldiery. A further reason for the stoppage of such needlework is the fact that women are engaged in countless forms of definite war work.

Upon the whole it is beyond question that the German women are not standing the losses as well as the British women. I have been honoured in England by conversations with more than one lady who has lost many dear ones. The attitude is quieter here than in Germany, and is not followed by the peace talk which such events produce in German households.

What surprises me in England is the fact that the word "peace" is hardly ever mentioned anywhere, whereas in any German railway train or tramcar the two dominant words are *Friede* (peace) and *Essen* (food). The peace is always a German idea of peace —for the extreme grumblers do not talk freely in public—and the food talk is not always the result of the shortage, but of the great difficulty in getting what is to be obtained, together with the increasing monotony of the diet.

It must not be supposed, however, that the life of feminine Germany is entirely a gloomy round of duty and suffering. Among the women of the poor, things are as bad as they can be. They are getting higher wages than ever, but the food usury and the blockade rob them of the increase.

The middle and upper classes still devote a good deal of time to the feminine pursuits of shopping and dressing. The outbreak of war hit the fashions at a curious moment. Paris had just abandoned the tight skirt, and a comical struggle took place between the Government and those women who desired to be correctly gowned.

The Government said, "In order to avoid waste of material, you must stick to the tight skirt," and the amount of cloth allowed was carefully prescribed. Women's desire to be in the mode was, however, too powerful for even Prussianism. Copies of French fashion magazines were smuggled in from Paris through Switzerland, passed from dressmaker to dressmaker, and house to house, and despite the military instructions and the leather shortage, wide skirts and high boots began to appear everywhere.

This feminine ebullition was followed by an appeal from the Government to abandon all enemy example and to institute new German fashions of their own making. Models were exhibited in shop windows of what were called the "old and elegant Viennese fashions." These, however, were found to be great consumers of material, and the women still continued to imitate Paris.

The day before I left Berlin I heard an amusing conversation in the underground railway between two women, one of whom was talking about her hat. She told her friend that she found the picture of the hat in a smuggled fashion paper, and had it made at her milliner's and she was obviously very pleased with her taste.

The women in the munition factories, who number millions, wear a serviceable kind of uniform overall.

The venom of the German women in regard to the war is quite in contrast to the feeling expressed by English women. They have read a great deal about British and American women and they cordially detest them. Their point of view is very difficult to explain. When I have told German women that in many States in my country women have votes, their reply is, "How vulgar!" Their attitude towards the whole question of women's franchise is that it is a form of Anglo-Saxon lack of culture and lack of authority.

The freedom accorded to English and American girls is entirely misunderstood. A Dutch girl who, in the presence of some German ladies, expressed admiration for certain aspects of English feminine life, was fiercely and venomously attacked by that never-failing weapon, the German woman's tongue. The poor thing, who mildly expressed the view that hockey was a good game for girls, and the fine complexions and elegant walk of English women were due to outdoor sports, was reduced almost to tears.

The intolerance of German women is almost impossible to express. I know a case of one young girl, a German-American, whose parents returned to Hamburg, who declined to repeat the ridiculous German formula, "Gott strafe England," and stuck to her point, with the result that she was not invited to that circle again.

To the cry "Gott strafe England" has been added "Gott strafe Amerika," the latter being as popular with the German women as the German men. The pastors, professors, and the Press have told the German women that their husbands and sons and lovers are being killed by American shells. A man who ought to know better, like Prince Rupert of Bavaria, made a public statement

that half of the Allies' ammunition is American. After
the British and French autumn offensive of 1915 the
feeling against America on the part of German women
became so intense that the American flag had to be
withdrawn from the American hospital at Munich, although that hospital, supported by German-American
funds, has done wonderful work for the German
wounded.

Arguments with German women about the war are
absolutely futile. They follow the war very closely
after their own method, and believe that any defeats,
such as on the Somme or Verdun, are tactical rear-
rangements of positions, dictated by the wisdom of the
General Staff, and so long as no Allied troops are upon
German soil so long will the German populace believe
in the invincibility of its army. I am speaking always
of the middle and upper classes, who are on the whole,
but with increasing exceptions, as intensely pro-war as
the lower classes are anti-war.

The modern German Bible is the *Zeitung* (the rough
translation of which is "newspaper") and German
women are even more fanatical than the men, if possible, in their worship of it.

On one occasion, when I candidly remarked that von
Papen and Boy-Ed came back to the Fatherland for
certain unbecoming acts, some of which I enumerated,
a Frau Hauptmann jumped to her feet and, after the
customary brilliant manner of German argument,
shrieked that I was a liar. She declared that their
Zeitung had said nothing about the charges I mentioned, therefore they were not true. She furthermore promised to report me to Colonel —— at the

Kriegsministerium (War Office), and she kept her word.

The neglect, and, in some cases refusal, to attend the British wounded by German nurses are a sign both of their own intensity of feeling in regard to the war and their entirely different mentality. Again and again I have heard German women say, "In the event of a successful German invasion of England the women will accompany the men, and teach the women of England that war is war." Their remarks in regard to the women of my own country are equally offensive. Indeed, States that Germany regards as neutral, and who are treated by the officially controlled German Press with a certain amount of respect, are loathed by German women. Their attitude is that all who are not on their side are their enemies. American women who are making shells for the British, French, and Russians are just as much the enemies of Germany as the Allied soldiers and sailors. One argument often used is that to be strictly neutral America should make no munitions at all, but it would not be so bad, say the Germans, if half the American ammunition went to Germany and half to the Allies.

I lost my temper once by saying to one elderly red-faced Frau, "Since you have beaten the British at sea, why don't you send your ships to fetch it?" "Our fleet," she said, "is too busy choking the British Fleet in its safe hiding places to afford time to go to America. You will see enough of our fleet one day, remember that!"

Summing up this brief and very sketchy analysis of German femininity in the war, I reiterate views expressed on previous visits to Germany, that German women are not standing the anxiety of the war as well as those of France and Britain.

They have done noble work for the Fatherland, but the grumblings of the lower third of the population are now such as have not been heard since 1848. German officials in the Press Department of the Foreign Office try to explain the unrest away to foreign correspondents like myself, but many thinking Germans are surprised and troubled by this unexpected manifestation on the part of those who for generations have been almost as docile and easily managed as children,

CHAPTER XX

THE WAR SLAVES OF ESSEN

Essen, the noisiest town in the world, bulks largely in the imagination of the Entente Allies, but "Essen" is not merely one city. It is a centre or capital of a whole group of arsenal towns. Look at your map of Germany, and you will see how temptingly near they are to the Dutch frontier. Look at the proximity of Holland and Essen, and you will understand the Dutch fear of Germany. You will grasp also the German fear, real as well as pretended, that the battle of the Somme may one day be accompanied by a thrust at the real heart of Germany, which is Westphalia—Westphalia with its coal and iron and millions of trained factory hands.

I saw when in Germany extracts from speeches by British politicians in which the bombing of Essen by air was advocated. Perhaps the task would have been easier if the bombing had come first and the speeches afterwards. Forewarned, forearmed; and Essen is now very much armed.

All German railroads seem to lead to this war monster. Attached to almost every goods train in Germany you will see wagons marked "Essen—special train." Wagons travel from the far ends of Austria and into Switzerland, which is showing its strict neutrality by making munitions for both sides.

On the occasion of my second visit to Essen during the war I arrived at night. It was before the time of the bombing speeches, and, though it was well into the hours when the world is asleep, the sky glowed red with a glare that could be seen for full thirty miles. My German companion glowed also, as he opened the carriage window and bade me join him in a peep at what we were coming to. "This is the place where we make the stuff to blow the world to pieces," he proudly boasted. "If our enemies could only see that the war would be over."

I suggested that Essen was not the only arsenal. There were, for instance, Woolwich, Glasgow, Newcastle, Creusot, and in my own strictly neutral country Bethlehem, Bridgeport, and one or two other humble hamlets. He brushed aside my remarks, "But we have also here in this very region Dortmund, Bochum, Witten, Duisburg, Krefeld, Düsseldorf, Solingen, Elberfeld and Barmen."

As we approached nearer, freight trains, military trains and passenger trains were everywhere. Officers and soldiers crowded the station platforms, and though it was night the activity of these Rhenish-Westphalian arsenal towns impressed me with the belief that unless the British blockade can strictly exclude essentials, such as copper and nickel, especially from their roaring factories, the war will be needlessly protracted.

It is not necessary to be long in Rhineland and Westphalia to realise that a shortage in these and other essentials is much more disturbing to the heads of these wonderful organisations than the fear of aerial bombs.

On the occasion of my first war-time visit to Essen

it would have been easy to have bombed it. There is an old saying that a shoemaker's children are the worst shod, and the display of anti-aircraft guns which has since manifested itself was then non-existent. The town was ablaze. It is still ablaze, but the lighting has been cunningly arranged to deceive nocturnal visitors, and any aeroplanes approaching Essen at a height of twelve or fifteen thousand feet would find it hard to discover which was Essen, and which Borbeck, and which was Steele.

Mülheim is easily found, because it is close to the River Ruhr. We had to halt a long time outside the station of Essen, so great was the pressure of traffic. The cordon surrounding the entrance to the city is some distance away, and having passed that safely I had no fear of being again interrogated.

I told the hotel manager that I was a travelling newspaper correspondent, and should like to see as many as possible of the wonders of his town. After praise of his hostelry, which, as the sub-manager said, was too good for the Essenites, I set out on my travels to see the sights of the city, foremost among them being the regulation statue of William I.

It was easy to find Krupps, for I had only to turn my steps towards the lurid panorama in the sky. As I came nearer, not only my sense of sight but my sense of hearing told me that Germany's great arsenal was throbbing with unwonted life. The crash and din of mighty steam hammers and giant anvils, the flame and flash of roaring blast furnaces, the rumbling of great railway trucks trundling raw and finished products in and out, chimneys of dizzy height belching forth mon-

ster coils of Cimmerian smoke, seem to transport one
from the prosaic valley of the Ruhr into the deafening
realm of Vulcan and Thor. The impression of Krupps
by night is ineffaceable. The very air exudes iron and
energy. You can almost imagine yourself in the midst
of a thunderous artillery duel. You are at any rate in
no doubt that the myriad of hands at work behind those
carefully guarded walls are even more vital factors in
the war than the men in the firing line. The blaze and
roar fill one with the overpowering sense of the Kaiser's
limitless resources for war-making. For you must roll
Sheffield and Newcastle-on-Tyne and Barrow-in-Fur-
ness into one clanging whole to visualise Essen-on-the-
Ruhr.

In some way Essen is unlike any other town I have
visited. It has its own internal network of railways,
running to and from the various branches of Krupps,
and as the trains pass across the streets they naturally
block the traffic for some minutes. They are almost
continuous and the pedestrians' progress is slow, but it
is exciting, for it is here that one realises what it means
to be at war with Germany. If the resolution of the
German people were as rigid as the steel in the great
cranes and rolling mills, the Allied task would be impossible.

The brief noon-tide rush of the workpeople resembles
our six o'clock rush in America towards Brooklyn
Bridge. I can say no more than that. There is nothing like it in London. The home-going crowd round
the Bank of England does not compare with the Essen
crowd, because the crowd at Essen is for a few minutes
more concentrated. Old and young, men and women,

refugees and prisoners of several nationalities (I saw
no British), Poles and Russians predominating, grimy,
worn, and weary, they pour out in a solid mass, and
cover the tramcars like bees in swarming time. The
pedestrians gradually break up into little companies,
most of them going to Kronenberg and other model colonies founded by Frau Krupp—"Bertha," as she is
affectionately called throughout Germany. The highest
honour the Germans can bestow upon her is to name
their 16-inch howitzer "Fat Bertha." Frau Bertha
Krupp, it may be well to recall, was the heiress to the
great Krupp fortune, and on her marriage in 1906 to
Herr von Bohlen und Halbach, a diplomatist, he
changed his name to Krupp von Bohlen und Halbach.

Though a private corporation with £12,500,000 share
capital owned by the "Cannon Queen" and her family, it is to all intents and purposes a Government Department just as Woolwich Arsenal is an adjunct of the
British War Office. In the past, as the elaborate cen-
tenary (1910) memorial proudly recites, fifty-two Governments throughout the world have bought Krupp
guns, armour, shells, and warships, with Germany by
far the biggest customer.

Out of the stupendous profits of war machines the
Krupps have built workpeople's houses that, as regards
material comfort, would not be easy to excel. These
houses are provided with ingenious coal-saving stoves,
that might well be copied elsewhere, for though Essen
is in the coal centre of Germany, they are just as careful about coal as though it were imported from the
other end of the world.

Frau Bertha and her husband (a simple and modest

man, who is, I was informed, entirely in the hands of his specialists, and who has the wisdom to let well alone) have put up a big fight with Batocki, the food dictator. The semi-famine had not reached its height when I was in Essen, and the suffering was not great there. A munition-maker working in any of the Rhenish-Westphalian towns is regarded by Germans as a soldier. As the war has proceeded he has been subject to continuous combing out.

The amount of food allowed to those engaged in these great factories and rolling mills is, I estimate, 33 per cent. more than that allowed to the rest of the civil population. In all the notices issued throughout Germany in regard to further food restrictions, there is appended the line, "This change is necessary owing to the need for fully supplying your brothers in the army and the munition works."

Essen is a town that before the war had a population exceeding 300,000. A conservative estimate makes the figure to-day nearly half a million. The Krupp Company employ about 120,000. A prevalent illusion is that Krupps confine their war-time effort exclusively to making war material. That is a mistake. A considerable part of Krupp's work is the manufacture of articles which can be exchanged for food and other products in neighbouring countries, thus taking the place of gold. At Lübeck, I saw the quays crowded with the products of Essen in the shape of steel girders and other building machinery going to Sweden in exchange for oil, lime from Gotland, iron ore, paper, wood, and food products.

A mining engineer of the great mines at Kiruna,

Lapland, told me that he had just given an order for steam shovels from the Westphalian manufacturers, who are also sending into Holland knives and scissors and other cutlery and tools.

Germany's principal bargaining commodities with contiguous neutral nations are steel building materials, coal, and dye-stuffs. Coal dug in Belgium by Belgian miners is a distinct asset for Germany, when she exchanges it for Swiss cattle, Dutch cheese, and Swedish wood. When we consider that the great industrial combinations of Rhineland and Westphalia are not only reaping enormous munition profits, but supply the steel and coal which form the bulk of German war-time exports, we can easily understand why some Social Democrats grew dissatisfied because the all-powerful National Liberals resisted a war profits tax for two years. It is noteworthy that several of the more outspoken German editors have been suspended for attacking these profiteers.

I should qualify this statement of exports slightly by saying that they pertained up to November, 1916. The effort to put more than ten million men into military uniform resulted not only in the slave-raids in Belgium but in a concentration in munition output that stopped further exports of steel products and coal on a large scale.

We should always remember in this great war of machinery that Germany secured a tremendous advantage at the expense of France at the outset when she occupied the most important French iron region of Longwy-Briey. The Germans, as I previously observed, have been working the French mines to the utmost—

indeed, they boast that they have installed improved machinery in them. They have, furthermore, been importing ore steadily from Sweden, some of the Swedish ore, such as Dannemora, being the best in the world for the manufacture of tool steel—so important in munition work.

Düsseldorf, probably the most attractive large manufacturing city in the world, had planned an industrial exhibition for 1915 or 1916, and the steel skeletons of many of the buildings had already been erected at the outbreak of war. But the Germans immediately set to work to tear down the steel frames to use them for more practical purposes. "We were going to call it a *German Fair*," said a native manufacturer to me early in the war; "but we can have it later and call it a *World's Fair*, as the terms will be synonymous."

Isolated near the Rhine is the immense reconstructed Zeppelin shed which British airmen in November, 1914, partly destroyed, together with the nearly completed Zeppelin within it. The daring exploit evidently work up the newly appointed anti-aircraft gunners, for they subsequently annihilated two of their own machines approaching from the West.

The badly paid war slaves of Essen are working the whole twenty-four hours, seven days a week, in three shifts a day of eight hours each, under strict martial law. The town is a hotbed of extreme Social Democracy, and as a rule the Socialists of Westphalia are almost as red as those of the manufacturing districts of Saxony. But Socialists though they be, they are just as anti-British as the rest of Germany, and they like to send out their products with the familiar hall-mark of "Gott strafe England," or "Best wishes for King George." It is the kind of Socialism that wants more money, more votes, less work, but has no objection to plenty of war. It is a common-sense Socialism, which knows that without war Essen might shrink to its pre-war dimensions.

Essen is very jealous of the great Skoda works near Pilsen in Austria. My hotel manager spoke with some acerbity of the amount of advertising the Austrian siege howitzers were receiving. "You can accept my assurance," he said, "that the guns for the bombardment of Dover were made here, and not at the skoda works, as the Austrians claim."

Every German in Essen seems to feel a personal pride in the importance of the works to the Empire at the fateful hour. The 42-centimetre gun "which conquered Belgium"—as the native puts it—is almost deified. Everybody struts about in the consciousness that he or she has had directly or indirectly something to do with the murderous weapon which has wrought such death and glory in Germany's name. "The Empire has the men, Essen has the armour-plate, the torpedoes, the shells, the guns. It is the combination which must win." That is the spirit in Kruppville.

CHAPTER XXI

O NE day the world will be flooded with some of the most dramatic, horrible, and romantic of narratives—the life-stories of the British soldiers captured in the early days of the war, their gross ill-treatment, their escapes, and attempts at escape. I claim to be the only unofficial neutral with any large amount of eye-witness, hand-to-hand knowledge of those poor men in Germany.

One of the most difficult tasks I assumed during the war was the personal and *unconducted* investigation of British prisoners of war. The visitor is only allowed to talk with prisoners when visiting camps under the supervision of a guide. My tramps on foot all over Germany gave me valuable information on this as on other matters.

My task was facilitated by the Germany policy of showing the hated British captives to as many people as possible; thus the 30,000 men have been scattered into at least 600 prison camps. In the depleted state of the German Army it is not easy to find efficient guards for so many establishments. Prisoners are constantly being moved about. They are conveyed ostentatiously and shown at railway stations *en route,* where until recently they were allowed to be spat upon by the public, and were given coffee into which the public were allowed to spit. These are but a few of the slights and abominations heaped upon them. Much of it is quite unprintable.

Many a night did I lie awake in Berlin cogitating how to get into touch with some of these men. I learned something on a previous visit in 1914, when I saw the British prisoners at one of the camps. At that time it was impossible to get into conversation with them. They were efficiently and continually guarded by comparatively active soldiers.

On this occasion I came across my first British prisoner quite by accident, and, as so often happens in life, difficult problems settle themselves automatically. In nothing that I write shall I give any indication of the whereabouts of the sixty prisoners with whom I conversed privately, but there can be no harm in my mentioning the whereabouts of my public visit, which took place in one of the regular neutral "Cook's tours" of the prisoners in Germany.

The strain of my work in so suspicious a place as Berlin, the constant care required to guard one's expressions, and the anxiety as to whether one was being watched or not got on my nerves sometimes, and one Sunday I determined to take a day off and go into the country with another neutral friend. There, by accident, I came across my first private specimen of Tommy in Germany.

We were looking about for a decent Gasthaus in which to get something to eat when we saw a notice high up in large type on a wall outside an old farmhouse building, which read:—

Jeder Verkehr der Zivilbevölkerung mit den Kriegsgefangenen ist STRENG VERBOTEN.

"Any intercourse of the civil population with the prisoners of war is strictly forbidden."

These notices, which threaten the civilian population with heavy penalties if they exchange any words with the prisoners, are familiar all over Germany, but I did not expect to find them in that small village.

My neutral friend thought it would make a nice photograph if I would stand under the notice, which I did after a cautious survey showed that the coast was clear.

As I did so a Russian came out of the barn and said, in rather bad German, "Going to have your photograph taken?" I replied, in German, "Yes."

He heard me speaking English to my friend, and then, looking up and down the street each way to see if we were being watched, he addressed me in English with a strong Cockney accent.

"You speak English, then?" I said.

"I am English," he replied. "I'm an English prisoner."

"Then what are you doing in a Russian uniform?"

"It is the only thing I could get when my own clothes wore out." Keeping a careful eye up and down the street, he told us his story. He was one of the old Expeditionary Force; was taken at Mons with five bullet wounds in him, and, after a series of unpublishable humiliations, had been drafted from camp to camp until he had arrived at this little village, where, in view of the German policy of letting all the population see an

Englishman, he was the representative of his race in that community. "The local M.P." he called himself, in his humorous way.

Robinson Crusoe on his island was not more ignorant of the truth about the great world than that man, for, while he had learnt a few daily expressions in German, he was unable to read it. The only information he could gather was from the French, Belgian, and Russian prisoners with him, and some he got by bribing one of the Landsturm Guards with a little margarine or sugar out of his parcel from England. He was full of the battle of Mons and how badly he and his comrades in Germany felt at the way they had been left unsupported there. None the less, though alone, with no Englishman for miles, living almost entirely on his parcels, absolutely cut off from the real facts of the war, hearing little but lies, he was as calmly confident of the ultimate victory of the Allies as I am.

I asked him if he heard from home.

"Yes," he said, "now and then, but the folks tell me nothing and I can tell them nothing. If you get back to England you tell the people there not to believe a word that comes from English prisoners. Those who write favourably do so because they have to. Every truthful letter is burned by the military censor. Tell the people to arrange the parcels better and see that every man gets a parcel at least once a week—not send five parcels to one man and no parcels to some poor bloke like me who is alone. How is the war going on, guv'nor?" he asked. I gave him my views. "I think it's going badly for the Germans—not by what they tell me here or what I gets in that awful *Continental Times* paper, but from what I notice in the people round about, and the officers who visit us. The people are not so abusive to the English as they used to be. The superior officers do not treat us like dogs, as they did, and as for the Landsturmers—well, look at old Heinrich here."

At that moment a heavy, shabby old Landsturm soldier came round the corner, and the Cockney prisoner treated him almost as though he were a performing bear.

"You're all right, ain't you, Heiny, so long as I give you a bit of sugar now and then?" he said to his decrepit old guardian in his German gibberish.

This state of affairs was a revelation to me, but I was soon to find that if the British prisoners are weary of their captivity their old German guardians are much more weary of their task. These high-spirited British lads, whom two years of cruelty have not cowed, are an intense puzzle to the German authorities.

"You see," remarked a very decent German official connected with the military censorship department, "everyone of these Britishers is different. Every one of them sticks up for what he calls his 'rights': many of them decline to work on Sunday, and short of taking them out on Sunday morning at the point of the bayonet we cannot get them to do it. We have to be careful, too, with these Englishmen now. As a man of the world, you will realise that though our general public here do not know that the English have captured many Germans lately, and the fact is never mentioned in the *communiqués,* we have had a hint from Headquarters that the British prisoners may one day balance ours, and that

hardship for these *verfluchte Engländer* may result in
hardship for our men in England."

That incident was long ago. It is important to relate
that since the beginning of the battle of the Somme
there is, if I was correctly informed, a marked improvement in the condition of English prisoners all over Germany—not as regards food supplied by the authorities,
because the food squeeze naturally affects the prisoners
as it does their guardians, but in other ways.

In addition to the British capturing numbers of German hostages on the Somme to hold against the treatment of their men in Germany, I think I may claim
without undue pride that much good work has been
done by the American Ambassador and his staff of
attachés, who work as sedulously on behalf of the prisoners as though those prisoners had been American.

The German authorities hate and respect publicity
and force in matters not to their liking, and Mr.
Gerard's fearlessness in reports of conditions and urgent
pleas for improvement have been of great service. All
the threats and bluster of Germany have failed to cow
him.

To continue my narrative of the Cockney soldier in
Russian uniform. So many Englishmen are in Russian uniform, Belgian uniform, French uniform, or a
mix-up uniform that there is no possibility of my Cockney Russian being recognised by the authorities, and
the photograph which my neutral friend took of him
and me was taken under the very eyes of his Landsturmer.

"Heiny," said the Russian Cockney, "is fed up with
the war. Aren't you, old Heiny? During the last few
weeks a fresh call for more men has cleared the district

of everything on two legs. We have had to work four-teen hours a day, and I wonder what my mates at home would think of 3s. pay for ten days' work?"

I was able to comfort him by giving him some cigars, and a great deal of really true and good news about the war, all of which he repeated to Landsturmer Heinrich. I suggested that this might be unwise. "Not a bit of it," he said. "Lots of these old Germans are only too anxious to hear bad news, because they think that bad news will bring the thing to a stop."

How true that remark was I knew from my minute investigations. The incident was closed by the distant appearence of a *Feldwebel* (sergeant-major). My Cockney vanished, and Heinrich patrolled onward.

This particular incident is not typical of the life of a British prisoner in Germany, but it is indicative of the position many of the 30,000 prisoners have taken up by reason of their strong individuality and extraordinary cheerfulness and confidence. My impression of them is of alert, resourceful men (their escapes have been wonderful)—men who never know when they are beaten. If Britain has sufficient of these people she cannot possibly lose the war.

*   *   *   *   *

The world does not need reminders such as that of Wittenberg or of such singularly accurate narratives as several in *Blackwood's Magazine* to know what *has* happened to British prisoners in Germany.

It is common knowledge throughout the German Empire that the most loathsome tasks of the war in connection with every camp or cage are given to the British. They have had to clean the latrines of negro prisoners, and were in some cases forced to work with implements which would make their task the more disgusting. One man told me that his lunch was served to him where he was working, and when he protested he was told to eat it there, or go without.

Conversations that I have had here in London about prisoners give me the impression that the British public does not exactly apprehend what a prisoner stands for in German eyes.

First, he is a hostage. If he be an officer his exact social value is estimated by the authorities in Berlin, who have a complete card index of all their officer prisoners, showing to what British families they belong and whether they have social or political connections in Britain. Thus when someone in England mistakenly, and before sufficient German prisoners were in their hands, treated certain submarine marauders differently from other prisoners, the German Government speedily referred to this card-index, picked out a number of officers with connections in the House of Lords and House of Commons, and treated them as convicts.

The other German view of the prisoner is his cash value as a labourer. I invite my readers to realise the enormous pecuniary worth of the two million prisoner slaves now reclaiming swamps, tilling the soil, building roads and railways, and working in factories for their German taskmasters.

The most numerous body of prisoners in Germany are the Russians. They are to be seen everywhere. In some cases they have greater freedom than any other prisoners, and often, in isolated cases, travel unguarded by rail or tramway to and from their work. If they are not provided with good Russian uniforms, in which, of course, they would not be able to escape, they are made conspicuous by a wide stripe down the trouser or on the back. They are easy, docile, physically strong, and accustomed to a lower grade of food than any other prisoners, except the Serbs.

The British, of course, are much the smallest number in Germany, but much the most highly prized for hate propaganda purposes.

"More difficult to manage," said one *Unteroffizier* to me, "than the whole of the rest of our two million." It is, indeed, a fact that the 30,000 British prisoners, though the worst treated, are the gayest, most outspoken, and rebellious against tyranny of the whole collection.

There is, however, a brighter side to prison life in Germany, I am happy to record. A number of really excellent camps have been arranged to which neutral visitors are taken. When I told the German Foreign Office that I would like to see the good side of prison life, I was given permission by the *Kriegsministerium* (War Office) to visit the great camp at Soltau with its 31,000 inmates with Halil Halid Bey (formerly Turkish Consul in Berlin) and Herr Müller (interested in Germany's Far Eastern developments).

Five hours away from Berlin, on the monotonous *Lüneberger Heide* (Lüneberg Heath), has sprung up this great town with the speed of a boom mining town in Colorado.

On arrival at the little old town of Soltau we were met by a military automobile and driven out on a road made by the prisoners to the largest collection of huts I have ever seen.

There is nothing wrong that I could detect in the camp, and I should say that the 200 British prisoners there are as well treated as any in Germany. The Commandant seems to be a good fellow. His task of ruling so great an assemblage of men is a large and difficult one, rendered the easier by the good spirit engendered by his tact and kindness.

I had confirmation of my own views of him later, when I came across a Belgian who had escaped from Germany, and who had been in this camp. He said:—"The little captain at Soltau was a good fellow, and if I am with the force that releases the prisoners there after we get into Germany, I will do my best to see that he gets extra good treatment."

Our inspection occupied six hours. Halil Halid Bey, who talks English perfectly, and looks like an Irishman, was taken for an American by the prisoners. In fact, one Belgian, believing him to be an American official, rushed up to him and with arms outstretched pleaded: "Do you save poor Belgians, too, as well as British?"

The physical comfort of the prisoners is well looked after in the neat and perfectly clean dormitories. The men were packed rather closely, I thought, but not more than on board ship.

One became almost dazed in passing through these miles of huts, arranged in blocks like the streets of an American town.

We visited the hospital, which was as good as many civilian hospitals in other countries. There I heard the first complaint, from a little red-headed Irishman, his voice wheezing with asthma, whose grievance was not against the camp itself, but against a medical order which had reversed what he called his promise to be sent to Switzerland.   He raised his voice without any fear, as our little group, accompanied by the Commandant and the interpreter, went round, and I was allowed to speak to him freely.   I am not a medical man, but I should think his was a case for release.   His lungs were obviously in a bad state.

We were also accompanied by an English sergeant, one Saxton—a magnificent type of the old Army, so many of whom are eating out their days in Germany. He spoke freely and frankly about the arrangements, and had no complaint to make except the food shortage and the quality of the food.

The British section reminded one now and then of England.   Portraits of wives, children, and sweethearts were over the beds; there was no lack of footballs, and the British and Belgians play football practically every day after the daily work of reclaiming the land, erecting new huts, making new roads, and looking after the farms and market gardens has been accomplished.

An attempt has been made to raise certain kinds of live stock, such as pigs, poultry, and Belgian hares—a large kind of rabbit.   There were a few pet dogs about —one had been trained by a Belgian to perform tricks equal to any of those displayed at variety theatres.

Apparently there is no lack of amusement.   I visited the cinematograph theatre, and the operator asked, "What would you like to see—something funny?"   He showed us a rather familiar old film.   The reels are those that have been passed out of service of the German moving picture shows.   In the large theatre, which would hold, I should think, seven hundred to a thousand people, there was a good acrobatic act and the performing dog, to which I have referred, with an orchestra of twenty-five instruments, almost all prisoners, but a couple of German Landsturmers helped out. The guarding of the prisoners is effected by plenty of barbed wire and a comparatively small number of oldish Landsturmers.

A special cruelty of the Germans towards prisoners is the provision of a lying newspaper in French for the Frenchmen, called the *Gazette des Ardennes.* The *Gazette des Ardennes* publishes every imaginable kind of lie about the French and French Army, with garbled quotations from English newspapers, and particularly *The Times,* calculated to disturb the relations of the French and English prisoners in Germany. For the British there is a paper in English which is quite as bad, to which I have already referred, called the *Continental Times,* doled out three times a week. The *Continental Times* is, I regret to say, largely written by renegade Englishmen in Berlin employed by the German Government, notably Aubrey Stanhope, who for well-known reasons was unable to enter England at the outbreak of war, and so remains and must remain in Germany, where, for a very humble pittance, he conducts this campaign against his own country.

For the Russians a special prevaricating sheet, called the *Russki Visnik,* is issued. All these newspapers pretend to print the official French, British, and Russian *communiqués.*

For a long time the effect on the British prisoners was bad, but little by little events revealed to them that the *Continental Times,* which makes a specialty of attacks on the English Press, was anti-British.

The arrival of letters and parcels is, of course, the great event for the prisoners and, so far as the *large* camps are concerned, I do not think that there are now any British prisoners unprovided with parcels. It is the isolated and scattered men, moved often from place to place for exhibition purposes, who miss parcels.

Soltau, although a model camp, is bleak and dreary and isolated. At the outset cases of typhus occurred there, and in a neat, secluded corner of the camp long lines of wooden crosses tell the tale of sadness. The first cross marked a Russian from far-away Vilna, the next a Tommy from London. East had met West in the bleak and silent graveyard on the heather. Close to them slept a soldier from some obscure village in Normandy, and beside him lay a Belgian, whose life had been the penalty of his country's determination to defend her neutrality. Here in the heart of Germany the Allies were united even in death.

As I made the long journey back to Berlin I reflected with some content on the good things I had seen at Soltau, and I felt convinced that the men in charge of the camp do everything within their power to make the life of the prisoners happy. But as the train pounded along in the darkness I seemed to see a face before me which I could not banish. It was the face of a Belgian, kneeling at the altar in the Catholic chapel, his eyes riveted on his Saviour on the Cross, his whole being tense in fervent supplication, his lips quivering in prayer. My companions had gone, but I was held spellbound, feeling "How long! How long!" was the anguish of his mind. He must have been a man who had a home and loved it, and his whole expression told unmistakably that he was imploring for strength to hold out till the end in that dreary, cheerless region of brown and grey.

His captors had given him a chapel, to be sure, but why was he in Germany at all?

* * * * *

Soltau and other camps are satisfactory—but there are others, many others, such as unvisited punishment camps. The average Britisher in confinement in Germany is under the care of an oldish guard, such as Heiny of the Landsturm, but the immediate authority is often a man of the notorious *Unteroffizier* type, whose cruelty to the *German* private is well known, and whose treatment of the most hated enemy can be imagined.

The petty forms of tyranny meted out to German soldiers such as making a man walk for hours up and down stairs in order to fill a bath with a wineglass; making him shine and soil then again shine and soil hour after hour a pair of boots; making him chew and swallow his own socks have been described in suppressed German books.

I believe that publicity, rigorous blockade and big shells are the only arguments that have any effect on the Prussians at present. It is publicity and the fear of opinion of certain neutrals that has produced such camps as Soltau. It is difficult for the comfortable sit-at-homes to visualise the condition of men who have been in the enemy atmosphere of hate for a long period. All the British soldiers whom I met in Germany were captured in the early part of the war when their shell-less Army had to face machine-guns and high explosives often with the shield of their own breasts and a rifle.

Herded like cattle many of the wounded dying, they travelled eastwards to be subject to the insults and vilifications of the German population. That they should retain their cheery confidence in surroundings and among a people so ferociously hostile so entirely un-British, so devoid of chivalry or sporting instinct, is a monument to the character of their race.

CHAPTER XXII

HOW THE PRUSSIAN GUARD CAME HOME FROM THE SOMME

E ARLY in August, 1916, I was in Berlin. The British and French offensive had commenced on July 1st. Outwardly it appeared to attract very little notice on the part of Germany and I do not believe that it attracted sufficient attention even in the highest military quarters. It was considered to be Great Britain's final "bluff." The great maps in the shop windows in every street and on the walls in every German house showed no change, and still show no change worth noticing. "Maps speak," say the Germans.

One hot evening in Berlin I met a young officer whom I had known on a previous visit to Germany, and who was home on ten days' furlough. I noticed that he was ill or out of sorts, and he told me that he had been unexpectedly called back to his regiment on the Western front. "How is that?" I said. He made that curious and indescribable German gesture which shows discontent and dissatisfaction. "These ——— English are putting every man they have got into a final and ridiculous attempt to make us listen to peace terms. My leave is cut short, and I am off this evening." We had a glass of beer at the Bavaria Restaurant in the Friedrichstrasse.

"You have been in England, haven't you?" he inquired. I told him that I had been there last year. "They seem to have more soldiers than we thought," he said. "They seem to be learning the business; my battalion has suffered terribly."

Within the next day or two there were other rumours in Berlin—rumours quite unknown to the mass. How and where I heard these rumours it would be unfair to certain Germans, who were extremely kind to me, to say, but it was suggested to me by a friend—a member of the Extreme Left of the Social Democratic Party —that if I wanted to learn the truth I should go out to Potsdam and see the arrival of the wounded men of the famous Prussian Guard, who had, he said, had a terrible experience at the hands of the English at Contalmaison on July 10th.

He drew me aside in the Tiergarten and told me, for he is, I am sure, a real German patriot, that the state of things in the Somme, if known throughout Germany, would effectively destroy the pretensions of the annexationist party, who believed that Germany has won the war and will hold Belgium and the conquered portion of France and Poland.

He told me to go out to Potsdam with caution, and he warned me that I should have the utmost difficulty in getting anywhere near the military sidings of the railway station there.

I asked another usually extremely well-informed friend if there was anything particular happening in the war, and told him that I thought of going to Potsdam, and he said, "What for? There is nothing to be seen there—the same old drilling drilling, drilling." So well are secrets kept in Germany.

The 4th of August is the anniversary of what is known in Germany as "England's treachery"—the day that Britain entered the war in what the German Government tells the people is "a base and cowardly attempt to try and beat her by starving innocent women and children."

On that sunny and fresh morning I looked out of the railway carriage window some quarter of a mile before we arrived at Potsdam and saw numerous brown trains marked with the Red Cross, trains that usually travel by night in Germany.

There were a couple of officers of the Guard Cavalry in the same carriage with me. They also looked out. *"Ach, noch 'mal"* ("What, again?") discontentedly remarked the elder. They were a gloomy pair and they had reason to be. The German public has begun to know a great deal about the wounded. They do not yet know all the facts, because wounded men are, as far as possible, hidden in Germany and never sent to Socialist centres unless it is absolutely unavoidable. The official figures which are increasing in an enormous ratio since the development of Britain's war machine, are falsified by manipulation.

And if easy proof be needed of the truth of my assertion I point to the monstrous official misstatement involved in the announcement that over ninety per cent. of German wounded return to the firing line! Of the great crush of wounded at Potsdam I doubt whether any appreciable portion of the serious cases will return to anything except permanent invalidism. They are suffering from shell wounds, not shrapnel, for the most part, I gathered.

As our train emptied it was obvious that some great spectacle was in progress. The exit to the station became blocked with staring peasant women returning from the early market in Berlin, their high fruit and vegetable baskets empty on their backs. When I eventually got through the crowd into the outer air and paused at the top of the short flight of steps I beheld a scene that will never pass from my memory. Filmed and circulated in Germany it would evoke inconceivable astonishment to this deluded nation and would swell the malcontents, already a formidable mass, into a united and dangerous army of angry, eye-opened dupes. This is not the mere expression of a neutral view, but is also the opinion of a sober and patriotic German statesman.

I saw the British wounded arrive from Neuve Chapelle at Boulogne; I saw the Russian wounded in the retreat from the Bukovina; I saw the Belgian wounded in the Antwerp retreat, and the German wounded in East Prussia, but the wounded of the Prussian Guard at Potsdam surpassed in sadness anything I have witnessed in the last two bloody years.

The British Neuve Chapelle wounded were, if not gay, many of them blithe and smiling—their bodies were hurt but their minds were cheerful; but the wounded of the Prussian Guard—the proudest military force in the world—who had come back to their home town decimated and humbled—these Guards formed the most amazing agglomeration of broken men I have ever encountered. As to the numbers of them, of these five Reserve regiments but few are believed to be unhurt. Vast numbers were killed, and most of the rest are back at Potsdam in the ever growing streets of hospitals that are being built on the Bornstädterfeld.

One of the trains had just stopped. The square was blocked with vehicles of every description. I was surprised to find the great German furniture vans, which by comparison with those used in England and the United States look almost like houses on wheels, were drawn up in rows with military precision. As if these were not enough, the whole of the wheeled traffic of Potsdam seemed to be commandeered by the military for the lightly wounded—cabs, tradesmen's wagons, private carriages—everything on wheels except, of course, motor-cars, which are non-existent owing to the rubber shortage. Endless tiers of stretchers lay along the low embankment sloping up to the line. Doctors, nurses, and bearers were waiting in quiet readiness.

The passengers coming out of the station, including the women with the tall baskets, stopped, but only for a moment. They did not tarry, for the police, of which there will never be any dearth if the war lasts thirty years, motioned them on, a slight movement of the hand being sufficient.

I was so absorbed that I failed to notice the big constable near me until he laid his heavy paw upon my shoulder and told me to move on. A schoolmaster and his wife, his *Rücksack* full of lunch, who had taken advantage of the glorious sunshine to get away from Berlin to spend a day amidst the woods along the Havel, asked the policeman what the matter was.

The reply was *"Nichts hier zu sehen"* ("Nothing to

be seen here. Get along!"). The great "Hush! Hush! Hush!" machinery of Germany was at work.

Determined not to be baffled, I moved out of the square into the shelter of a roadside tree, on the principle that a distant view would be better than none at all, but the police were on the alert, and a police lieutenant tackled me at once. I decided to act on the German military theory that attack is the best defence, and, stepping up to him, I stated that I was a newspaper correspondent. "Might I not see the wounded taken from the train?" I requested. He very courteously replied that I might not, unless I had a special pass for that purpose from the *Kriegsministerium* in Berlin.

I hit upon a plan.

I regretfully sighed that I would go back to Berlin and get a pass, and retracing my steps to the station I bought a ticket.

A soldier and an Unteroffizier were stationed near the box in which stood the uniformed woman who punches tickets.

The Unteroffizier looked at me sharply. "No train for an hour and a half," he said.

"That doesn't disturb me in the least when I have plenty to read," I answered pleasantly, at the same time pointing to the bundle of morning papers which I carried, the *Norddeutsche Allgemeine Zeitung* of the Foreign Office, on the outside.

I knew Potsdam thoroughly, and was perfectly familiar with every foot of the station. I knew that there was a large window in the first and second-class dining-room which was even closer to the ambulances in the square than were the exit steps.

I did not go directly to the dining-room, but sat on one of the high-backed benches on the platform and began to read the papers. The Unteroffizier looked out and found me fairly buried in them. He returned a little later and saw me asleep—or thought he did.

When he had gone I sauntered along the platform into the dining-room, to find it vacant save for a youthful waiter and a barmaid. I walked straight to the window—where the light would be better for reading—and ordered bread and Edam cheese, tearing off a fifty gram amount from my Berlin bread ticket, which was fortunately good in Potsdam.

My position enabled me to look right out upon the square below, but rendered me inconspicuous from the street.

By this time the wounded were being moved from the train. The slightly wounded were drawn up in double ranks, their clean white arm- and head-bandages gleaming in the noonday light. They stood dazed and dejected, looking on at the real work which was just beginning—the removal of the severely wounded.

Then it was that I learned the use of those mammoth furniture vans. Then it was, I realised that these vans are part of Germany's plans by which her wounded are carried—I will not say secretly, but as unobtrusively as possible. In some of the mammoths were put twelve, into others fourteen; others held as many as twenty.

The Prussian Guard had come home. The steel corps of the army of Germany had met near Contalmaison the light-hearted boys I had seen drilling in Hyde Park last year, and in a furious counter-attack, in which they had attempted to regain the village, had been wiped out.

These were not merely wounded, but dejected wounded. The whole atmosphere of the scene was that of intense surprise and depression. Tradition going back to Frederick the Great, nearly two hundred years ago, had been smashed—by amateur soldiers. The callow youth of sixteen who served my lunch was muttering something to the barmaid, who replied that he was lucky to be in a class that was not likely to be called up yet.

The extreme cases were carried at a snail's pace by bearers, who put their feet down as carefully as if they were testing very thin ice, and who placed the comfortable spring stretchers in the very few vehicles which had rubber or imitation rubber tyres. The work was done with military precision and great celerity. The evacuation of this train was no sooner finished than another took its place, and the same scene was repeated. Presently the great furniture vans returned from having deposited their terrible loads, and were again filled. One van was reserved for those who had expired on the journey, and it was full.

This, then, was the battered remnant of the five Reserve regiments of the Prussian Guard which had charged the British lines at Contalmaison three weeks before in a desperate German counter-attack to wrest the village from the enemy, who had just occupied it. Each train discharged between six and seven hundred maimed passengers. Nor was this the last day of the influx.

The Guard had its garrisons chiefly in Potsdam, but also partly in Berlin, and represents the physical flower of German manhood. On parade it was inspiring to look at, and no military officer in the world ever doubted its prowess. Nor has it failed in the war to show splendid courage and fighting qualities. English people simply do not understand its prestige at home and among neutrals.

The Guard is sent only where there is supreme work to be done. If you hear that it has been hurled into a charge you may rest assured that it is striving to gain something on which Germany sets the highest price—for the life-blood of the Guard is the dearest that she can pay.

In the battle of the Marne the active regiments of the Guard forming a link between the armies of von Bülow and von Hausen were dashed like spray on jagged cliffs when they surged in wave after wave against the army of Foch at Sézanne and Fère Champenoise.

Germany was willing to sacrifice those superb troops during the early part of the battle because she knew that von Kluck had only to hold his army together, even though he did not advance, and the overthrow of Foch would mean a Teuton wedge driven between Verdun and Paris.

One year and ten months later she hurled the Guard Reserve at Contalmaison because she was determined that this important link in the chain of concrete and steel that coiled back and forth before Bapaume-Péronne must remain unbroken. The newly-formed lines of Britain's sons bent but did not break under the shock. They were outnumbered, but, like all the rest of the British that the back-from-the-front German soldiers have told me about, these fought on and on, never thinking of surrender.

I know from one of these that in a first onslaught the Guard lost heavily, but was reinforced and again advanced. Another desperate encounter and the men from Potsdam withered in the hand-to-hand carnage. The Germans could not hold what they had won back, and the khaki succeeded the field grey at Contalmaison.

The evacuation of the wounded occupied hours. I purposely missed my train, for I knew that I was probably the only foreign civilian to see the historic picture of the proudest soldiery of Prussia return to its garrison town from the greatest battle in history.

Empty trains were pulled out of the way, to be succeeded by more trains full of wounded, and again more. Doctors and nurses were attentive and always busy, and the stretcher-bearers moved back and forth until their faces grew red with exertion.

But it was the visages of the men on the stretchers that riveted my attention. I never saw so many men so completely exhausted. Not one pair of lips relaxed into a smile, and not an eye lit up with the glad recognition of former surroundings.

It was not, however, the lines of suffering in those faces that impressed me, but that uncanny sameness of expression, an expression of hopeless gloom so deep that it made me forget that the sun was shining from an unclouded sky. The dejection of the police, of the soldier onlookers, of the walking wounded, and those upturned faces on the white pillows told as plainly as words could ever tell that the Guard had at last met a force superior to themselves and their war machine. They knew well that they were the idol of their Fatherland, and that they had fought with every ounce of their great physical strength, backed by their long traditions. They had been vanquished by an army of mere sportsmen.

My thoughts went back to Berlin and the uninformed scoffings at the British Army and its futile efforts to push back the troops of Rupprecht on the Somme. Yet here on the actual outskirts of the German capital was a grim tribute to the machine that Great Britain had built up under the protection of her Navy.

In Berlin at that moment the afternoon editions were fluttering their daily headlines of victory to the crowds on the Linden and the Friedrichstrasse, but here the mammoth vans were moving slowly through the streets of Potsdam.

To the women who stood in the long lines waiting with the potato and butter tickets for food on the other side of the old stone bridge that spans the Havel they were merely ordinary cumbersome furniture wagons.

How were they to know that these tumbrils contained the bloody story of Contalmaison?

CHAPTER XXIII

GERMANY, according to Reichstag statements, is spending millions of pounds upon German propaganda throughout the universe. The trend of that propaganda is:—

1. To attempt to convince the neutral world that Germany cannot be beaten; and

2. Above all, to convince Great Britain (the chief enemy) that Germany cannot be beaten.

The only factors really feared by the Germans of the governing class are the Western front and the blockade.

I went into Germany determined to try to find out the truth, and to tell the truth. I had an added incentive to be thorough and work on original lines, since I was fortunate enough to secure possession of an official letter which advised those whom it concerned to give no information of value to Americans in general. I also got accurate information that the Wilhelmstrasse had singled me out as one American in particular to whom nothing of value was to be imparted.

The German, with his cast-in-a-mould mind, does not understand the trait developed among other peoples of seeing things for themselves. He is unacquainted with originality in human beings. He thinks a corre-

276

spondent does not observe anything unless it is pointed out to him.

Last summer, for example, one could learn in the Wilhelmstrasse that the potato crop was a glittering success. By walking through the country and pulling up an occasional plant, also talking to the farmers, I concluded that it was a dismal failure, which conclusion I announced in one of the first newspaper articles I wrote after I had left Germany. Recent reports from that country show that I was right, which increases my conviction that the *confidential tips* given by Germany's professional experts, who instruct neutral visitors, do very well to make Germany's position seem better than it actually is, but they seldom stand the acid test of history.

Seeking to invent excuses is not peculiar to the Germans, but it is more prevalent among them than among any other people that I know. In this one respect the German Government is a Government of the people. Some of the diplomatic explanations which have emanated from Berlin during the war have been weird in their absurdity and an insult to the intelligence of those to whom they were addressed.

President Wilson did not accept the official lie concerning the sinking of the *Arabic,* in view of the positive proof against Germany, and Germany backed down. President Wilson did not accept the official lie concerning the sinking of the *Sussex.* Incomprehensible as it is to the Teutonic mind, he attached greater weight to the first-hand evidence of reliable eye-witnesses, plus fragments of the torpedo which struck the vessel, than to the sacred words of the German Foreign Office, which had the impertinence to base its case on a sketch, or alleged sketch, hastily made by a U-boat manipulator whose artistic temperament should have led him to Munich rather than to Kiel. The crime and the lie were so glaring that Germany once more backed down.

Germany lied about the Dutch liner *Tubantia.* As in the case of the *Sussex,* the evidence of the fragments of torpedo was so incontrovertible that Berlin had to admit that a German torpedo sank the *Tubantia.* Indeed, one fragment contained the number of the torpedo. During my travels in the Fatherland at that time I found no doubt in the minds of those with whom I discussed the matter that a German submarine sank the vessel, though many were of the opinion that it was a mistake.

The Wilhelmstrasse is tenacious, however, and we awoke one morning to read what was probably its most remarkable excuse. To be sure, a German torpedo sank the *Tubantia,* but it was not fired by the Germans. The expert accountant who was in charge of the U-boat learned upon consulting his books that he fired that torpedo on March 6. It did not strike the *Tubantia* until March 16. So that it had either been floating about aimlessly and had encountered the liner, or perhaps the cunning British had corraled it and made use of it. At any rate, Berlin disclaimed all responsibility for its acts subsequent to the day it parted company with the German submarine.

The path of the torpedo, however, had been observed from the bridge of the *Tubantia.*

I remarked to one of my well-informed confidants among the Social Democratic politicians that although it is perfectly true that a rolling stone gathers no moss, it is equally true that a moving torpedo leaves no wake.

"Yes," he said with a twinkle in his eye, "our Foreign Office is well aware of that. Have you not noticed the significance of the two dates, March 6, when the torpedo is said to have been fired, and March 16, when it struck? Do you not see that our diplomats have still one more loop-hole in case they are pressed? Is it not clear that they could find a way out of their absurd explanation by shifting the responsibility to the man or the men who jotted down the date and transferred it? The question in my mind is: Who lost the 1 from the 16?"

Be that as it may, little Holland, enraged at the wanton destruction of one of her largest vessels, was not in a position to enforce her demands. Therefore Germany did not back down—that is, not publicly.

My description of the return of the Prussian Guard to Potsdam naturally aroused the wrath of a Government which strives incessantly to hide so much from its own people and the outside world.

Directly the article reached Germany the Government flashed a wireless to America that no members of the *Potsdam* Guard returned to Potsdam from Contalmaison. This is a typical German denial trick. I never mentioned the *Potsdam* Guard.

I had referred to the *Prussian* Guard.

If any reader of this chapter cares to look into the files of English newspapers at the time of the Contalmaison battle, for such it was, they will find confirmation of my statements as to the presence of the Prussian Guard in the English despatches published in the second week in July.

The Contalmaison article has in whole or in part been circulated in the United States, and also in the South-American Republics, and probably in other neutral countries. This has now called forth a semi-official detailed denial, which I print herewith.

It is signed by the Head Staff Doctor at Potsdam, one Géronne, by name. He divides his contradiction into ten clauses. Each of the first nine contains an absolute untruth.

The last is a mere comment on a well-known German statesman, who told me that as I was seeking the truth in Germany I had better go and find it at Potsdam.

I wish to deal with the denials one by one, as each is a revelation of German psychology.

1. The hospital train, which reached Potsdam on August 4, and was there unloaded, brought wounded men from various troop divisions. There were no Prussian Guards among them.

This says "Hospital *train*" (singular). I described hospital *t r a i n s* (plural). It may be true that *one* train did not contain any Prussian Guards. I did not happen to see that train. All the trains that I saw unloaded Prussian Guard Reserves.

2. No wounded man is kept concealed in Germany. All are consigned to public hospitals or lazarets, where they may at any time be visited by their relatives and friends.

I have never said that any wounded *man* was kept concealed in Germany. I have pointed out that the whole system of the German placing of the wounded is to hide from

3. Hospital trains travel by day as well as by night, and, in accordance with instructions, are unloaded only in the daytime. In case they reach their destination during the night, the regulations provide that they are to wait until the following morning before unloading.

the German population, and especially in Social Democrat districts, the extent of their wounded.

This is absolutely untrue. The number of wounded arriving at the depots in Germany is now so great that the trains are obliged to be unloaded whenever they arrive, by day or by night. I have witnessed both.

4. In order that the loading or unloading of the vehicles which transport the wounded to the lazarets may proceed as rapidly as possible, it is necessary to keep the surroundings of the train clear. The wounded must also be spared all annoyance and curiosity on the part of the public.

The whole of this paragraph is a transparent distortion of fact. What happens at Potsdam and what happens everywhere else is that a cordon of police surrounds the scene and drives the public by force in the usual Prussian way, if necessary, from the scene. I described the method by which I witnessed what was going on at the railway station from the railway station refreshment room itself.

5. Dead men have never been unloaded from the lazaret trains at Potsdam—therefore there could have been none on

I saw the dead men removed.

August 4, 1916. The principle of transporting the wounded is based upon the ability of the wounded to bear transportation. All those who suffer during the journey are removed to a hospital at the frontier.

6. The furniture vans used for transporting wounded to the hospitals at Potsdam and other cities have proved a great success. These vans, moreover, all bear the sign of the Red Cross, and may easily be recognised as hospital vehicles.

A transparent untruth on the face of it. If only one train came into Potsdam why use furniture vans at all? The furniture vans are used for purposes of concealment, and because the very large ambulance supply always on duty at the great military hospitals at Potsdam was unequal to the task. I saw no Red Cross indications.

7. That men who are seriously wounded should give one an impression of weariness goes without saying. Lightly wounded men who travel from the Somme to Boulogne may make a better appearance than the seriously wounded who have made the long journey from the West front to Potsdam.

My statement is that all the German wounded at the present stage of the war, lightly or otherwise, compare badly with the English and French wounded, whom I have seen. They are utterly war weary and suffering not so much from shell shock as from surprise shock, the revelation of the creation of a British Army that had never occurred to the German soldiers.

8. As to the great "Hush! hush! machinery"—what is one to call the attempt to keep the truth from neutrals by closing English harbours near the Channel to neutral shipping for whole days at a time—during which the English ship-transports of wounded proceed to England?

I have made inquiries of British officials, and they tell me that it is absolutely untrue that the channel is closed to neutral shipping when the English hospital transports proceed to England. This untruth is on a par with the others.

9. The figures published by the Ministry of War concerning the numbers of men dismissed from lazarets (hospitals) are based upon unquestionable statistics. These statistics remain as given —despite all the aspersions of our enemies.

An interesting revelation as to German casualty lists. It is stated by this head medical officer of Potsdam that these lists are drawn up from the men *dismissed* from lazarets (hospitals), that is to say, this doctor admits that the custom is now to keep back the casualty lists until the man is *discharged,* whereas your British lists, I am informed on authority, are published as speedily as possible after the soldier is *wounded.* The whole of the German wounded now in hospitals have not yet, therefore, been included in casualty lists—the casualties which are forcing the Germans to employ every kind of labour they can enslave or enroll from Belgium, Poland, France, and now from their own people from sixteen up to sixty years of age of both sexes.

10. It would prove interesting to learn the name of the "patriotic German Statesman," who is said to cherish the same opinions as this writer in the *Daily Mail*.

For obvious reasons I decline to subject my friend to the certain punishment that would follow disclosure of his name.

I regret to burden readers with a chapter so personal to myself, but I think that anyone who studies these German denials with the preceding chapter on the Contalmaison wounded will learn at least as much about the German mind as he would by studying the famous British White paper of August, 1914.

CHAPTER XXIV

GERMANY'S HUMAN RESOURCES

THREE factors are of chief importance in estimating German man-power. First, the number of men of military age; second, the number of these that are indispensable in civil life; third, the number of casualties. Concerning the last two there are great differences of opinion among military critics in Allied and neutral countries. As regards the first there need be little difference, although I confess surprise at the number of people I have met who believe the grotesque myth that Germany has systematically concealed her increase in population, and that instead of being a nation of less than seventy millions she has really more than one hundred millions.

It is safe to say that at the outbreak of war Germany was a nation of 68,000,000, of whom 33,500,000 were males. Of these nearly 14,000,000 were between 18 and 45; 350,000 men over 45 are also with the Colours. The boys who were then 16 and 17 can now be added, giving us a grand total of some 15,000,000.

Normally Germany employed men of between 18 and 45 as follows:—Mines, 600,000; metals, 800,000; transport, 650,000; agriculture, 3,000,000; clothing, food preparation, 1,000,000, making a total of 6,-050,000.

Up to this point there can be little difference of

opinion. From this point on, however, I must, like others who deal with the subject, make estimates upon data obtained. During my last visit to Germany I systematically employed a rough check on the figures derived through the usual channels. Concentrated effort to obtain first-hand information in city, village, and countryside, north, east, south, and west, with eyes and ears open, and vocal organs constantly used for purposes of interrogation, naturally yielded considerable data when carried over a period of ten months. The changes from my last visit and from peace time were also duly observed as were the differences between Germany and the other nations I had visited during the war. Walking, of which I did a colossal amount, was most instructive, because it afforded me an opportunity to study conditions in the villages. Discreet questioning gave me accurate statistics in hundreds of these that I visited, and of many more hundreds that I asked about from people whom I met on my travels. For example, in Oberammergau, which had at the beginning of the war 1,900 inhabitants, about 350 had been called to the Colours when I was there, and of these thirty-nine had been killed.

My investigations in the Fatherland convinced me that of the 3,000,000 men between 18 and 45 formerly engaged in agriculture, considerably fewer than 100,-000 continue to be thus occupied. This work is done by prisoners and women. Mine and metal work have kept from 60 to 70 per cent. of their men of military age; but transport, already cut somewhat, lost 25 per cent. of the remainder when Hindenburg assumed supreme command, which would reduce 650,000 to about

300,000. More than 90 per cent. of those engaged in the preparation of food and the making of clothing have been called up. Thus of the 6,050,000 engaged in the occupations given above, about 1,750,000 remain, which means that more than 4,000,000 have been called to the Colours.

From building and allied trades at least 90 per cent. are in military uniform. Assuming that some 2,000,-000 men of military age are included in indispensable engineers, fishermen, chemists, physically unfit, and so forth, we conclude on this basis that Germany can enrol in her Army and Navy more than 11,000,000 men.

We may approach the subject from a somewhat different angle by considering what percentage of her total population Germany could call to the Colours under stress—and she is to-day under stress. Savage tribes have been known to put one-fifth under arms. An industrial State such as Germany cannot go to this extreme. Yet by using every means within her power she makes a very close approach to it. In practically every village of which I secured figures in Saxony, Bavaria, Posen, East Prussia, West Prussia, Pomerania, Mecklenburg, and Oldenburg, a fifth or nearly a fifth have been called up. In some Silesian and Rhenish-Westphalian districts, however, not more than from a seventh to a tenth. If we allow for all Germany a little less than one-sixth, we get 11,000,000.

What are the factors which enable Germany to call this number or a little more than this number to the Colours? First, the organisation of the women. I have seen them even in the forges of Rhineland doing the work of strong men. "The finest women in the world, these Rhinelanders," as one manager put it. "Just look at that one lift that weight. Few men could do better." And his eyes sparkled with enthusiasm.

Second, and of tremendous importance, are the huge numbers of prisoners in Germany, and her sensible determination to make them work. She has taken about one and two-third millions on the field of battle. *There also happen to be in Germany nearly a million other prisoners, buried alive, whose existence has apparently escaped the notice of the outside world.* These are the Russian civilians who were caught in the German trap when it snapped suddenly tight in the summer of 1914. Before the war 2,000,000 Russians used to go to Germany at harvest time. The war began at harvest time. The number of these men, which from my own first-hand investigations in the remote country districts I estimate at nearly a million, would have escaped my notice also, had I not walked across Germany.

Another important factor in the labour problem in Germany is the employment of the Poles. Not only are they employed on the land, but great colonies of them have grown up in Düsseldorf and other industrial centres. I saw an order instructing the military commandants throughout Germany to warn the Poles, whose discontent with the food conditions in Germany made them desire to return home, that conditions in Poland were much worse. This, then, is an official German admission that there is starvation in Poland, for *much worse* could mean nothing else. Germany is keeping Poland a sealed book, although I admit that she occasionally takes tourists to see the German-fostered university at Warsaw. Just before I left Germany still another order was issued for the regulation of neutral correspondents. Under no circumstances were they to be allowed to talk with the natives in Poland. From unimpeachable authority I learned that the Poles were intensely discouraged at the thoroughness with which the Prussians stripped the country after the last harvest, and that in some sections the people are actually dying of hunger. Even in Warsaw, the death-rate in some neighbourhoods has increased from 700 to 800 per cent. I was witness to German rage when Viscount Grey stipulated that food could be sent there only if the natives were allowed to have the produce of their own land. Prussia wanted that produce, and she got it.

I mention these supplies here because the Poles who worked to produce them must be included in German labour estimates just as much as though they had been working in Germany.

Germany also adds to her man-power by utilising her wounded so far as possible. Her efforts in this direction are praiseworthy, since they not only contribute to the welfare of the State, but benefit the individual. I have seen soldiers with one leg gone, or parts of both legs gone, doing a full day's work mending uniforms. The blind are taught typewriting, which enables them to earn an independent living in Government employ. In short, work is found for everybody who can do anything at all.

In a previous chapter I have spoken of the organisation of the children, a factor which should not be left out of consideration.

*   *   *   *   *

Having considered the assets, let us turn to the debits.

The German casualty lists to the end of 1916 total 4,010,160, of which 909,665 have been killed or died of wounds. My investigations in Germany lead me to put the German killed or died of wounds at 1,200,000, and the total casualties at close to 5,000,000. If we assume that 50 per cent. of *all* wounded return to the front and another 25 per cent. to service in the interior, we must also consider in computation of man-power that the casualty lists do not include the vast numbers of invalided and the sick, which almost balance those that return to the front. This means, in short, that the net losses are nearly as great at any one time as the gross losses. Consequently, according to my estimates there must be at least 4,500,000 Germans out of action at this moment.

In a war of attrition it is the number of men definitely out of action which counts, for the German lines can be successfully broken, and only successfully broken, when there are not enough men to hold them. The Germans now have in the West probably about 130 divisions.

Hindenburg's levies in the late summer were so enormous that I am convinced from what I saw in Germany that she has now called almost everything possible to the Colours. One of Hindenburg's stipulations in taking command was that he should always have a force of half a million to throw wherever he wished. We have seen the result in Rumania, and the men skimmed from the training units then have been replaced by this last great levy from civilian life.

Therefore, with something over 11,000,000 men

called up, Germany has now 6,000,000, or a little more all told, many of whom are not at all suited for service at the front.

Germany on the *defensive* at the Somme certainly lost at least 600,000 men. Attrition, to be sure, works both ways, but if the Germans are out-gunned this year in the West to the extent expected their position must become untenable. The deadly work of reducing German man-power continues even though the Allied line does not advance. I know of a section of the German front opposite the French last winter which for five months did not have an action of sufficient importance to be mentioned by either side in the official reports, yet the Germans lost 10 per cent. of their effectives in killed.

The more munitions the Allies make Germany use, the more fat she must use for this purpose, and the less she will have for the civil population, with a consequent diminution of their output of work. Germany simply cannot burn the candle at both ends.

CHAPTER XXV

THE poor of Berlin live in the north and east of the city. I have seen Berlin's East-end change from the hilarious joy of the first year of the war to an ever-deepening gloom. I have studied conditions there long and carefully, but I feel that I can do no better than describe my last Saturday in that interesting quarter of the German capital.

Late in the morning I left the Stettiner Bahnhof in the north and walked eastward through the Invaliden-strasse. There was practically no meat in the butchers' shops, just the customary lines of empty hooks. A long *queue* farther on attracted my attention and I crossed the street to see what the people were waiting for. A glance at the dark red carcases in the shop told me that this was horse-meat day for that district.

The number of vacant shops of all descriptions was increasing. The small shoemaker and tailor were clos-ing up. The centralisation of food distribution is greater here than in the better-class districts, with the result that many small shopkeepers have been driven out of business. In parts of Lothringerstrasse a quar-ter of the shops were vacant, in other parts one-half. The bakers' shops are nearly empty except at morning and evening. In fact, after my long sojourn in block-aded Germany I *still* find myself after two months in

England staring in amazement at the well-stocked shop windows of every description.

Shortly before noon I reached the *Zentral Viehund-Schlachthof* (the slaughter-houses). Through a great gateway poured women and children, each carrying some sort of a tin or dish full of stew. Some of the children were scarcely beyond the age of babyhood, and their faces showed unmistakable traces of toil. The poor little things drudged hard enough in peace time, and in war they are merely part of the big machine.

The diminishing supply of cattle and pigs for killing has afforded an opportunity to convert a section of the slaughter-houses into one of the great People's Kitchens. Few eat there, however. Just before noon and at noon the people come in thousands for the stew, which costs forty pfennigs (about 5d.) a quart, and a quart is supposed to be enough for a meal and a half.

I have been in the great *Schlachthof* kitchen, where I have eaten the stew, and I have nothing but praise for the work being done. This kitchen, like the others I have visited, is the last word in neatness. The labour-saving devices, such as electric potato-parers, are of the most modern type. In fact, the war is increasing the demand for labour-saving machinery in Germany to at least as great an extent as high wages have caused such a demand in America. Among the women who prepare the food and wait upon the people there is a noticeable spirit of co-operation and a pride in the part they are playing to help the Fatherland *durchhalten* (hold out). Should any of the stew remain unsold it is taken by a

well-known restaurant in the Potsdamer Platz, which
has a contract with the municipal authorities.   Little
was wasted in Germany before the war; nothing, absolutely nothing, is wasted to-day.

As at the central slaughter-house, so in other districts
the poor are served in thousands with standard stew.
The immense Alexander Market has been cleared of
its booths and tables and serves more than 30,000
people.   One director of this work told me that the
Berlin authorities would supply nearly 400,000 people
before the end of the winter.

The occasional soldier met in the streets looked shab-
bier in the shabby surroundings of the East.   The German uniform, which once evoked unstinted praise, is
suffering sadly to-day owing to lack of raw materials.
I was in a Social Democratic district, but the men in
uniform who were home on leave were probably "good"
Social Democrats, since it is notorious that the regular
variety are denied this privilege.

The faces of the soldiers were like the rest of the
faces I saw that day.   There was not the least trace
of the cheerful, confident expression of the days when
all believed that the Kaiser's armies would hammer
their way to an early peace—"in three months," as
people used to say during the first year and a quarter of
the war.   Verdun had been promised them as a certain
key to early peace, and Admiral Scheer was deified as
the immortal who tore loose the British clutch from the
German throat.   But Verdun and Jutland faded in
succeeding months before the terrible first-hand evidence that the constant diminution of food made life a
struggle day after day and week after week.   The news

from Rumania, though good, would bring them no cheer until it was followed by plenty of food.

In the vicinity of the Schlesischer Bahnhof occurred a trifling incident which gave me an opportunity to see the inside of a poor German home that day. A soldier in faded field-grey, home on leave, asked me for a match. During the conversation which followed I said that I was an American, but to my surprise he did not make the usual German reply that the war would have been ended long ago if it had not been for American ammunition. On the contrary, he showed an interest in my country, as he had a brother there, and finally asked me if I would step into his home and explain a few things to him with the aid of a map.

Though I was in a district of poverty the room I entered was commendably clean. An old picture of William I. hung on one wall; opposite was Bismarck. Over the low door was an unframed portrait of "unser Kaiser," while Hindenburg completed the collection. Wooden hearts, on which were printed the names Liége, Maubeuge, and Antwerp, recalled the days when German hearts were light and German tongues were full of brag.

A girl of ten entered the room. She hated the war because she had to rush every day at noon from school to the People's Kitchen to fetch the family stew. In the afternoon she had to look after the younger children while her mother stood in the long lines before the shops where food was sold. The family were growing tired of stew day after day. They missed the good German sausage and unlimited amount of bread and butter.

The mother looked in on her way to the street, basket under arm. She was tired, and was dulled by the daily routine of trying to get food. She talked bitterly about the war, but though she blamed the Agrarians for not doing their part to relieve the food situation, she expressed no animosity against her own Government. The father had been through Lodz in Hindenburg's two frontal assaults on Warsaw, where he had seen the slopes covered with forests of crosses marking the German dead, and his words were bitter, too, when he talked of his lost comrades. And then, the depressing feeling of returning from an army pursuing the mirage of victory to find his family and every other family struggling in the meshes of that terrible and relentless blockade!

It never had occurred to him that his Government might be in the least responsible for the misery of his country. Like the great bulk of the German people he is firmly convinced that the Fatherland has been fighting a war of defence from the very beginning. "To think that one nation, England, is responsible for all this suffering!" was the way that he put it. He is a "good" Social Democrat.

When I once more resumed my walk I saw the lines of people waiting for food in every street. Each time I turned a corner great black masses dominated the scene. I paused at a line of more than three hundred waiting for potatoes. Ten yards away not a sound could be heard. The very silence added to the depression. With faces anxious and drawn they stood four abreast, and moved with the orderliness of soldiers. Not a sign of disturbance, and not a policeman in sight.

Some women were mending socks; a few, standing on
the edge of the closely packed column, pushed baby carriages as they crawled hour after hour toward the narrow entrance of the shop.

Every line was like the rest. The absence of police-
men is particularly noteworthy, since they had to be
present in the early days—a year ago—when the butter
lines came into being. Drastic measures were taken
when the impatient women rioted. Those days are over.
The Government has taught the people a lesson. They
will wait hour after hour, docile and obedient henceforth, if necessary until they drop—make no mistake
of that.

But the authorities also learned a lesson. "People
think most of revolution when they are hungry," was
what one leader said to me. On this Saturday of which
I write not a potato was to be bought in the West-end
of Berlin, where the better classes live. Berlin had
been without potatoes for nearly a week. To-day they
had arrived, and the first to come were sent to the East-
end. In the West-end the people are filled with more
unquestioning praise of everything the Government
does; they applaud when their Kaiser confers an Order
upon their Crown Prince for something, not quite clear,
which he is supposed to have accomplished at Verdun.
Therefore they can wait for potatoes until the more
critical East-end is supplied.

I went farther eastward through the Kottbuser district to the Kottbuser Ufer on the canal, along which
a couple of hundred people waited in an orderly calumn
without any guardian—another evidence of the success
of the drastic measures of July and early August, when

the demonstrations against the war were nipped in the bud. These people were waiting for the free advertisement sheets from the gaudily painted yellow Ullstein newspaper building across the square. They had to stand by the side of the canal because a *queue* of several hundred people waiting for potatoes wound slowly before Ullstein's to the underground potato-shop next door.

I had not heard a laugh or seen anybody smile all day, and when darkness fell on the weary city I went to a cheap little beer-room where several "bad," but really harmless, Social Democrats used to gather. Among them was the inevitable one who had been to America, and I had become acquainted with them through him. They talked in the new strain of their type, that they might as well be under the British or French as under their own Government.

Their voices were low—a rare event where Germans gather at table. They did not plot, they merely grumbled incessantly. The end of the war had definitely sunk below their horizon, and peace, not merely steps to peace, was what they longed for. There was the customary cursing of the Agrarians and the expressions of resolve to have a new order of freedom after the war, expressions which I believe will not be realised unless Germany is compelled to accept peace by superior forces from without.

I left the dreary room for the dreary streets, and turned towards the centre and West-end of Berlin, where the *café* lights were bright and tinkling music made restricted menu-cards easier to bear.

Suddenly the oppressive feeling of the East-end was

dispelled by the strains of military music drawing
closer in a street near by. I hurried towards it, and
saw a band marching at the head of two companies of
wounded soldiers, their bandages showing white under
the bright street lights of Berlin.

The men were returning to their hospital off the
Prenzlauer Allée from a day's outing on the River
Spree. Scores of followers swelled to hundreds. The
troubles of the day were forgotten. Eyes brightened
as the throng kept step with the martial music. A roll
of drum, a flare of brass, and the crowd, scattered voices
at first, and then swelling in a grand *crescendo,* sang
Deutschland über Alles. To-morrow they would complain again of food shortage and sigh for peace, but to-
night they would dream of victory.

CHAPTER XXVI

IN THE DEEPENING SHADOW

A LITTLE, bent old woman, neat, shrivelled, with clear, healthy eye and keen intelligence, was collecting acorns in the park outside the great Schloss, the residence of von Oppen, a relative of the Police President of Berlin.

I had walked long and was about to eat my picnic lunch, and stopped and spoke with her. We soon came to the one topic in Germany—the war. She was eighty-four years of age, she told me, and she worked for twelve hours a day. Her mother had seen Napoleon pass through the red-roofed village hard by. She well remembered what she called "the Bismarck wars." She was of the old generation, for she spoke of the Kaiser as "the King."

"No," she said, "this war is not going like the Bismarck wars—not like the three that happened in 1864, 1866, 1870, within seven years when I was a young woman." She was referring, of course, to Denmark, Austria, and France. "We have lost many in our village—food is hard to get." Here she pointed to the two thin slices of black bread which were to form her midday meal. She did not grumble at her twelve hours' day in the fields, which were in addition to the work of her little house, but she wished that she could have half an hour in which to read history.

Her belief was that the war would be terminated by the Zeppelins. "When our humane King really gives the word, the English ships and towns will all be destroyed by our Zeppelins. He is holding back his great secret of destruction out of kindness."

The remark of that simple, but intelligent old woman as to the restraint imposed by the Kaiser upon the Zeppelins constituted the universal belief of all Germany until the British doggedly built up an air service under the stress of necessity, which has brilliantly checked the aerial carnival of frightfulness. People in Great Britain seem to have no conception of the great part the Zeppelins were to play in the war, according to German imagination. That simple old peasant lady expressed the views that had been uttered to me by intelligent members of the Reichstag—bankers, merchants, men and women of all degrees. The first destruction of Zeppelins—that by Lieutenant Warneford, and the bringing down of L Z77 at Révigny, did not produce much disappointment. The war was going well in other directions. But the further destruction of Zeppelins has had almost as much to do with the desire for peace, in the popular mind, as the discomfort and illness caused by food shortage and the perpetual hammerings by the French and British Armies in the West.

It should be realised that the Zeppelin has been a fetish of the Germans for the last ten years. The Kaiser started the worship by publicly kissing Count Zeppelin, and fervently exclaiming that he was the greatest man of the century. Thousands of pictures have been imagined of Zeppelins dropping bombs on

Buckingham Palace, the Bank of England, and the Grand Fleet. For a long time, owing to the hiding of the facts in England of the Zeppelin raids, even high German officials believed that immense damage had been done. The French acted more wisely. They allowed full descriptions of the aeroplane and Zeppelin raids in France to be published, and the result was discouraging to the Germans. I remember studying the British Zeppelin *communiqués* with Germans. At that time the London Authorities were constantly referring to these raids taking place in the "Eastern counties," when the returned Germans knew exactly where they had been. The result was great encouragement. Nothing did more to depress the Germans than the humorous and true accounts of the Zeppelin raids which were eventually allowed to appear in the English newspapers.

The Germans have now facts as to the actual damage done in England. They know that the British public receive the Zeppelins with excellent aircraft and gun-fire. They know that anti-aircraft preparations are likely to increase rather than decrease, and while, for the sake of saving the nation's "face," it will be necessary that Zeppelins be further used, the people who are directing the war know that, so far as land warfare is concerned, they are not a factor.

There have been more mishaps than have been published; more wounded and damaged Zeppelins than the Germans have ever announced. I was informed that the overhauling and repair of many Zeppelins after a successful or unsuccessful raid was a matter, not of days, but of weeks. There was great difficulty in obtaining crews. Most of them are sailors, as are the officers. There have been suppressed mutinies in connection with the manning of the Zeppelins.

Count Zeppelin, who, up to a year ago, was a national hero, is already regarded by a large section of the population as a failure. The very house servants who subscribed their pfennigs and marks in the early days to help conduct his experiments now no longer speak of him with respect. They have transferred their admiration to Hindenburg and the submarines.

The majority of Germans of all classes believe what they are officially instructed to believe, no more, no less. The overmastering self-hypnotism which leads the present-day German to believe that black is white, if it adds to his self-satisfaction, is one of the most startling phenomena of history. But what of Ballin, Heineken, von Gwinner, Gutmann, Thyssen, Rathenau, and other captains of industry and finance? Some of them have expressed opinions in interviews, but what do they *really* think? I am not going to indulge in any guesswork on this matter. I am simply going to disclose some important statements made at a secret meeting attended by many of the business directors of the German Empire. The meeting was for the purpose of discussing actual conditions in a straightforward manner, therefore no member of the Press, German or foreign, was present.

In striking contrast with custom when the war is discussed, nothing was said of *Kultur,* of German innocence or enemy guilt, of an early and victorious peace, of British warships hiding always in safety, or of the omniscience and infallibility of the Supreme Military Command.

The little circle of Germans who have displayed such brilliant organising ability in commerce and industry are practical men, who look at the war and the days to follow the war in the cold light of debit and credit. This being the case, the honest opinions expressed by Arthur von Gwinner, President of the Deutsche Bank, are worthy of serious consideration. His chief points were:—

1. The belief cherished by the mass of the nation that a Central Europe Economic Alliance will amply compensate us for any shortcomings elsewhere, and enable us to sit back and snap our fingers at the rest of the world is too absurd to be entertained by serious men. Our trade, import and export, with Austria-Hungary was as great as it could be for many years to come, and it was only a small part of our total trade. After the war, as before, the bulk of our trade must be with countries now neutral or enemy, and we must seriously consider how to hold and add to this trade in the future.

2. The solution of the labour problem will be vital in the work of reconstruction. We must make every provision in order to forge rapidly ahead immediately after the close of the war.

No German, except for necessary reasons of State, should be allowed to leave the country for a number of years after the war.

3. Before the war 2,000,000 Russians came to us every year at harvest time. These must continue to come.

4. We have done wonderful work in scientific agriculture, but the limit of productivity of the soil has undoubtedly been reached.

5. Do not place too much hope in an early war between the United States and Japan.

6. There is great rejoicing over the sinking of enemy ships. It should also be remembered, however, that we are not paying any dividends at present.

In the discussion which followed the statements of Herr von Gwinner and from various channels of reliable information which I made use of in Germany, I found a serious view taken of these and other topics, of which the great body of Germans are quite unaware.

Take the labour problem, for example. For years Germany has recognised the necessity of a rapid increase of population, if a nation is to smash rivals in industry and war. Not for a moment during this struggle has Germany lost sight of this fact. Many times have I heard in the Fatherland that the assurance of milk to children is not entirely for sentimental but also for practical reasons. Official attempts are being made at present to increase the population in ways which cannot be discussed in this book. "You get yourself born and the State does all the rest" was an accurate analysis of Germany before the war; but the State looks after everything now.

When men go home on leave from the army, married or single, they are instructed in their duty of doing their part to increase the population so that Germany will have plenty of colonists for the Balkans, Turkey and Asia in the great economic development of those regions. To impress this they argue that Germany and France had nearly the same number of inhabitants in 1870. "See the difference to-day," says the German.

"This difference is one of the chief causes of our greatly superior strength."

Working girls in Dresden have not only been encouraged but quietly advised to serve the State "by enabling Deutschland to achieve the high place in the world which God marked out for it, which can only be done if there are a sufficient number of Germans to make their influence felt in the world." They have been told not to worry, that the State will provide for the offspring. In fact, societies of godfathers and godmothers are growing all over Germany. They do not necessarily have to bring up the child in their own home; they can pay for its maintenance. Thus the rich woman who does not care to have many children herself is made to feel in ultra-scientific Germany that she should help her poorer sister.

The Germans treat the matter very lightly. In Bremen, for example, where the quartering of Landstürmers (the oldest Germans called to military service) among the people resulted in a large batch of illegitimate children, I found it the custom, even in mixed society of the higher circles, to refer to them jokingly as "young Landstürmers."

A serious consideration of what Germany, or any other belligerent, will do after the war is usually of little value, as conditions *after* the war depend upon what is done *during* the war. The amount of freedom which the German people attain in the next few years is in direct proportion to the amount of thrashing administered to their country by the Allies. Perhaps they will have something to say about the frontier regulations of Germany; but assuming that the training of centuries will prevent their hastily casting aside their docility, it is extremely probable that few, if any, Germans will be allowed to leave Germany during the first years of reconstruction.

This will disappoint several million Germans. Despite the snarling rage displayed everywhere in the Fatherland, except in diplomatic circles, against the United States, I heard an ever-increasing number of malcontents declare that, immediately after the close of war, they would go to the States to escape the burden of taxation. One hears two words—*Friede* (peace) and *Essen* (food)—constantly. The third word I should add is *Steuern* (taxes). It is all very well to sit by some neutral fireside reading Goethe or Schopenhauer, while listening to the *Meistersinger von Nürnberg,* or the "Melody in F," and lull yourself into the belief that the Germans are a race of idealists. This touch is used to a considerable extent in German propaganda. Any one familiar, however, with conditions in modern Germany knows that Germans are ultra-materialistic.

I have heard them talk of the cost of the war from the very beginning. They gloated over the sweeping indemnities they would exact. After they realised the possibilities of State-organised scientific burglary in Belgium they were beside themselves in joyful anticipation of what Paris, London, and a score of other cities would yield. When the war became a temporary stalemate, I heard it said, particularly by army officers, that Germany was taking no chances with the future, but was exacting indemnities now from the occupied districts. When taxes rose and food shortage increased, the possibility that the Germans themselves would have to pay some of their own costs of the war in various forms of taxation determined a rapidly growing number to seeek a way out by emigrating at the first opportunity.

As Herr Ballin said, "The world will find us as strongly organised for peace as we were organised for war." The labour problem, however, not only now, but for the days of reconstruction, is viewed very seriously, how seriously may be gathered from the fact that there is so much apprehension that Russia may refuse to allow her workers to go to Germany for some years after the war, that nearly everyone at the secret conference mentioned above was in favour of making concessions at the peace conference, should Russia insist. Indeed one Rhinelander was of the opinion that it would be worth while giving up Courland to get an unlimited supply of labour.

In the meantime the Germans have not been idle in other directions. Until Hindenburg called up his immense levies in the late summer, Germany exported steel building materials and coal to contiguous neutral countries, but she can no longer do this. Nevertheless, she did make elaborate preparations to "dump" into Russia on a colossal scale immediately after the resumption of intercourse. Immense supplies of farming implements and other articles of steel have been stored in the Rhineland, Westphalia, and Silesia, ready for immediate shipment to Russia, thus enabling Germany to get ahead of all rivals in this field.

Germans also derive comfort from the fact that their

ships will be ready at once to carry cargoes and passengers, while so many of those of the Allies will be
used for the transport of troops after the close of the
war, and must then refit.

With such plans for "getting the jump" on competitors it is only natural that I saw more and more ir-
ritability on the part of the financial men with each
month of the war after last April.

Von Gwinner's remark about the improbability of
war between Japan and the United States in the near
future would, if known to the German people, cause
still another keen disappointment, since one of their
solaces has been the thought that they would soon have
an opportunity of reaping a munition harvest themselves.

When Germany tried to make a separate peace with
Russia, Japan was also approached—how far, I do not
know. The Wilhelmstrasse still maintains a Japanese
department, and any possible thread, however light,
which may be twisted from a Tokyo newspaper to
show that perhaps Japan may be won over, is pounced
upon most eagerly. Germany, Japan, and Russia was
the combination whispered in Berlin at the time of the
unsuccessful attempt to separate the Allies.

Absolute governments have certain advantages in
war. They have also disadvantages. When things are
not running smoothly in Germany the Germans worry
more than do the English when things are not going
well in England. When the German leaders began to
disagree as to the best methods to conduct the war, the
effect upon the people was demoralising. Only their
gullibility saved them from complete dismay.

Month after month the great struggle raged, under the surface for the most part, but occasionally boiling over. Would it be to the best interests of Germany to go the limit with the submarines or not? Not once did I hear the subject discussed on ethical grounds. Some remarks made to me by Doctor Stresemann, one of the powerful National Liberals behind the mammoth industrial trust in Germany, and the most violent apostle of frightfulness in the Reichstag, aptly express the sentiment in favour of unrestricted submarine warfare. He and the rest of the men behind Tirpitz had fought and lost in the three Committee Assemblies called to discuss U-boat policy in 1916.

As the day set for the September meeting of the Reichstag approached I noticed that Herr Stresemann was growing more and more excited. "This war is lasting too long," he declared to me in great agitation. "The Kaiser's most glaring fault is that of trying to fight Great Britain with one foot in the grave of chivalry. If the Chancellor continues to sway him, we will wreck the Chancellor at all costs. The only way to win this war is to publish again, and this time enforce, the decree of February 4th, 1915, warning all neutrals to keep out of the submarine zone."

"But, according to the 'Sussex Ultimatum,' that will cause a break with the United States," I said.

"We cannot let that deter us," he declared. "Britain is the keystone of our enemies. If she falls they all fall. We must attack her where she is vulnerable. *We must starve her out.* As for America, we have little to fear from her. In the first place, although she may break off diplomatic relations, she will not enter the war if we are careful not to sink *her* ships. As American ships play a small part in the carrying trade to England, we can thus refrain from sinking them—although we naturally should not proclaim this.

"In the second place, if America does declare war upon Germany, it would have little effect. The war will be over before she can organise after the manner of Great Britain. Herr Helfferich (former Minister of Finance and now Vive-Chancellor) feels that we should do everything possible to keep America out, inasmuch as thereby we shall be in a better position to conclude commercial treaties after the war. Herr Helfferich exerted powerful influence in the meeting at Great Headquarters at the time of the *Sussex* Crisis. But our duty to ourselves is to win the war. If we starve out England we win, no matter how many enemies we have. If we fail, another enemy, even the United States, would not make our defeat more thorough. We are justified, for our existence is at stake. The only way we can escape defeat is by a successful U-boat war against England. That would change defeat into overwhelming victory. I am absolutely confident; that is why the slow methods of the Chancellor make me so angry. It will take at least half a year to bring England to her knees, and with our increased privations he may wait too long. But we shall compel him; we shall compel him."

Herr Stresemann later requested me not to publish these statements—at least, not until a decision had been reached. I did, however, lay the matter before the American Embassy in London as soon as I arrived in England, since my investigations in Germany left no

doubt in my mind that she would play two great cards
—one, to work for peace through negotiation; the other,
the last desperate recourse to the submarine.

As I write (January 21st, 1917) I am convinced
that it is only a question of time until Germany is
reduced to this last desperate resort. The men who will
decide that time will be Hindenburg and Batocki. The
successful siege of Germany is a stupendous though not
impossible task.

On the other hand, the human system is a very
elastic piece of mechanism, and modern man, far from
being the degenerate which some admirers of cave-man
hardihood have pictured him, is able to undergo a
tremendous amount of privation. Besieged cities have
nearly always held out longer than the besiegers expected. In the besieged city the civilian population
is for the most part a drag on the military, but in besieged Germany the civilian population, reinforced by
slave labour from Belgium, France and Poland, continues working at high pressure in order to enable the
military to keep the field. Fat is the vital factor. The
more munitions Germany heaps up the more fat she
must use for this purpose, and the less she will have for
the civil population, with a consequent diminution of
their output of work. Germany simply cannot burn
the candle at both ends. It is my personal opinion that
Verdun marks the supreme culmination of German
military offensive in the West, and the West is the
decisive theatre of war. If that is Hindenburg's
opinion, then he realises that another colossal German
offensive in the West would not bring a victorious
peace. There remains only the alternative of building

up a defensive against the coming Allied attacks—an alternative depending for its success upon sufficient food for the mass of the people. Thus the U-boat decision clearly rests upon the Chief of Staff and the Food Dictator, since their advice to the Imperial Chancellor and the All Highest War Lord must be determinative.

When the day comes for Germany to proclaim to the world that she will sink at sight all ships going to and from the ports of her enemies, that day will be one of the great moments of history. Germany's last card will be on the table. It will be war to the knife. Either she will starve Great Britain or Great Britain will starve her.

These are problems for the leaders, who have the further task of keeping the population hopeful on an alarmingly decreasing diet. Superficially, or until you want something to eat, or a ride in a taxicab, Berlin at night is gay. But you somehow feel that the gaiety is forced. London at first sight is appallingly gloomy is the evening, and foreigners hardly care to leave their hotels. But I find that behind the gloom and the darkness there is plenty of spontaneous merriment at the theatres and other places of entertainment. There is plenty of food, little peace talk, and quiet confidence.

Across the North Sea, however, great efforts are made by the German Government to keep up the spirits of the people. No public entertainer need go to the war at all, and the opera is carried on exactly as in peace time, though I confess that my material soul found it difficult to enjoy *Tristan* on a long and monotonous diet of sardines, potatoes, cheese and freshwater fish—chiefly pike and carp. A humorous

American friend used to laugh at the situation—the brilliantly dressed house, officers in their extremely handsome grey uniforms, ladies, some of them with too many diamonds, and—very little to eat.

At the slightest military gain the bells of victory peal wildly, and gay flags colour mile after mile of city streets, flags under which weary, silent women crawl in long lines to the shops where food is sold. A bewildering spectacle is this crawling through victory after victory ever nearer to defeat.

Early in the war a Norwegian packer, who had not had much demand for his sardines in Germany, put the picture of Hindenburg on the tins and christened them the "Hindenburg Sardines." When he changed the trade-mark the Germans bought them as fast as he could supply them—not because they were short of food at that time, but through the magic of a name. To-day all that is changed. Norwegians no longer have to flatter the Germans, who are anxious to buy anything in the way of food. They flood Germany now with impunity with sardines whose merits are extolled in the hated English language, sardines which had originally been intended for Britain or America, but which are now eagerly snapped up at four and five times the peace price by people who invariably bid one another good-bye with *"Gott strafe England."* I saw the gem of the collection in a Friedrichstrasse window. It was entitled: "Our Allies Brand," on a bright label which displayed the flags of Great Britain, France, Russia, Italy, Belgium and Japan.

In Germany you feel that the drama of the battlefield has changed to the drama of the larder. Hope and despair succeed one another in the determination to hold out economically while soldier and sailor convince the world that Germany cannot be beaten. People laugh at the blockade, sneer at the blockade and curse the blockade in the same breath. A headline of victory, a mention of the army, the army they love, and they boast again. Then a place in the food line, or a seat at table, and they whine at the long war and rage against "British treachery." Like a cork tossing on the waves —such is the spirit of Germany.

The majority struggle on in the distorted belief that Germany was forced to defend herself from attack planned by Great Britain, while the minority are kept in check by armed patrols and "preventive arrest."

The spirit of "all for the Fatherland" is yielding to the spirit of self-preservation of the individual. Everywhere one sees evidence of this. The cry of a little girl running out of a meat shop in Friedenau, an excellent quarter of Berlin, brought me in to find a woman, worn out with grief over the loss of her son and the long waiting in the *queue* for food, lying on the floor in a semiconscious condition. It is the custom to admit five or six people at a time. I was at first surprised that nobody in the line outside had stirred at the appeal of the child, but I need not have expected individual initiative even under the most extenuating circumstances from people so slavishly disciplined that they would stolidly wait their turn. But the four women inside—why did they not help the woman? The spirit of self-preservation must be the answer. For them the main event of the day was to secure the half-pound of meat which would last them for a week. They simply would not be turned from that one objective until it was reached.

And the soldiers passing through Berlin! I saw some my last afternoon in Berlin, loaded with their kit, marching silently down Unter den Linden to the troop trains, where a few relatives would tearfully bid them good-bye.   There was not a sound in their ranks— only the dull thud of their heavy marching boots. They didn't sing nor even speak.   The passers-by buttoned their coats more tightly against the chill wind and hurried on their several ways, with never a thought or a look for the men in field-grey, moving, many of them for the last time, through the streets of the capital. The old man who angered the war-mad throng before the *Schloss* on August 1st, 1914, with his discordant croak of "War is a serious business, young man," lives in the spirit of to-day.   And he did not have to go to the mountain!

CHAPTER XXVII

A FTER my last exit from Germany into Holland I was confronted by a new problem. I had found going to England very simple on my previous war-time crossings. Now, however, there were two obstacles in my path—first, to secure permission to board a vessel bound for England; secondly, to make the actual passage safely.

The passport difficulty was the first to overcome. The passport with which I had come to Europe before the war, and which had been covered with frontier *visées,* secret service permissions and military permissions, from the Alps to the White Sea and from the Thames to the Black Sea, had been cancelled in Washington at my request during my brief visit home in the autumn of 1915. On my last passport I had limited the countries which I intended to visit to Germany and Austria-Hungary. I purposed adding to this list as I had done on my old passport, but subsequent American regulations, aimed at restricting travellers to one set of belligerents, prevented that.

I was not only anxious to return to London to continue my work with Lord Northcliffe on *The Times* and the *Daily Mail,* but I was encouraged by two American officials in Germany and Austria-Hungary to write the truth about Germany—a feat quite impossible, as one of them said to me, for a correspondent remaining in the zone of the Central Powers. The official in Austria-Hungary had become righteously indignant at the sneering German remarks about how they could "play with Washington in the U-boat question." He asked me to learn all possible news of submarines. The official in Germany had been impressed by my investigations among the men behind Tirpitz, men who never for a moment ceased in their efforts to turn on frightfulness in full force. When I mentioned the new American passport regulations which would delay me getting to England, he said: "In Holland fix it with the British. I hope you will do some good with all this information, for you have the big scoop of the day. Now is the time."

I tried to "fix it" with the British authorities in Rotterdam, but as they did not know me my progress was slow for a few days. Then I went to Amsterdam to my old newspaper friend, Charles Tower, correspondent for the *Daily Mail,* a man of broad experience, and in close touch with affairs in Holland, a country which war journalists have grown to look upon as an important link in the news chain between Germany and England. I realised that this move might confirm the suspicions of von Kühlmann's spies who were on my trail. However, the free air of Holland was making me a little incautious, a little over-confident.

"There is the man who is following you," said Tower, as we stepped in the evening from his home on to the brightly lighted street and made our way along the edge of the canals. The tall, round-shouldered German shadowed us through the crowded streets to the Amstel

Hotel. Then we shadowed *him,* while he telephoned for help which came in the form of a persistent Hollander, who insisted in sitting at the table next to us, although it had just been vacated by diners and needed re-arranging, whereas many other tables were entirely free.

That is a sample of the manner in which we were systematically spied upon. In order to make arrangements it was necessary for us to travel together so that we could talk, as our time was limited. It was absolutely impossible for us to go into a restaurant or get into a railway compartment without having a satellite at our elbow. They were very persistent and very thorough; but the system in Holland has the same glaring flaw that is common to the German system everywhere—too much system and not sufficient cleverness in the individual.

Von Kühlmann, the German Minister, certainly does not lack men. We encountered them everywhere. Travelling first class gives one more or less privacy in Holland, so that it was decidedly irritating to have a listener make for our compartment, while adjoining first-class compartments were entirely empty. If the intrusion resulted in our going to another compartment, an ever-ready *Kamerad* would quickly join us.

In all countries Germany considers certain telephone connections to be of great strategic importance. It is practically impossible to be connected with the British Consulate at Rotterdam until the "interpreter" is put on. Mr. Tower experiences the same annoyance. Indeed, the Germans are extremely attentive to him. Although he needs only a small flat, since he lives alone, he has to protect himself by hiring the floor above and the floor below, as the Germans are continually trying to get rooms as close to him as possible. The German Government has for years been pouring out money like water to conquer the world. If I were a German taxpayer I should feel much like the man who discovers that the Florida land which some smooth-talking combination travelling book-agent and real estate agent persuaded him to buy is several feet under water.

Tower and the British authorities finally obtained permission for me to land in England, but they insisted that it would be worse than useless for me to attempt to go on a Dutch steamer, as I should be taken off. Within a week two of these steamers had been conducted by the Germans to Zeebrugge.

After I had left word that I wished to go at the first possible opportunity, and had received some further instructions, Tower and I left for Rotterdam on our last train ride together in Holland. The little man with the book who sat beside us in the tram to the Central station turned us over to a big man with whitish eyebrows and reddish hair and moustache, who followed us into a second-class compartment, which we had entered purposely, although we had bought first-class tickets. We then pretended to discover our mistake and changed to a vacant first-class compartment. Through some rare oversight there was no *Kamerad* on hand, whereupon the man with the reddish hair followed us with the pathetically feeble explanation that he, too, had made the same mistake.

When Tower and I had talked *ad nauseam* on such fiercely neutral subjects as Dutch cheese and Swiss scenery, I felt an impelling desire to "get even" with the intruder, and began to complain to Tower of the injustice of the British not allowing me to return to America via England, which I wished to see for a few days. He took the cue readily, and accused me of being "fed-up like all neutral correspondents in Berlin." He frankly expressed his disgust at the enthusiasm which he declared that I had been showing for everything German since I met him in Holland. As the train pulled into the Hague, where I prepared to leave him, he concluded by saying, "After all, you ought not to blame the British authorities for refusing you permission to go to England. I have done my best and have failed; there is nothing more that I can do. I did get one concession for you, however. You will not be roughly handled or otherwise maltreated when your vessel touches at Falmouth."

I had to make a serious effort to keep a straight face while leaving the train with this last realistic touch of "British brutality" ringing in my ears. Tower, I might add, had voiced the extraordinary myth one hears in the Fatherland about the terrible manner in which the British treat passengers on neutral steamers touching at their ports.

The man with the reddish hair followed me to the office of the Holland-America Line, where I made application for a reservation on the boat which would sail in a week or ten days. From there I went to a small restaurant. He seemed satisfied and left me, whereupon I followed him. He hurried to the large Café Central, stepped straight to a table in the front room, which is level with the street, and seated himself beside a thin, dark German of the intellectual type who appeared to be awaiting him. From my seat in the shadows of the higher room I watched with amusement the increasingly puzzled expression on the face of the intellectual German while the man with the reddish hair unfolded his tale. When they parted my curiosity caused me to trail after the thin, dark man. He went straight to the German Legation.

For two days I nervously paced up and down the sands at Scheveningen looking out upon the North Sea and waiting for the call. It came one short drizzly afternoon. The Germans, of course, knew the whereabouts of the vessel on which I should embark for England, though it is highly improbable that they knew the sailing time, and they did not know when I should go on it.

I did everything possible to throw any possible spies off the trail as I made my way in the dark to a lonely wharf on the Maas River where I gave the password to a watchman who stepped out of a black corner near the massive gates which opened to the pier.

I went aboard a little five hundred ton vessel with steam up, and stood near two other men on the narrow deck, where I watched in considerable awe the silent preparations to cast away.

A man stepped out of the cabin. "I presume, sir, that you are the American journalist," he said. He explained that he was the steward. From the bridge came the voice of the captain, "We can give them only a few minutes more," he said.

Two minutes of silence, broken only by the gentle throbbing of the engines. Then from the blackness near the street gate came the sound of hurrying feet. I could make out three stumbling figures, apparently urged along by a fourth. "Who are they?" I asked the steward.

"They must be the three Tommies who escaped from Germany. Brave lads they are. A couple more days and we'll have them back in England."

"A couple of days?" I exclaimed. "Why, it's only eight hours to the Thames estuary, isn't it?"

"Eight hours in peace time; and eight hours for Dutch boats now—when the Germans don't kidnap them away to Zeebrugge. But the course to the Thames is not our course. The old fourteen-hour trip to Hull often takes us forty now. Every passage is different, too. It isn't only on the sea that the Germans try to bother us; they also keep after us when we are in port here. Only yesterday the Dutch inspectors did us a good turn by arresting five spies monkeying around the boat—three Germans and two Dutchmen."

The little vessel was headed into the stream now, the three Tommies had gone inside, followed a little later by the two men who were on the deck when I arrived, men who talked French. When the steward left I was alone on the deck.

I watched the receding lights of Rotterdam till they flickered out in the distance. The night was misty and too dark to make out anything on shore. My thoughts went back to the last time, nearly a year before, when I had been on that river. I saw it then, in flood of moonlight as I stepped on the boat deck of the giant liner *Rotterdam*. The soft strains of a waltz floated up from the music room, adding enchantment to the windmills and low Dutch farmhouses strung out below the level of the water.

At that time my thoughts were full of my coming attempt to get into Germany, a Germany which was smashing through Serbia, and already planning the colossal onslaught against Verdun, the onslaught which she hoped would put France out of the war. I had got into Germany, but for a long time I had almost despaired of getting out; twice I had been turned back courteously but firmly from the frontiers, once when I tried to cross to Switzerland and again when I started for Denmark. A reliable friend had told me that the Wilhelmstrasse had suspected me but could prove nothing against me. The day before I felt Germany I was called to the Wilhelmstrasse, where I received the interesting and somewhat surprising information that the greatest good that a correspondent could do in the world be to use his influence to bring the United States and Germany to a better understanding. I made neither comment nor promise. I was well aware that the same Wilhelmstrasse, while laying the wires for an attempt to have my country play Germany's game, was sedulously continuing its propaganda of *Gott strafe Amerika* among the German people. As in the hatred sown against Great Britain hate against America was sown so that the Government would have a united Germany behind them in case of war.

I was at last out of Germany, but the lights of the Hook of Holland reminded me that a field of German activity lay ahead—floating mines, torpedoes, submarines, and swift destroyers operating from Ostend and Zeebrugge. They are challenging British supremacy in the southern part of the North Sea, through the waters of which we must now feel our way.

We were off the Hook running straight to the open sea. The nervous feeling of planning and delay of the last few days gave way now to the exhilaration which comes of activity in danger. If the Germans should get us, the least that would happen to me would be internment until the end of the war. I was risking everything on the skill and pluck of the man who paced the bridge above my head, and on the efficiency of the British patrol of the seas.

The little steamer suddenly began to plunge and roll with the waves washing her decks when I groped my way, hanging to the rail, to the snug cabin where six men sat about the table. The pallor of their faces made them appear wax-like in the yellow light of the smoking oil lamp which swung suspended overhead. Three of them were British, two were Belgian, and one was French, but there was a common bond which drew them together in a comradeship which transcends all barriers of nationality, for they had escaped from a common enemy.

They welcomed me to the table. It is surprising what a degree of intimacy can spring up between seven men, all with histories behind, and all with the same hope of getting to England. They were only beginning to find themselves, they were indeed still groping to pick up the threads of reality of a world from which they had been snatched two years before.

The Englishman at my right, a corporal, had been taken prisoner with a bullet in his foot at the retreat from Mons. In the summer of 1916 he had been sent to a punishment work camp near Windau in Courland. I had already heard unsavoury rumours of this camp while I was in Germany, of men forced to toil until they dropped in their tracks, of an Englishman shot simply because his guard was in bad temper. But the most damning arraignment of Windau came from a young Saxon medical student, who told me that after he had qualified for a commission as second lieutenant he declined to accept it. This was such an unusual occurrence in a country where the army officer is a semi-deity that I was naturally curious to know why.

"I am loyal to the Fatherland," the young Saxon said to me, "and I am not afraid to die. I was filled with enthusiasm to receive a commission, but all that enthusiasm died when I saw the way Russian prisoners were treated in East Prussia and at Windau. I saw them stripped to the waist under orders from the camp officers, tied to trees and lashed until the blood flowed. When I saw one prisoner, weak from underfeeding, cut with switches until he died in the presence of a Berlin captain, my mind was made up. My country has gone too far in making the army officer supreme. I now could see the full significance of Zabern, a significance which I could not realise at the time. During the first part of the war I became angry when outsiders called us barbarians; now I feel sad. I do not blame them. But it is our system that is at fault, and we must cor-rect it. Therefore, although I am an insignificant indi-vidual and do not count, I shall, as I love my country, obey the dictates of my conscience. I will not be an officer in the German system."

I thought of that sincere young student while the boat staggered under the onslaughts of heavy seas, and the corporal told of how twelve hours' daily toil on the railway in Courland with rations entirely inadequate for such work, finally put him on the sick list, and he was sent back to Münster in western Germany.

He was then sent into the fields with two companions—the two who were in the group about the table—and with them he seized a favourable opportunity to escape. His companions had tried on previous occasions, each separately, but had been caught, sent back and put into dark cells and given only one meal a day for a long and weakening period. That did not daunt them. The Germans thought that men who had gone through that kind of punishment would not try to escape again. Yet as soon as their strength was restored through their food parcels from home they were off, but in an entirely different direction.

I asked one of them, a little Welshman, where he got the waterproof rubber bag on the floor at his feet, in which were all his earthly belongings. "That used to be the old German farmer's tablecloth," he said.

To-day in Europe there are millions of civilians dressed in military uniform, which fails to hide the fact that their main work of life is not that of the soldier. But the three British soldiers sitting under the smoky brass lamp were of a different sort. Twelve years of service had so indelibly stamped them as soldiers of the King that the make-shift clothing given them in Holland could not conceal their calling. Their faces were an unnatural white from the terrible experiences which they had undergone, but, like the rest of the

Old Army, they were always soldiers, every inch of them.

The two men whom I had heard talking French on the deck were Belgians. The one had been a soldier at Liége, and had managed to scramble across a ditch after his three days' tramp to Holland, although the sentry's bullet whistled uncomfortably close. He said that his strongest wish was to rejoin the Belgian army so that he might do his part to avenge the death of seven civilian hostages who had been shot before his eyes.

The other Belgian was just over military age, but he wanted to reach England to volunteer. His nerve and resource are certainly all right. He knew of the electrified wire along the Belgian-Dutch frontier, so he brought two pieces of glass with him, and thus held the current of death away from his body while he wriggled through to freedom.

We talked until after midnight. The French captain, formerly an instructor of artillery at Saint Cyr—the West Point and the Sandhurst of France—taken prisoner in the first autumn of the war, was the last to tell his story.

At Torgau, Saxony, in the heart of Germany, he plunged into the Elbe in the darkness of night, stemmed the swift waters, and on landing, half-drowned, rose speedily and walked fast to avoid a fatal chill.

For twenty-nine days he struggled on towards liberty. Nothing but the tremendous impulse of the desire for freedom could have carried him on his own two feet across Germany, without money, through countless closely-policed villages and great cities, in a country where everyone carries an identity book (with which, of course, he was unprovided), without a friend or accomplice at any point of the journey, with only a map torn from a railway time-table, and no other guides than the sun, moon, and stars and direction posts.

I will give the rest of the man's story in his own words.

"I came to the conclusion that my brain would not stand the captivity. I knew some of the difficulties before me, but I doubt whether I would have started if I had known them all. I lived on unthreshed wheat and rye, apples, blackberries, bilberries, carrots, turnips and even raw potatoes. I did not taste one morsel of cooked food or anything stronger than water till I arrived in Holland. I did not speak one word to any human being. On two occasions I marched more than thirty miles in the twenty-four hours. I slept always away from the roadside, and very often by day, and as far as possible from any inhabited house. I am, as you see, weak and thin, practically only muscle and bone, and during the last three days, while waiting in Holland for the boat, I have had to eat carefully to avoid the illness that would almost certainly follow repletion."

After I had lain down for a few hours' sleep, I thought, as I had often thought during the past thirty months, that although this is a war of machinery there is plenty of the human element in it, too. People who tell only of the grim-drab aspect of the great struggle sometimes forget that romances just as fine as were ever spun by Victor Hugo happen around them every day.

At dawn I hung to the rail of the wildly tossing ship, looking at the horizon from which the mists were clearing. Two specks began to grow into the long low black lines of destroyers. Our most anxious moment of the voyage had come. We waited for the shot that would show them to be German.

"They're all right. They're the escort!" came a voice on the winds that swept over the bridge.

They grew rapidly large, lashed the sea white as they tore along one on each side of us, diving through the waves when they could not ride them. When abreast of us they seemed almost to stop in their own length, wheel and disappear in the distance. Somehow the way they wheeled reminded me of the way the Cossacks used to pull their horses sharply at right angles when I saw them covering the rearguard in the retreat through the Bukovina.

The rough soldier at my side looked after them, with a mist in his eyes that did not come from the sea. "I'll be able to see my wife again," he said, more to the waves than to me. "I didn't write, because I didn't want to raise any false hopes. But this settles it, we're certain to get home safe now. I suppose I'll walk in and find her packing my food parcel for Germany—the parcel that kept me alive, while some of them poor Russian chaps with nobody to send them parcels are going under every day."

We ran close to two masts sticking up out of the water near the mouth of the Humber, the mast of our sister ship, which had gone down with all on board when she struck a mine.

That is the sort of sight which makes some critics say, "What is the matter with the British Navy?" Those critics forget to praise the mine-sweepers that we saw all about, whose bravery, endurance and noble spirit of self-sacrifice lead them to persevere in their perilous work and enable a thousand ships to reach port to one that goes down.

On that rough voyage across the North Sea, through the destroyer and armed motor launch patrol, maintained by men who work unflinchingly in the shadow of death, I felt once again the power of the British Navy. I cast my lot with that Navy when I left Holland. I know what its protection means, for I could not have crossed on a neutral Dutch vessel.

It is all very well to complain about a few raiders that manage in thirty months to pierce the British patrols, or the hurried dash of swift destroyers into the Channel, but when you look from the white chalk cliffs of the Kentish coast at hundreds of vessels passing safely off the Downs, when you sail the Atlantic and the Mediterranean and see only neutral and Allied ships carrying on commerce, when you cross the Rhine and stand in food lines hour after hour and day after day, where men and women who gloried in war now whine at the hardships it brings, when you see a mighty nation disintegrating in the shadow of starvation, and then pass to another nation, which, though far less self-sustaining in food, has plenty to eat, you simply have to realise that there are silent victories which are often farther reaching than victories of *éclat*.

CHAPTER XXVIII

THE LITTLE SHIPS

I HAVE been particularly impressed with two misconceptions which have existed, and to some extent still exist, not only in Germany but in neutral countries. The first is that England lacks virility, is degenerate, has had her day of greatness; the second, that in the present war she is continuing what is alleged to have been her policy in the past, namely, pulling the strings and reaping the benefit while other nations do the fighting. Through personal investigation I find these contentions so thoroughly refuted that to develop the point would be to commence another book instead of finishing this one.

As I write I can look from my desk in the Alexandra Hotel, Bridlington, on to the North Sea where it washes the "Frightfulness Coast," for Bridlington lies between Hull and Scarborough.

I see trawlers fishing and mine-sweeping whenever I raise my eyes from my writing. Their crews know that they work in the shadow of death in what they describe in the dock-side taverns as the greatest sport in the world. Praise of the big ships often causes us to forget the little ships. I admire the one and reverence the other. For if the men on the humbler craft could be intimidated, the doctrine of Frightfulness would be justified by victory.

Intimidation is a favourite weapon of the people across the Rhine. I was among them when their airmen dropped bombs on Paris early in the war. "It is really humane," they said, "for it will frighten the civilian population into imploring the military to yield to us to save them." They thought the same of Zeppelin raids over England. Intimidation was their guiding star in Belgium. The first I heard of the massacre of Louvain was from one of its perpetrators.

Intimidation was again their weapon in the case of Captain Fryatt. "We planned it well," snarled a member of the Reichstag, incensed over my expression of disapproval. "Before we sent our ships to intercept the *Brussels* we determined to capture him, try him quickly and execute him. Since our submarines will win the war we must protect them by all possible means. You see, when the next British captain thinks of ramming one of our submarines he will remember the fate of Captain Fryatt and think twice!"

Once more Germany is attempting intimidation, and seeking to make neutrals her ally in an attempt to starve Britain into defeat. The American Ambassador is leaving Berlin, hundreds of neutral vessels hug havens of safety all over the world, but the women in Grimsby and Hull still wave farewell to the little trawlers that slip down the Humber to grapple with death. Freighters, mine-sweepers, trawlers, and the rest of the unsung toilers of the sea continue their silent, all-important task. They know that for them Germany has declared the law off, that they will be slaughtered at sight. They know also that despite the Grand Fleet and the armies in France, the Allies and their cause will go down in complete defeat if Germany succeeds in blocking the routes of commerce. The insurmountable obstacle in her path is the simple, old-fashioned dogged courage of the average British seaman.

The Germans have developed to an astounding degree the quality of incorrectly diagnosing other peoples, due partly to the unbounded conceit engendered by their three wars of unification and their rapid increase of prosperity. Their mental food in recent years has been war, conquest, disparagement of others and glorification of self. They entered the struggle thinking only in army corps and siege artillery. Certain undefinable moral qualities, such as the last-ditch spirit of the old British Army on the Yser, did not come within their scope of reckoning.

British illusions of the early part of the war are gone. The average Briton fully appreciates Germany's gigantic strength, and he coldly realises that as conditions are at present, his country must supply most of the driving force—men, guns, and shells—to break it. He thinks of the awful cost in life, and the thought makes him serious, but he is ready for any sacrifice. He welcomes help from Allies and neutrals, but whether the help be great or small, he is willing and resolved to stand on his own feet, and carry on to the end. It is this spirit which makes Britain magnificent to-day.

When losses are brought home to the Germans they generally give vent to their feelings by hurling maledictions upon their enemies. The Briton, under similar circumstances, is usually remarkably quiet, but, unlike the German, he is *individually* more determined, in consequence of the loss, to see the thing through. Somehow the German always made me feel that his war determination had been organised for him.

Organisation is the glory and the curse of Germany. The Germans are by nature and training easily influenced, and as a mass they can be led as readily in the right path as in the wrong. Common-sense administration and co-operation have made their cities places of beauty, health, comfort and pleasure. But when you stop for a moment in your admiration of the streets, buildings, statues, bridges, in such a city as Munich and enter a crowded hall to sit among people who listen with attention, obedience and delight to a professor venomously instructing them in their duty of "hating with the whole heart and the whole mind," and convincing them that "only through hate can the greatest obstacles be overcome," you begin to suspect that something is wrong.

It is part of the Prussian nature to push everything to extremes, a trait which has advantages and disadvantages. It has resulted in brilliant achievements in chemical and physical laboratories, and in gout, dyspepsia and flabbiness in eating establishments. A virtue carried too far becomes a vice. In Germany patriotism becomes jingoistic hatred and contempt for others, organisation becomes the utilisation of servility, obedience becomes willingness to do wrong at command.

Americans and British are inclined to ascribe to the Germans their own qualities. In nothing is this more obvious than in the English idea that the fair treatment of Germans in England will beget fair treatment of the English in Germany. The Prussians, who have many Oriental characteristics—and some of them, a good deal of Oriental appearance—think orientally and attribute fair, or what we call sportsmanlike, treatment to fright and a desire to curry favour.

When Maubeuge fell I heard Germans of all classes boast of how their soldiers struck the British who offered to shake hands after they surrendered to the Germans. Nearly two years later, during the Battle of the Somme, some Berlin papers copied from London papers a report of how British soldiers presented arms to the group of prisoners who had stubbornly defended Ovillers. I called the attention of several German acquaintances to this as an evidence of Anglo-Saxon sporting spirit, but I got practically the same response in every case. "Yes, they are beginning at last to see what we can do!" was the angry remark.

The Germans have become more and more "Prussianised" in recent years. State worship had advanced so far that the German people entered the conflict in the perverted belief that the German Government had used every means to avert war. It is a mistake, however, to suppose that the German people entered the war reluctantly. They did not. There was perfect unity in the joyful thought of German invincibility, easy and complete victory, plenty of plunder, and such huge indemnities that the growing burden of taxation would be thrown off their shoulders.

A country where the innocent children are scientifically inoculated with the virus of hate, where force, and only force, is held to be the determinant internationally of mine and thine, where the morals of the farmyard are preached from the professorial chair in order to manufacture human cogs for the machine of militarism, is an undesirable and a dangerous neighbour and will continue so until it accepts other standards. A victorious Germany would not accept other standards.

That is why I look on the little ships with so much admiration this morning. They sail between Germany and victory, for if they could be intimidated Britain would be starved out. Then the gospel that "only through hate can the greatest obstacles be overcome," would be the corner-stone of the most powerful Empire of history.